Introduction to ITIL®

Based on a product previously published by Van Haren Publishing on behalf of itSMF Netherlands.

Office of Government Commerce

ITIL® Managing IT Services

London: TSO

Published by TSO (The Stationery Office) and available from:

Online
www.tsoshop.co.uk

Mail, Telephone, Fax & E-mail
TSO
PO Box 29, Norwich NR3 1GN
Telephone orders/General enquiries: 0870 6005522
Fax orders: 0870 600 5533
E-mail: customer.services@tso.co.uk
Textphone: 0870 240 3701

TSO Shops
123 Kingsway, London WC2B 6PQ
020 7242 6393 Fax 020 7242 6394
16 Arthur Street, Belfast BT1 4GD
028 9023 8451 Fax 028 9023 5401
71 Lothian Road, Edinburgh EH3 9AZ
0870 606 5566 Fax 0870 606 5588

TSO@Blackwell and other Accredited Agents

Titles within the ITIL series include:

Service Support (Published 2000)
Service Desk and the Process of Incident Management,
Problem Management, Configuration Management,
Change Management and Release Management   ISBN 0 11 330015 8

Service Delivery (Published 2001)
Capacity Management, Availability Management,
Service Level Management, IT Service Continuity, Financial Management
for IT Services and Customer Relationship Management   ISBN 0 11 330017 4

ICT Infrastructure Management   ISBN 0 11 330865 5
Application Management   ISBN 0 11 330866 3
Planning to Implement Service Management   ISBN 0 11 330877 9
Security Management   ISBN 0 11 330014 X
Business Perspective: The IS View on Delivering Services to the Business   ISBN 0 11 330894 9

ITIL back catalogue - an historical repository available as PDF downloads from www.tso.co.uk/ITIL
The managers' set
The complementary guidance set
Environmental management, strategy and computer operations set

First edition, second impression December 2005
First edition, third impression, April 2006
First edition, fourth impression January 2007
First edition, fifth impression June 2007

ISBN 978 0 11 330973 3

Printed for TSO in the Netherlands by Wilco Printers. Prepress: DTPresto Design & Layout, Zeewolde - NL

CONTENTS

Foreword OGC

This new introduction to OGC's IT Infrastructure Library (ITIL®) is well timed, as organizations respond to increasing pressures to rationalize their structures whilst improving their delivery of services.

ITIL is globally accepted best practice in service management, with large and small users in both private and public sectors. It is actively practiced in most countries around the world and is aligned with formal British, Hungarian and Australian Standards. ITIL is supported internationally by a user forum for IT Service Management (itSMF) with over 30 participating countries. For professional development, there is a formal, official ITIL qualification scheme offering individual certification at three levels, recognized by IT industry world-wide and provided by accredited training organizations. This scheme is operated by ISEB and EXIN and supported by trade mark and copyright agreements for accredited training providers. Finally, ITIL has been embedded in products and services from major suppliers such as HP, IBM and Microsoft.

I am sure that organizations across the world are experiencing the same pressures as the UK public sector to be more efficient and accountable. This leads us to search for ways to reduce costs whilst increasing value in service provision in every area including IT. A clear framework for the management of IT enabled services and capable professionals committed to a common approach across the organization and its partners, will appreciably reduce the risks of failure. Without the clear underpinning of standards and key best practice frameworks such as ITIL, attempts at performance improvement and service aggregation are more likely to result in increased costs and a reduction in net service performance across the organization. ITIL provides the consistent information, repeatable processes and common understanding that assure management control of successful service delivery. These are essential prerequisites of any attempt at managed improvement in IT based service delivery.

I welcome this new book as an entry level introduction to the language and concepts of ITIL. It is an essential part of enabling people to get to grips with effective service delivery.

Peter Fanning
Deputy Chief Executive
Office of Government Commerce

August 2005

Foreword itSMF

It is with great pride that these words are added to the Foreword of this book. The release of this Introduction to ITIL marks a significant event in the itSMF world-wide community.

The International itSMF organization, through its International Publications Executive Sub-Committee (IPESC), comprised of a council of members from global itSMF chapters has given its formal itSMF International endorsement to this book, which was based on a previously endorsed itSMF publication.

Through the efforts and dedication of its committee members, the objective of itSMF International's Publications ESC is to create added value to the community of ITSM professionals, by enabling the development of a common global library that supports *a uniform standard* of ITSM knowledge and best practices.

The review process itself is a rigorous one, with stringent endorsement criteria that any ITSM-related publication must meet before it can be endorsed by the IPESC.

The Acknowledgements on the following pages identify many itSMF chapter representatives who were involved in the review and endorsement of this book.

On behalf of the itSMF global community I wish to thank the IPESC for their dedication, effort and commitment to participating in the review and endorsement of this book. I hope you find this book enjoyable, informative and a useful introduction to ITSM.

Sharon Taylor,
Chair, International Publications Executive Sub-Committee
itSMF International

ACKNOWLEDGEMENTS

Title: Introduction to ITIL

Editors: Jan van Bon (Inform-IT, chief editor)
            Mike Pieper (Inform-IT, editor)
            Annelies van der Veen (Inform-IT, editor)
            Tieneke Verheijen (Inform-IT, editor)

This publication is the result of the cooperation of many experts from the field, in many different countries, representing users, providers, government, trainers, examiners, and itSMF chapters. It was based on an itSMF publication in the Netherlands, developed as an introduction to IT Service Management, first published in April 1999. The book was originally initiated by Georges Kemmerling (Quint Wellington Redwood), and built by a Dutch itSMF project team, under the guidance of chief editor Jan van Bon (Inform-IT). Since 1999, this project team of reviewers and co-authors has extended and improved the book, in a series of new editions. The following experts from the Netherlands contributed to the project:

Rolf Akker (BHVB)
Jan Bakx (IT's ME Management Solutions)
Koos Berg (Capgemini)
Aad Brinkman (Aranea Consult)
Bob Driessen (Achmea Active)
Lex Hendriks (EXIN)
Jan Heunks (Multitasking Competence Services)
Ton van den Hoogen (TotZ)
Georges Kemmerling (Quint Wellington Redwood)
Louk Peters (Getronics PinkRoccade)
Dick Pondman (ISES International)
Bart van Rooijen (IBM Global Services)

In May 2002 the first translation was published, in English. This first global edition was soon followed by a second, improved, version, audited by selected itSMF members, cooperating in the itSMF International Publications Executive Sub Committee, each representing an itSMF chapter. In addition to that, the global edition was reviewed by several experts from vendor and user organizations, and by representatives of the OGC. This resulted in the very first internationally endorsed itSMF publication, supported by the entire itSMF community, and accepted as a high quality standard introduction to ITIL. The book provided excellent services as an aid in the preparation for ITIL examination, specifically for the Foundations exam, in many countries.

Since 2002, several other translations appeared. Each of these translations was developed and audited by a team of experts in the targeted language region, if possible under the guidance of an itSMF chapter. In all cases, a terminology translation table was determined, before translating the text. Translations were delivered in German, French, Spanish, Russian, Chinese and Japanese, and several other languages will follow. Now, in 2005, this book is published by TSO as the official introduction to ITIL. Two additional chapters, on ITIL books that were not yet covered in the itSMF edition, were written by Chris Littlewood (Parity Training Ltd, UK) and Ivor Macfarlane (Guillemot Rock, UK), and pre-edited by Ashley Hanna (HP, UK). The book was then reviewed by the team that was responsible for the English, itSMF endorsed, edition.

The following experts contributed to the English edition:

Jan Bakx (IT's ME Management Solutions, NL)
Ivo Barros (itSMF Portugal)
Klaus Berghoffer (itSMF Romania)
Aad Brinkman (Aranea Consult, NL)
Bernd Broksch (itSMF Germany)
Hal Dally (Fujitsu Consulting, Canada)
Vincent Douhairie (itSMF France)
Bob Driessen (Achmea Active, NL)
Martin Erb (Capitol One, US)
Karen Ferris (ProActive, Australia)
John Gibert (Southcourt, UK)
John Groom (UK)
Peter Haberl (itSMF Austria)
Ashley Hanna (HP, UK)
Mark Haddad (Directions, UK)
John Ib Hansen (itSMF Denmark)
Lex Hendriks (EXIN)
Signe Marie Hernes (itSMF Norway)
Klaas Hofkamp (IBM, Canada)
Ton van den Hoogen (TotZ, NL)
Brian Johnson (CA, USA)
Chris Jones (itSMF Australia)
Georges Kemmerling (Quint Wellington Redwood, NL)
Graham Kennedy (ProActive, Australia)
Glenn LeClair (Fujitsu Consulting, Canada)
Chris Littlewood (Parity Training, UK)
Ivor Macfarlane (itSMF International)
Steve Mann (itSMF Belgium)
Jürgen Müller (itSMF South Africa)
Christian Nissen (ITILLIGENCE, Denmark)
Dave Pultorak (Fox IT, USA)
Barclay Rae (e2e, UK)
Mart Rovers (InterProm, USA)
Colin Rudd (itSMF UK)
Philip Stubbs (Sheridan College, Ontario Canada)
Sharon Taylor (itSMF Canada)
Walter Vogt (itSMF Switzerland)
Wilfred Wah (itSMF Hong Kong)
Ken Wendle (itSMF USA)
Takashi Yagi (itSMF Japan)

Given the desire for a broad consensus in the ITIL field, new developments, additional material and contributions from ITIL professionals are welcome. They will be discussed by the editors and where appropriate incorporated into new editions.

Contact information

Full details of the range of material published under the ITIL banner can be found at www.itil.co.uk/.
For further information on this and other OGC products, please visit the OGC website at
www.ogc.gov.uk/. Alternatively, please contact:
OGC Service Desk
Rosebery Court
St Andrews Business Park
Norwich
NR7 0HS
United Kingdom
Tel: +44 (0) 845 000 4999
Email: ServiceDesk@ogc.gsi.gov.uk

I INTRODUCTION

In recent decades IT developments have had a major impact on business processes. The introduction of the PC, LAN, client/server technology and the Internet has enabled organizations to bring their products and services to markets more quickly. These developments have ushered in the transition from the industrial to the information age. In the information age, everything has become faster and more dynamic. Traditional hierarchical organizations often find it difficult to respond to rapidly changing markets, which has led to a trend towards less hierarchical and more flexible organizations. Similarly, emphasis within organizations has shifted from vertical functions or departments, to horizontal processes that run across the organization, and decision-making authority is increasingly granted to personnel at a lower level. The IT Service Management processes were developed against this background.

In the 1980s, the quality of the IT services provided to the British government was such that the then CCTA (Central Computer and Telecommunications Agency, now Office of Government Commerce, OGC) was asked to develop an approach for efficient and cost-effective use of IT resources by British public sector organizations. The aim was to develop an approach independent of any supplier. This resulted in the **Information Technology Infrastructure Library (ITIL®)**. ITIL[1] grew from a collection of best practices observed in the IT service industry.

ITIL gives a detailed description of a number of important IT practices, with comprehensive checklists, tasks, procedures and responsibilities which can be tailored to any IT organization. Where possible, these practices have been defined as processes covering the major activities of IT service organizations. The broad subject area covered by the ITIL publications makes it useful to refer to them regularly and to use them to set new improvement objectives for the IT organization. The organization can grow and mature with them.

A number of other IT Service Management frameworks have been developed on the basis of ITIL, generally by commercial organizations. Examples include Hewlett-Packard (HP ITSM Reference model), IBM (IT Process Model), Microsoft (MOF) and many others. This is one of the reasons why ITIL has become the de facto standard for describing a number of fundamental processes in IT Service Management. This adoption and adaptation of ITIL directly reflects the ITIL philosophy, and is a welcome development as ITIL has become a force for industry alignment that is sorely needed in today's heterogeneous and distributed IT environment.

This publication, developed and endorsed by itSMF, is aimed at anyone involved in IT Service Management or interested in the subject. Given the broad target group, the IT Service Management Forum (itSMF) provides the perfect channel as a non-profit industry organization. The objectives of this book are to create an accessible and practical reference book on IT Service Management, covering the core ITIL publications.

ITIL is primarily a collection of best practices developed in the industry, and theory and practice are not always in step. Given the rapid developments in this field, the generic guidance in the core ITIL books can not always describe the latest developments. For that reason the set of core books is extended with a 'Complementary' portfolio of titles on more detailed subjects. The first title in this Complementary portfolio was Software Asset Management. Together with additional titles, available from other publishers and from itSMF chapters, ITIL provides the

---

[1] ITIL ® is a Registered Trade Mark and a Community Trademark of the Office of Government Commerce.

source for enabling adoption of best practices in IT Service Management, keeping the market place up to date on the latest standards. This way the Introduction to ITIL can be used both as a self-study guide, and as a general introduction to the broader area of IT Service Management, with a strong focus on ITIL. Each of the ITIL core books is described in one or more separate chapters. In Chapter 2 'IT Service Management - Background' the book addresses, in a more general way, relevant matters in IT Service Management, in terms of quality, processes and policies.

2 IT SERVICE MANAGEMENT - BACKGROUND

This chapter addresses issues such as services, quality, organization, policy and process management. These concepts provide the backdrop for the development of a systematic approach to IT Service Management.

The IT Service Management processes described in this book (also referred to as IT Management) are best understood against the background of the concepts of the organizations, quality and services which influenced the development of the discipline. Familiarity with these terms also helps to understand the links between the elements of the IT Infrastructure Library (ITIL). ITIL is by far the best-known description of IT Service Management and is therefore used as the foundation for this book.

This chapter introduces the following subjects:
- **Services and quality** - This section addresses the relationship between the quality experienced by the customer's organization and users, and quality management by the provider of the IT services.
- **Organization and policies** - This section addresses concepts such as vision, objectives, and policies, and discusses issues such as planning, corporate culture and Human Resource Management. This section also discusses the coordination between the business processes of a company and the IT activities.
- **Process management** - This section addresses the control of IT service processes.

2.1 Services and Quality

Organizations are often greatly dependent on their IT services and expect the IT services not only to support the organization, but also to present new options to implement the objectives of the organization. Furthermore, the high expectations of customers of IT services tend to change significantly over time and require constant review. Providers of IT services can no longer afford to focus on technology and their internal organization, they now have to consider the quality of the services they provide and focus on the relationship with their customers.

The provision of IT services refers to the full management - maintenance and operation - of the IT infrastructure.

Before buying a **product** in a store, we normally assess the quality such as its appearance, usefulness and robustness. In a store, the customer has few opportunities to influence the product quality. This is because the product is produced in a factory. By effectively controlling the production plant, the manufacturer will try to deliver a fairly constant quality. In this example, manufacture, sales and consumption of the product are quite separate.

However, **services** are provided through interaction with the customer. Services cannot be assessed in advance, but only when they are provided. The quality of a service depends to some extent on the way in which the service provider and the customer interact. In contrast to the manufacturing process, the customer and provider can still make changes when the services are being delivered. How the customer perceives the service and what the provider thinks they supply both depend largely on their personal experiences and expectations.

The process of providing a service is a combination of production and use, in which the provider and customer participate simultaneously.

The perception of the customer is essential in the provision of services. Customers will generally use the following questions to assess the quality of the service:
■ Does the service meet expectations?
■ Can I expect a similar service the next time?
■ Is the service provided at a reasonable cost?

Whether or not the service fulfills the **expectations** depends primarily on how effectively the deliverables were agreed upon in any dialogue with the customer, rather than on how well the supplier provides the service.

A **continuing dialogue** with the customer is essential to refine the services and to ensure that both the customer and the supplier know what is expected of the service. In a restaurant, the waiter will first explain the menu, and ask if everything is satisfactory when serving a new course. The waiter actively coordinates supply and demand throughout the meal. And this experience with customers is then used to improve future customer contact.

*The **quality** of a service refers to the extent to which the service fulfills the requirements and expectations of the customer. To be able to provide quality, the supplier should continuously assess how the service is experienced and what the customer expects in the future. What one customer considers normal could be considered a special requirement by another customer, and eventually a customer may get used to something considered special at the start. The results of the assessment can be used to determine if the service should be modified, if the customer should be provided with more information, or if the price should be changed.*

"Quality is the totality of characteristics of a product or service that bear on its ability to satisfy stated and implied needs" (ISO-8402).

Reasonable costs may be considered as a derived requirement. Once it has been agreed on what is to be expected of the service, the next step is to agree on the cost. Cost can also be considered as a quality attribute that needs to be considered in conjunction with other quality attributes, to reach an overall balance on which the customer will be more than happy. At this stage the service provider has to be aware of the costs they incur, and the current market rates for comparable services.

A customer will be dissatisfied about a service provider who occasionally exceeds the expectations but disappoints at other times. Providing a constant quality is one of the most important, but also one of the most difficult aspects of the service industry.

For example, a restaurant will have to purchase fresh ingredients, the chefs will have to work together to provide consistent results, and hopefully there are no major differences in style among the waiting staff. A restaurant will only be awarded a three-star rating when it manages to provide the same high quality over an extended period. This is not always the case: there are changes among the waiting staff, a successful approach may not last, and chefs leave to open their own restaurants. Providing a constant high quality also means that the component activities have to be coordinated: the better and more efficiently the kitchen operates, the more quickly the guests can be served.

Thus, when providing a service, the overall quality is the result of the quality of a number of component processes that together form the service. These component processes form a chain, and the links affect each other and the quality of the service. Effective coordination of the component processes requires not only adequate quality when performing each process, but also consistent quality.

2.1.1 Quality assurance

Supplying products or services requires activities. The quality of the product or service depends greatly on the way in which these activities are organized. Deming's Quality Circle (Figure 2.1) provides a simple and effective model to control quality. The model assumes that to provide appropriate quality, the following steps must be undertaken repeatedly:

■ **Plan** - what should be done, when should it be done, who should be doing it, how should it be done, and by using what?
■ **Do** - the planned activities are implemented.
■ **Check** - determine if the activities provided the expected result.
■ **Act** - adjust the plans based on information gathered while checking.

Effective and timely intervention means that the activities are divided into processes with their own plans and opportunities for checking. It must be clear who is responsible in the organization and what authority they have to change plans and procedures, not only for each of the activities, but also for each of the processes.

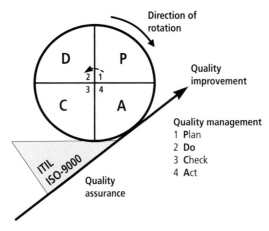

Figure 2.1 - Deming's Quality Circle

Dr. Edward Deming was an American statistician brought to Japan by General Douglas MacArthur after the Second World War to help rebuild the destroyed economy. He had developed theories about the best possible use of expertise and creativity in organizations in the United States in the 1930s, but because of the Depression his ideas were not accepted in the US. However, his optimization methods were successfully adopted in Japan.

Some of Deming's typical statements:
- *'The customer is the most important part of the production line.'*
- *'It is not enough to have satisfied customers, the profit comes from returning customers and those who praise your product or service to friends and acquaintances.'*
- *'The key to quality is to reduce variance.'*
- *'Break down barriers between departments.'*
- *'Managers should learn to take responsibility and provide leadership'*
- *'Improve constantly.'*
- *'Institute a vigorous program of education and self-improvement.'*
- *'Institute training on the job.'*
- *'The transformation is everybody's job.'*

Quality management is the responsibility of everyone working in the organization providing the service. Every employee has to be aware of how their contribution to the organization affects the quality of the work provided by their colleagues, and eventually the services provided by the organization as a whole. Quality management also means continuously looking for opportunities to improve the organization and implementing quality improvement activities.

Quality assurance is a policy matter within the organization. It is the complete set of the measures and procedures used by the organization to ensure that the services provided continue to fulfill the expectations of the customer and the relevant agreements. Quality assurance ensures that improvements resulting from quality management are maintained.

The quality system is the organizational structure related to responsibilities, procedures and resources for implementing quality management.

The ISO 9000 series of standards is often used to develop, define, assess and improve quality systems.

ISO 9000 quality standard:

Some organizations require their suppliers to hold an ISO 9001 or ISO 9002 certificate. Such a certificate proves that the supplier has an adequate quality system whose effectiveness is regularly assessed by an independent auditor.

ISO is the International Organization for Standardization. A quality system that complies with the ISO standard ensures that
- *the supplier has taken measures to be able to provide the quality agreed with the customers;*
- *the management regularly assesses the operation of the quality system, and uses the results of internal audits to implement improvement measures where necessary;*
- *the supplier's procedures are documented and communicated to those affected by them;*
- *customer complaints are recorded, dealt with in a reasonable time, and used to improve the service where possible;*
- *the supplier controls the production processes and can improve them.*

An ISO certificate does not provide an absolute guarantee about the quality of the service provided, however, it does indicate that the supplier takes quality assurance seriously and is prepared to discuss it.

The new ISO 9000 series of standards, ISO-9000-2000, puts even greater emphasis than the previous standard on the ability of an organization to learn from experience and to implement continuous quality improvement.

2.1.2 Organizational maturity

Experience with improving the quality of IT services has shown that it is rarely sufficient to structure and define current practices. The causes of a mismatch between the service provided and the customer's requirements are often related to the way in which the IT organization is managed. Permanent quality improvement demands a certain degree of maturity of the organization.

The European Foundation for Quality Management was set up in 1988 by fourteen large European companies, with the support of the European Commission. The objective of the EFQM is to promote Total Quality Management, aimed at excelling in customer satisfaction, employee satisfaction, and appreciation by society, and performance results.

The EFQM 'Model of Business Excellence', generally known simply as the EFQM model, is widely accepted as the major strategic framework for managing an organization aimed at the balanced, continuing improvement of all aspects relevant to the business. Over 600 European businesses and research organizations have now joined the EFQM. For further information: http://www.efqm.org.

The European Foundation for Quality Management (EFQM) model (Figure 2.2) can be useful in determining the maturity of an organization. It identifies the major areas to be considered when managing an organization.

Deming's Quality Circle is incorporated in the EFQM model. Based on the outcomes from the result areas actions are taken (strategy, policies). These actions serve to underpin the planning (e.g. the structure of the processes) which should then lead to the desired results. The EFQM identifies nine areas.

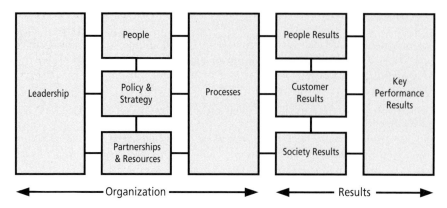

Figure 2.2 - EFQM© model (The EFQM Excellence Model is a registered trademark)

As an additional tool, the Dutch quality organization, INK, divided the EFQM model into stages indicating to what extent a company has implemented Total Quality Management, either in a particular area, or in general.

There are five stages:
- **Product-focused** - also known as ad hoc, output-focused; everyone in the organization works hard but their efforts show little direction.
- **Process-focused** - also known as 'we know our business'; the performance of the organization is planned and repeatable.
- **System-focused** - or 'cooperation between departments'.
- **Chain-focused** - also known as 'external partnership'; the organization is focused on the value it adds in the supplier-customer chain it forms a part of.
- **Total quality-focused** - also known as 'heaven on earth'; the organization has reached the stage where a continuous and balanced focus on improvement has become second nature.

The areas covered by the EFQM model can be combined with the levels of organizational maturity. Questionnaires can be used to determine how mature the organization is in each of these areas. Internal or external auditors can carry out such an assessment.

When an organization determines its maturity, it can develop a strategy for improvement that can then be further developed into a plan. The plan, based on the model and covering a period of one year, describes what improvements should be made to specific aspects in each area and how. By repeating this process of self-assessment and planning, every year the organization becomes more aware how it is maturing. Major benefits of this approach are that the organization can improve its quality step by step, that the intermediate results are visible, and that the management can steer the organization on the basis of its strategy.

There are many other health checks and types of self-assessment in addition to the EFQM approach. Some focus primarily inwardly. One should bear in mind that improvements to parts of the internal organization might only have a limited effect on the results, for example if there is no improvement in the relationships with the customers, employee satisfaction and leadership, or if the strategy and policy of the organization is unclear.

In the IT industry, the process maturity improvement process is best known in the context of the Capability Maturity Model (CMM). This process improvement method was developed by the Software Engineering Institute (SEI) of Carnegie Mellon University. CMM is concerned with improving the maturity of the software creation processes. CMM provides a staged model, including the following levels:

- **Initial** - the processes occur ad hoc.
- **Repeatable** - the processes have been designed such that the service quality should be repeatable.
- **Defined** - the processes have been documented, standardized and integrated.
- **Managed** - the organization measures the results and consciously uses them to improve the quality of its services.
- **Optimizing** - the organization consciously optimizes the design of its processes to improve the quality of its services, or to develop new technology or services.

Since 2002 this staged model has been followed up by CMMI: CMM Integrated. This new model is still based on the well-known approach of CMM, but it now contains a more flexible continuous maturity model as well. Maturity models based on the CMM levels of maturity have also been developed for IT Service Management.

Developing and maintaining a quality system which complies with the requirements of the ISO 9000 (ISO-9000-2000) series can be considered a tool for the organization to reach and maintain the system-focused (or 'managed' in IT Service CMM) level of maturity. These ISO standards emphasize the definition, description and design of processes.

When assessing the maturity of an organization, we cannot restrict ourselves to the service provider. The level of maturity of the customer (Figure 2.3) is also important. If there are large differences in maturity between the supplier and the customer, then these will have to be considered to prevent a mismatch in the approach, methods and mutual expectations. Specifically, this affects the communication between the customer and the supplier.

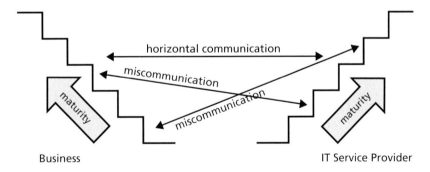

Figure 2.3 - Communication and maturity levels: customer and supplier (source: itSMF)

2.2 Organization and Policies

The preceding sections clearly illustrated that service quality is closely associated with the quality of an organization and its policies. This section will discuss several important aspects of organization and policies that are relevant to process management.

2.2.1 Vision, objectives and policies

An organization is a form of cooperation between people. Any organization, from a darts club to a multinational company, depends upon a shared concept of why it is worth cooperating in the organization. The **vision** might be that you could make money by selling PCs. However, to be attractive to all stakeholders (e.g. customers, investors, personnel) your organization will have to communicate why they should do business with you, for example because you are the best, cheapest or most fun. Thus, you will want to build up a suitable image. Just think of slogans such as 'Let's make things better' or 'You'll never walk alone'.

To communicate its vision, the organization can be defined in the form of a **Mission Statement** (Figure 2.4). The mission statement is a short, clear description of the objectives of the organization and the values it believes in.

The **objectives** of the organization describe in greater detail what it wants to accomplish. Good objectives have five essential elements: they have to be **S**pecific, **M**easurable, **A**ppropriate, **R**ealistic and **T**ime-bound (SMART).

The **policy** of the organization is the combination of all decisions and measures taken to define and realize the objectives. In its policies, the organization will prioritize objectives and decide how the objectives will be reached. Of course, priorities may change over time, depending on the circumstances. The clearer the organization's policies are to all stakeholders, the less needs to be defined about how personnel are supposed to do their work. Instead of detailed procedures, personnel can independently use the policies as their guideline. Clearly formulated policies contribute to a flexible organization, as all levels in the organization can respond more quickly to changing circumstances.

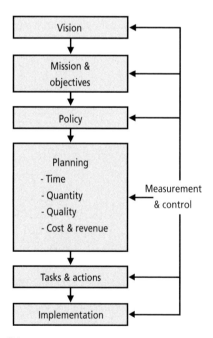

Figure 2.4 - Vision, objectives and policies

Implementing policies in the form of specific activities requires **planning**. Plans are usually divided into stages to provide milestones where progress can be monitored. For example, the policies can be used to draw up an annual plan, which is then used to develop the budgets. An annual plan can be developed in greater detail into departmental plans, quarterly plans or project plans. Each of these plans contains a number of elements: an activity schedule, the required resources, and agreements about the quality and quantity of the products or services to be delivered.

Realization of the planned activities requires **action**. Actions are allocated to personnel as **tasks**, or outsourced to external organizations.

When translating the mission of the organization into objectives, policies, planning and tasks, there is the risk that after some time, the mission, objectives or policies are forgotten. It is therefore important that at every stage we **measure** if the organization is still moving in the right direction, and to take remedial action where necessary.

Thus, we have to measure if the organization or processes fulfill the objectives, and there are various methods available for this. One of the most common methods in business is the **Balanced Score Card**, or BSC. In this method, the objectives of the organization or process are used to define **Critical Success Factors** (CSF). CSF's are defined for a number of areas of interest or perspectives: customers/market, business processes, personnel/innovation and finance. The parameters determined to measure if the CSF's meet the standard are known as **Key Performance Indicators** (KPI). Where necessary, these can be subdivided into Performance Indicators (PI).

Key performance indicators, or KPI's, are parameters for measuring progress relative to key objectives or Critical Success Factors (CSF) in the organization.

The outcome of the measurements and changing circumstances can lead to **modification** of the processes, tasks, plans, and policies, and even to a change in the objectives, mission and vision of the organization. The more mature the organization is, the better it deals with such changes. If the IT department supports the interests of the business, the objectives of the IT department will be derived from the business objectives. The IT department, for example, might have the following objective: 'To contribute to the competitive strength of the business'. The specific objectives of the IT department will then be developed on the basis of this general objective. Depending on the nature of the business, objectives will be defined for the IT department with respect to safety, accessibility, response speed, technical sophistication, and so forth.

2.2.2 Planning horizon

When considering the policies and planning of an IT department, we should be aware of the links between planning for the business as a whole, the application systems and the technical infrastructure. When planning the network and applications of a business, the IT department will have to stay ahead of the overall planning to ensure that the business has an IT infrastructure in which it can develop. Figure 2.5 gives an example of the links between the various plans.

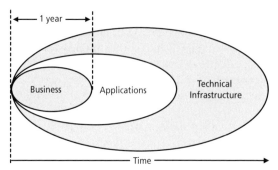

Figure 2.5 - Planning horizons

Technical infrastructure has the longest planning horizon and in its support role it has fewer clear links with the substantive business activities. It takes time to develop a technical infrastructure and the fact that information systems and the business depend on the technical infrastructure limits the speed at which changes can be implemented. Furthermore, developing a technical infrastructure demands significant investment and the period over which it can be depreciated has to be considered.

The planning horizon is shorter for **applications** as they are designed for specific business purposes. Application life cycle planning is primarily based on the business functions to be provided by the system, after which the underlying technology is considered.

Business plans, based on the organization's strategy, normally cover one calendar or financial year. Budget, planning and progress reports all fall within this period. In some markets, the planning cycle time has become even shorter as the cycle time for product development is also being cut.

Planning should address four elements:
- **Time** - this is the easiest factor to determine. It is defined by a start date and end date, and is often divided into stages.
- **Quantity** - the objectives have to be made measurable to monitor progress. Terms such as 'improved' and 'quicker' are insufficient for planning purposes.
- **Quality** - the quality of the deliverables (results) should be appropriate for the objective.
- **Costs and revenues** - the deliverables must be in proportion to the expected costs, efforts and revenues.

Differences between the planning horizons occur not only between areas, but also between the various levels of activities and processes (strategic, tactical and operational).

2.2.3 Culture

Organizations that want to change, for example to improve the quality of their services, will eventually be confronted with the current organizational culture. The organizational culture, or corporate culture, refers to the way in which people deal with each other in the organization; the way in which decisions are made and implemented; and the attitude of employees to their work, customers, suppliers, superiors and colleagues.

Culture, which depends on the standards and values of the people in the organization, cannot be controlled, but it can be influenced. Influencing the culture of an organization requires leadership in the form of a clear and consistent policy and a supportive personnel policy.

The corporate culture can have a major influence on the provision of IT services. Businesses value innovation in different ways. In a stable organization, where the culture places little value on innovation, it will be difficult to adjust its IT services in line with changes in the organization of the customer. If the IT department is unstable, then a culture which values change can pose a serious threat to the quality of its services. In that case, a free for all can develop where many uncontrolled changes lead to a large number of faults.

2.2.4 Human Resource Management

Personnel policy plays an important and strategic role in fulfilling the long-term objectives of an organization (see also the EFQM model). It can also be used as an instrument to change the corporate culture. The objective of modern personnel management is to optimize the performance of all personnel across the organization, for which it uses instruments such as recruitment and selection, training and career development, motivation and reward.

Human Resource Management (HRM) is the major form of modern personnel management. Human Resource Management is based on two premises:
■ Personnel management should contribute to the objectives of the organization. If organizations have to respond better and more quickly in an environment which changes ever more quickly, then this will affect the deployment, quality and number of personnel.
■ Giving employees in the organization the opportunity to develop and use their skills will benefit the organization.

There are three approaches to HRM:
■ **The hard approach** sees human resources as means of production which have to be organized as effectively and efficiently as possible. As the corporate strategy is determined by economic, technical and market factors, the same applies to personnel policy. This approach places different values on employees. Some core employees are strategically more important than peripheral employees who are easily replaceable. For example, a company might choose to permanently employ only core personnel, and for the rest use a pool of contract personnel.
■ **The soft approach** emphasizes that making the best possible use of human potential and opportunities will benefit the business. Modern employees are highly educated, ambitious and prepared to invest a lot in their work. For this reason, their potential must be identified early and developed continuously (career development, training policy). When selecting its strategy and policy, the business must base its choices on the talent and potential of its employees.
■ **The integrated approach** looks at the shared interests of personnel and management in an organization. To reach the objectives of the organization there will have to be good inflow, movement and outflow of personnel. Changes in the market and the organization (e.g. developments in technology) lead to constant changes in the need for skills.

All aspects of personnel policy have to be carefully coordinated. The movement of employees in the organization, determining and developing skills (competence), and promoting mobility in the internal labor market are becoming increasingly important in organizations.

The quality of service provided by an organization will benefit if the best use is made of the potential of its employees. This facilitates continuous improvement. Instruments for quality management in personnel policy include:
■ **Policy Deployment** - communicating to each employee how and to what extent their task contributes to realizing the objectives of the organization. An important condition for the success of policy deployment is that it extends to all layers of management.

- **Empowerment** - giving employees the opportunity to organize and implement their task in consultation with the organization. The degree of empowerment determines the extent to which employees can be held responsible for the quality of the work they provide.
- **Accountability** - as the result of policy deployment and empowerment. If an employee has had explained what is expected of them, and if they have had the opportunity to arrange and implement the task as they wanted, then they can be held accountable for it. This could be used as a basis for assessing and rewarding employees. The reward may be tangible (salary) or intangible, for example appreciation, new opportunities for development and career opportunities.
- **Competence Management** - this is both a means to use the competence available in an organization as effectively as possible, and as a way to systematically develop the competence the organization needs. This approach charts the competence required by the processes and projects as well as the competence of the employees. When organizing employees, the focus is not only on obtaining a good match between the required and available competence, but also on the opportunities to develop competence, transfer expertise, and learn skills. Mentors or coaches may support employees. Setting up skills groups can also support the exchange of experience and encourage the development of new competence.

2.2.5 IT Customer Relationship Management

The quality of IT services largely depends on good relationships with the customers of the IT organization. These relationships provide the basis for making and updating agreements. IT Customer Relationship Management addresses maintaining a relationship with customers and coordinating with customer organizations, at the strategic, tactical and operational levels. Figure 2.6, a diagram of customer relationships, illustrates the horizontal communication between the customers and the IT organization, regarding support and coordination. The vertical communication concerns policies, control and reporting.

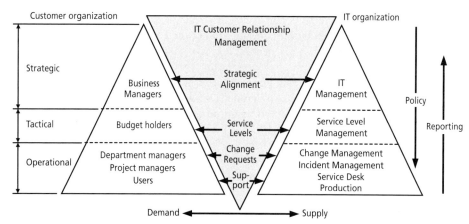

Figure 2.6 - IT Customer Relationship Management

In IT Customer Relationship Management, the major challenge is to ensure that there are good and effective relationships between the IT organization and the customer organization at all levels. However, the extent of IT Customer Relationship Management will be different at each level. For instance, most Service Desks act on an operational level, while the control of Service Levels is a task for Service Level Management, at a more tactical level of the organization. IT Customer Relationship Management may also play a supportive role, for example, by organizing surveys among customers and users, providing information, and so forth.

*The **user** is the 'hand on the keyboard' user, the employee who uses IT services for their routine activities.*

*The **customer** is the 'pay the bills' customer, the person who is authorized to conclude an agreement with the IT organization about the provision of IT services (for example a Service Level Agreement, or SLA) and who is responsible for ensuring that the IT services are paid for.*

Obviously the 'pay the bills' customer can also play the role of the 'hands on the keyboard' user in many situations.

IT Customer Relationship Management plays an important role in developing the Strategic Alignment between the IT organization and the organization purchasing the IT services. In practice, this is primarily a matter of staying in touch with the customer organization, and exploring the options for linking the strategic objectives of both organizations. This can provide the basis for a long-term relationship, in which the IT organization focuses on the customer and proposes IT solutions that help the customer reach their business objectives. Given the dynamic nature of both the customer organization and the IT organization, the rate of change in both organizations should also be coordinated.

The agreements with the customer about the services to be provided are then developed into service level proposals through Service Level Management. For example, if the customer wants to introduce an Intranet, then the availability, user support, implementation of change requests and cost all have to be agreed. These agreements are laid down in a Service Level Agreement (SLA). If the customer organization wants changes (expansion or modification) to the IT services that fall within the agreements laid down in the SLA, then a **Request For Change** will be submitted. Change Management then processes the request. Changes outside the current agreements are introduced into the Service Level Management process.

In most cases, users can contact a **Service Desk** for such operational requests and questions, and to report problems.

Figure 2.6 not only provides information about the horizontal and vertical communication, but also about the **planning horizon** of the processes. Coordination at a strategic level has a planning horizon of several years. Service Level Management concerns agreements at the tactical level, with a planning horizon of approximately one year. Change Management, Service Desk and Incident Management all concern the operational level, with a planning horizon of months, weeks, days or even hours.

2.3 Process Management

Every organization aims to realize its vision, mission, objectives and policies, which means that appropriate activities have to be undertaken. To return to the example of the restaurant, appropriate activities include buying vegetables, bookkeeping, ordering publicity material, receiving guests, cleaning tables, peeling potatoes, and making coffee.

With just such an unstructured list, something will be left out and we will easily become confused. It is therefore a better idea to structure the activities. Preferably they should be arranged such that we can see how each group of activities contributes to the objectives of the business, and how they are related.

Such groups of activities are known as **processes**. If the process structure of an organization is clearly described, it will show:

■ What has to be done.
■ What the expected result is.
■ How we measure if the processes deliver the expected results.
■ How the results of one process affect those of another process.

The questions in Figure 2.7 arise constantly in the process-based approach typical of modern IT Service Management. The tools to answer these questions are shown on the right in Figure 2.7.

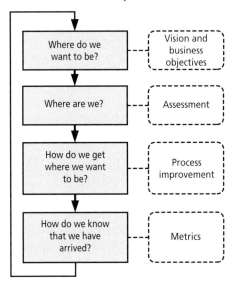

Figure 2.7 - A simple process improvement model

2.3.1 Processes

When arranging activities into processes, we do not use the existing allocation of tasks, nor the existing departmental divisions. This is a conscious choice. By opting for a process structure, we can often show that certain activities in the organization are uncoordinated, duplicated, neglected, or unnecessary.

*A **process** is a logically related series of activities conducted toward a defined objective.*

Instead, we look at the objective of the process and the **relationships** with other processes. A process is a series of activities carried out to convert input into an output (Figure 2.8). We can associate the **input** and **output** of each of the processes with **quality characteristics** and **standards** to provide information about the results to be obtained by the process. This produces chains of processes which show what goes into the organization and what the result is, as well as monitoring points in the chains to monitor the quality of the products and services provided by the organization.

The standards for the output of each process have to be defined such that the complete chain of processes meets the corporate objective, if each process complies with its process standard. If the result of a process meets the defined standard, then the process is **effective**. If the activities in the process are also carried out with the minimum required effort and cost, then the process is **efficient**. The aim of process management is to use planning and control to ensure that process-es are effective and efficient.

We can study each process separately to optimize its quality. The **process owner** is responsible for the process results. The **process manager** is responsible for the realization and structure of the process, and reports to the process owner. The **process operatives** are responsible for defined activities, and these activities are reported to the process manager.

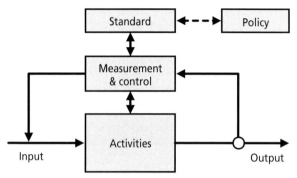

Figure 2.8 - Process diagram

The logical combination of activities results in clear transfer points where the quality of processes can be monitored. In the restaurant example, we can separate responsibility for purchasing and cooking, so that the chefs do not have to purchase anything and possibly spend too much on fresh ingredients that do not add value.

The management of the organization can provide control on the basis of the quality of the process as demonstrated by data from the results of each process. In most cases, the relevant **performance indicators** and standards will already be agreed upon. The day-to-day control of the process can then be left to the process manager. The process owner will assess the results based on a report of performance indicators and whether they meet the agreed standard. Without clear indicators, it would be difficult for a process owner to determine whether the process is under control, and if planned improvements are being implemented.

Processes are often described using **procedures** and work **instructions**.

*A **procedure** is a description of logically related activities, and who carries them out. A procedure may include stages from different processes. A procedure defines who does what, and varies depending on the organization.*

*A set of **work instructions** defines how one or more activities in a procedure should be carried out.*

Figure 2.9 shows the process model based on the ITIL approach which forms the foundation for the IT Service Management processes described in this book.

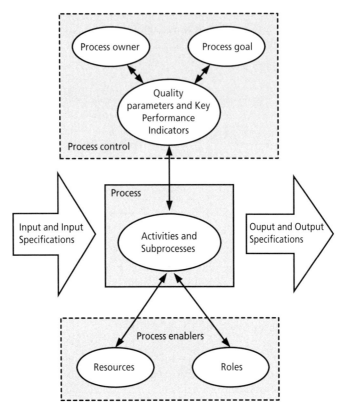

Figure 2.9 - Generic ITIL process model

2.3.2 Processes and departments

Most businesses are hierarchically organized. They have departments that are responsible for a group of employees. There are various ways of structuring departments, for example by customer, product, region or discipline. IT services generally depend on several departments, customers or disciplines. For example, if there is an IT service to provide users with access to an accounting program on a central computer, this will involve several disciplines. The computer center has to make the program and database accessible, the data and telecommunications department has to make the computer center accessible, and the PC support department has to provide users with an interface to access the application.

Processes that span several departments can monitor the quality of a service by monitoring certain aspects of quality, such as availability, capacity, cost and stability. A service organization will then try to match these quality aspects with the customer's demands. The structure of such processes can ensure that good data is available about the provision of services, so that the planning and control of services can be improved.

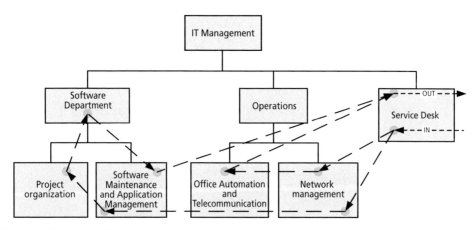

Figure 2.10 - Processes and departments (example)

Figure 2.10 shows a basic example of the combinations of activities in a process (indicated by the dashed lines).

2.3.3 IT Service Management

IT Service Management is primarily known as the process and service-focused approach of what was initially known as IT Management. In this chapter we demonstrated that processes should always have a defined objective. The objective of IT Service Management processes is to contribute to the quality of the IT services. Quality management and process control form part of the organization and its policies.

With a process-focused approach we also have to consider the situation within an organization (policies, culture, size, etc.).

ITIL, the best known approach to IT Service Management, does not prescribe the type of organization, but instead describes the relationships between the activities in processes, which are relevant to any organization. This provides a framework for exchanging experiences between organizations. This approach also provides a framework for learning from the experience of dynamic organizations.

3 INTRODUCTION TO ITIL

This chapter describes the structure and objectives of the IT Infrastructure Library (ITIL) and the organizations that contribute to maintaining ITIL as the best practice standard for IT Service Management.

3.1 Background

ITIL was developed in recognition of the fact that organizations are becoming increasingly dependent on IT to fulfill their corporate objectives. This increasing dependence has resulted in a growing need for IT services of a quality corresponding to the objectives of the business, and which meet the requirements and expectations of the customer. Over the years, the emphasis has shifted from the development of IT applications to the management of IT services. An IT application (sometimes referred to as an information system) only contributes to realizing corporate objectives if the system is available to users and, in the event of fault or necessary modifications, it is supported by maintenance and operational management.

In the overall life cycle of IT products, the operations phase amounts to about 70 to 80% of the overall time and cost, the rest is spent on product development (or procurement). Thus, effective and efficient IT Service Management processes are essential to the success of IT. This applies to any type of organization, large or small, public or private, with centralized or decentralized IT services, with internal or outsourced IT services. In all cases, the service has to be reliable, consistent, of a high quality, and of acceptable cost.

IT Service Management addresses the provision and support of IT services tailored to the needs of the organization. ITIL was developed to disseminate proven IT Service Management best practices systematically and cohesively. The approach is based on service quality and developing effective and efficient processes.

ITIL offers a common framework for all the activities of the IT department, as part of the provision of services, based on the IT infrastructure. These activities are divided into processes, which when used together provide an effective framework to make IT Service Management more mature. Each of these processes covers one or more tasks of the IT department, such as service development, infrastructure management, and supplying and supporting the services. This process approach makes it possible to describe the IT Service Management best practices independently from the structure of the organization.

Many of these best practices are clearly identifiable and are indeed used to some extent in most IT organizations. ITIL presents these best practices coherently. The ITIL books describe how these processes, which have sometimes already been identified, can be optimized, and how the coordination between them can be improved. The ITIL books also explain how the processes can be formalized within an organization. Finally, the ITIL books provide a frame of reference within the organization for the relevant terminology, and help to define the objectives and to determine the required effort.

By using a process approach, ITIL primarily describes what must be included in IT Service Management to provide IT services of the required quality. The structure and allocation of tasks and responsibilities between functions and departments depends on the type of organization, and these structures vary widely among IT departments and often change. The description of the process structure provides a common point of reference that changes less rapidly, which can help maintain the quality of IT services during and after reorganizations and among suppliers and partners as they change.

The list below identifies some benefits and possible problems of using ITIL best practices. This list is not intended to be definitive, but is provided here as a basis for considering some of the benefits that can be achieved and some of the mistakes that can be made when using ITIL.

Benefits of ITIL to the customer/user:
- The provision of IT services becomes more customer-focused and agreements about service quality improve the relationship.
- The services are described better, in customer language, and in more appropriate detail.
- The quality, availability, reliability and cost of the services are managed better.
- Communication with the IT organization is improved by agreeing on the points of contact.

Benefits of ITIL to the IT organization:
- The IT organization develops a clearer structure, becomes more efficient, and more focused on the corporate objectives.
- The IT organization is more in control of the infrastructure and services it has responsibility for, and changes become easier to manage.
- An effective process structure provides a framework for the effective outsourcing of elements of the IT services.
- Following the ITIL best practices encourages a cultural change towards providing service, and supports the introduction of quality management systems based on the ISO 9000 series or on BS15000.
- ITIL provides a coherent frame of reference for internal communication and communication with suppliers, and for the standardization and identification of procedures.

Potential problems/mistakes with using ITIL:
- The introduction can take a long time and require significant effort, and may require a change of culture in the organization. An overambitious introduction can lead to frustration because the objectives are never met.
- If process structures become an objective in themselves, the service quality may be adversely affected. In this scenario, unnecessary or over-engineered procedures are seen as bureaucratic obstacles that are to be avoided where possible.
- There is no improvement in IT services due a fundamental lack of understanding about what the relevant processes should provide, what the appropriate performance indicators are, and how processes can be controlled.
- Improvement in the provision of services and cost reductions are insufficiently visible, because no baseline data was available for comparison and/or the wrong targets were identified.
- A successful implementation requires the involvement and commitment of personnel at all levels in the organization. Leaving the development of the process structures to a specialist department may isolate that department in the organization and it may set a direction that is not accepted by other departments.
- If there is insufficient investment in appropriate training and support tools, justice will not be done to the processes and the service will not be improved. Additional resources and personnel may be needed in the short term if the organization is already overloaded by routine IT Service Management activities which may not be using 'best practices'.

These potential problems and mistakes could of course be avoided by understanding and using ITIL best practices in line with the needs of the business that the IT organization is there to support.

3.2 Organizations

3.2.1 OGC (CCTA)

ITIL is UK Crown Copyright and was originally created by CCTA. CCTA was the Central Computer and Telecommunications Agency of the UK government. On 1 April 2001 the CCTA ceased to be an organization in its own right and became part of the OGC (Office of Government Commerce), which is an office of the UK Treasury and now the new owner of ITIL. The objective of the OGC is to help UK government to achieve best value for money in all its commercial relationships, through the use of best practices. 'OGC aims to modernize procurement in government, and deliver substantial value for money improvements.' The OGC promotes the use of 'best practices' in many areas (e.g. project management, procurement and IT Service Management). The OGC publishes several series of best practice material written by UK and international experts from a range of public and private sector user and vendor organizations.

OGC's ITIL is a coherent set of clear, thorough and proven best practices to provide efficient and effective IT services.

3.2.2 itSMF

The Information Technology Service Management Forum (itSMF), originally known as the Information Technology Infrastructure Management Forum (ITIMF), is the only internationally recognized and independent user group dedicated to IT Service Management. It is owned and operated solely by its membership. The itSMF is a major influence and contributor to Industry Best Practice and Standards worldwide.

The first chapter of itSMF was set up in the UK in 1991. The Dutch itSMF (itSMF The Netherlands) was the next chapter, set up in November 1993. There are now itSMF chapters in more than 30 countries all over the world, which cooperate in itSMF International, and new chapters of itSMF are emerging every year.

itSMF chapters promote the exchange of information and experience which enables IT organizations to improve the services they provide. They organize seminars, conferences, special subject evenings, and other events about current IT Service Management subjects. They also publish newsletters and operate a website for information sharing. Task forces also contribute to the development of ITIL.

3.2.3 EXIN and ISEB

The Dutch foundation 'Exameninstituut voor Informatica' (EXIN) and the UK 'Information Systems Examination Board' (ISEB) jointly developed a professional certification system for IT Service Management (ITSM). This was done in cooperation with the OGC and itSMF. EXIN and ISEB cooperate to offer a full range of ITSM qualifications at three levels:
- **Foundation Certificate** in IT Service Management.
- **Practitioner Certificate** in IT Service Management.
- **Manager Certificate** in IT Service Management.

The certification system is based on the requirements for effectively fulfilling the relevant role within an IT organization. To date, Foundation Certificates have been awarded to over 250.000 IT professionals in more than 100 countries.

The Foundation Certificate is intended for all personnel who have to be aware of the major activities in IT service support and delivery, and the relationships between them. The Practitioner Certificate is aimed at the practical level of how to perform a specific ITIL process and the tasks within that process.

The Manager Certificate is intended for those who are required to control all the ITSM processes, to advise on the structure and optimization of the processes, and to implement them in a way that meets the business needs of the organization. Today, ITIL is recognized as the global de facto standard for IT Service Management and represents much more than a series of useful publications. The framework of ITIL best practices in IT Service Management is an entire industry of user and vendor organizations, formal training and qualification providers, tools and consulting services.

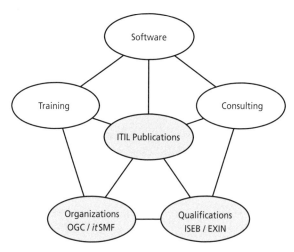

Figure 3.1 - ITIL environment

Figure 3.1, the ITIL environment, shows that the organizations involved also provide feedback between current practice (white ellipses) and theory (grey ellipses) to keep ITIL up-to-date. Furthermore, extensions and alternatives have been developed, some of which may be considered as IT Service Management methods in their own way. These alternatives often address the needs of certain groups or organizations whose specific problems are not adequately covered by ITIL.

The unique aspect of ITIL is that it offers a generic framework based on the practical experience of a global infrastructure of professional users.

3.3 The ITIL publications

Each of the ITIL publications addresses part of the framework. Each provides:
- An outline description of what is needed to organize IT Service Management.
- A definition of the objectives, activities, inputs and outputs of each of the processes required in an IT organization.

However, ITIL does not prescribe how these activities should be implemented, as this will be different in every organization. The emphasis is on an approach that has been proven in practice, but that, depending on the circumstances, may be implemented in a number of ways. ITIL is not a method, instead it offers a framework for planning the essential processes, roles and activities, indicating the links between them and what lines of communication are necessary.

ITIL is based on the need to supply high-quality services, with an emphasis on customer relationships. The IT organization will have to fulfill the agreements with the customer which means maintaining good relationships with customers and partners such as suppliers.

Part of the ITIL philosophy is based on quality systems, such as the ISO 9000 series, and Total Quality frameworks, such as that of the EFQM. ITIL supports such quality systems with a clear description of the processes and best practices in IT Service Management. This can significantly reduce the time required to obtain ISO certification.

Originally, ITIL consisted of a large number of books, each of which described a specific area of the maintenance and operation of IT infrastructure. Ten books describing Service Support and Service Delivery were considered as the core of ITIL. There were approximately 40 other books on supplementary subjects that related to IT Service Management, from cabling to managing customer relationships. However, the original series of books in the IT Infrastructure Library mostly approached IT Service Management from the IT perspective. The Business Perspective Set, containing three different titles, was introduced to bridge the gap between the business and the IT organization.

Furthermore, certain aspects of ITIL had a slightly dated approach. All of these older publications have been replaced by more recent editions. Figure 3.2 shows the current set of ITIL best practice publications. The Service Management processes, at the center of the ITIL framework, are divided into the two core areas of Support and Delivery.

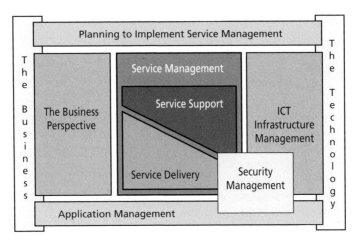

Figure 3.2 - The ITIL publication framework

The current set of seven publications will be updated in a new version of ITIL (v3), which is planned for the end of 2006.

3.3.1 Service Delivery

As indicated above, Service Support and Service Delivery are considered to be at the heart of the ITIL framework for IT Service Management. The ITIL book on Service Delivery describes the services the customer needs to support their business, and what is needed to provide these services.

The following subjects are addressed in the Service Delivery book:
- Service Level Management.
- Financial Management for IT Services.
- Capacity Management.
- IT Service Continuity Management.
- Availability Management.

The complex interrelationship between the processes described in the books on Service Support and Service Delivery is almost impossible to show in a diagram. The simplified diagram in Figure 3.2 illustrates the main outlines.

Service Level Management

The objective of Service Level Management is to make clear agreements with the customer about the type and quality of IT services to be delivered, and to implement these agreements. Consequently, Service Level Management needs information about the customer needs, facilities provided by the IT organization, and the financial resources available.

Service Level Management addresses the service provided to the customer (customer focus). By creating services based on the needs of the customer (demand pull) rather than solely on the basis of what is currently technically feasible (supply push), the IT organization can improve customer satisfaction. The chapter on Service Level Management in the Service Delivery book describes:
- How clearly defining the agreements in a Service Level Agreement can optimize the IT services at a cost that can be justified to the customer.
- How the service can be monitored, discussed and where necessary improved.
- How the service can be supported by Underpinning Contracts with suppliers to the IT organization.

Financial Management for IT Services

Financial Management addresses the prudent provision of IT services. For example, Financial Management provides information about the costs incurred while providing IT services. This enables a proper consideration of costs and benefits (price and performance) when deciding on changes to the IT infrastructure or IT services. The identification, allocation, forecasting and monitoring of the costs, as discussed in the chapter on Financial Management in the Service Delivery book, are all covered by the term 'costing', which in the current edition of ITIL is referred to as Budgeting and Accounting. These activities support cost awareness (what cost is incurred where?) and can also be used in drawing up budgets. With respect to the revenue stream of the IT organization, Financial Management for IT Services describes various charging methods, including setting goals for charging and pricing, as well as budgeting aspects.

Capacity Management

Capacity Management is the process of optimizing the cost, timing of acquisition, and deployment of IT resources, to support the agreements made with the customer. Capacity Management addresses resource management, performance management, demand management, modeling, capacity planning, load management and application sizing. Capacity Management emphasizes planning, and aligning to demand, to ensure that the agreed Service Levels can also be fulfilled in the future.

Availability Management
Availability Management is the process of ensuring the appropriate deployment of resources, methods and techniques, to support the availability of IT services agreed with the customer. Availability Management addresses issues such as optimizing maintenance, and design measures to minimize the number of incidents.

IT Service Continuity Management
This process addresses the preparation and planning of disaster recovery measures for IT services in the event of a business interruption. Known as Contingency Planning in the previously published book in ITIL, it emphasizes the links with all the measures necessary to safeguard the continuity of the customer organization in the event of a disaster (Business Continuity Management) as well as the measures to prevent such disasters. IT Service Continuity Management is the process of planning and coordinating the technical, financial and management resources needed to ensure continuity of service after a disaster, as agreed with the customer.

3.3.2 Service Support
The ITIL book on Service Support describes how customers and users can get access to the appropriate services to support their activities and the business, and how those services are supported.

This book covers the following subjects:
- Service Desk.
- Incident Management.
- Problem Management.
- Configuration Management.
- Change Management.
- Release Management.

Service Desk
The Service Desk is the initial point of contact with the IT organization for users. Previously, earlier ITIL books referred to it as the Help Desk. The major task of the Help Desk was recording, resolving and monitoring problems. A Service Desk can have a broader role (for example receiving Requests For Change - RFC's) and it can carry out activities belonging to several processes. It is the initial point of contact with the IT service provider for users.

Incident Management
The distinction between incidents and problems is possibly one of the best known, but not always the most popular, contribution made by ITIL to the IT Service Management field. Although this distinction may sometimes be confusing, it has a major advantage in that a distinction is made between the rapid return of the service, and identifying and remedying the cause of an incident.

The Incident Management process aims to resolve the incident and restore the provision of services quickly. Incidents are recorded, and the quality of the records determines the effectiveness of a number of other processes.

Problem Management

If a problem is suspected within the IT infrastructure, Problem Management aims to identify the underlying cause. A problem may be suspected because there are incidents, but obviously the objective is to be proactive and prevent disturbances where possible.

Once the causes have been identified and a workaround has been identified, the problem is classified as a known error and a business decision is taken whether or not to make a permanent fix to prevent new incidents. The process for making the fix is through a RFC If there is no business justification for a fix, but a temporary workaround or a permanent alternative has been identified, then the problem remains classified as a known-error.

Configuration Management

Configuration Management addresses the control of a changing IT infrastructure (standardization and status monitoring); identifying all significant components within the infrastructure; collecting, recording and managing details about the components; and providing information about them to all other processes.

Change Management

Change Management addresses the approval and controlled implementation of changes to the IT infrastructure. The objective of the process is to assess changes, and make sure they can be implemented with a minimum adverse impact on the IT services, while at the same time ensuring the traceability of changes, by effective consultation and coordination throughout the organization. Changes are made in consultation with the status monitoring activities of Configuration Management; with the initiator of the Request For Change; with Problem Management and with several other processes. Changes are implemented by following a specific path of definition, planning, building and testing, acceptance, implementation and evaluation.

Release Management

A release is a set of configuration items (CI's) that are tested and introduced into the live environment together. The main objective of Release Management is to ensure the successful rollout of releases, including integration, testing and storage. Release Management ensures that only tested and correct versions of authorized software and hardware are provided. Release Management is closely related to Configuration Management and Change Management activities. The actual implementation of changes is often carried out through Release Management activities.

3.3.3 Security Management

The objective of Security Management is to protect the value of the information, in terms of confidentiality, integrity and availability. This is based on security requirements laid down in Service Level Agreements, which relate to contractual requirements, legislation and organizational policy. Security Management aims at providing a basic level of security, independent of external requirements.

3.3.4 ICT Infrastructure Management

ICT Infrastructure Management is concerned with the processes, organization and tools needed to provide a stable IT and communications infrastructure that is aligned with business needs at acceptable cost. ICT Infrastructure Management is concerned with the flow of work from the definition of the business requirements through to the deployment and delivery of the final ICT business solutions. ICT Infrastructure Management is technology-focused.

The processes include the management and administration of the required resources, personnel, skills and training levels. The book covers the following life cycle stages: Design and Planning, Deployment, Operations, and Technical Support.

3.3.5 Application Management
Application Management provides an outline of the Application Management life cycle and is a guide for business users, developers and service managers of how applications can be managed from a service management perspective.

This book positions service management at the heart of the provision of information services to the business. Based on this perspective, applications should be managed throughout their life cycle with the business objectives in mind.

3.3.6 Business Perspective
This book is concerned with helping business managers to understand IT service provision. Issues covered include Business Continuity Management, Partnerships and Outsourcing, Surviving Change and Transformation of business practices through radical change.

3.3.7 Planning to Implement Service Management
There is now much experience throughout the world with planning and implementing programs to optimize IT Service Management. The main aims of this book are to give practical guidance on the key issues that need to be considered when planning for the implementation of IT service management, and to explain the essential steps needed to implement or improve service provision.

Guidance is given on assessing the alignment between the business needs and the services provided, and on how to implement a program of changes that will lead to measurable and continuous improvements.

Analyzing the current and future needs of the organization and implementing the required solution should be considered as a project, or as a series of projects in an improvement program. A key advantage of this approach is that it will provide the organization with clear decision points where it can decide to terminate, continue, or modify the project/program. In this context, the ITIL books recommend the adoption of a formal project management method, such as PRINCE2 (Projects IN Controlled Environments, 2nd version), to manage such projects.

Each project is based on an analysis of the current situation, the desired situation, and the path in between. In most cases, the alternatives will be compared on the basis of:
- Benefits to the organization.
- Risks, obstacles and potential problems.
- Transition costs and long-term costs.
- Costs of continuing the current approach.

Identifying the potential alternatives may well be a project in itself. Experience shows that you should be aware that ITIL is no magic formula.

You should be particularly wary of so-called ITIL implementation projects that have a hidden agenda, such as a reorganization or merger. ITIL describes the best practice for improving IT Service Management, it is not an organizational cookbook. ITIL primarily provides a frame of reference for process structures, roles and responsibilities in the IT organization and, to a much lesser extent, a guideline for the structure of that organization. If a project aims to improve the organization as such, it is advisable to involve experts in this field.

A baseline measurement or health check can provide a good start for process improvements. Such an assessment of the IT Service Management processes can help identify the strengths and weaknesses of the organization, and define clear objectives for an improvement project. After some time the measurement can be repeated to show the progress of the project or program.

4 INCIDENT MANAGEMENT

4.1 Introduction

Incident Management is a reactive task, i.e. reducing or eliminating the effects of actual or potential disturbances in IT services, thus ensuring that users can get back to work as soon as possible. For this reason, incidents are recorded, classified and allocated to appropriate specialists; incident progress is monitored; and incidents are resolved and subsequently closed.

Because this requires close contacts with the users, the focal point of the incident management process is usually through the Service Desk function, which serves as a front office for the back office of underlying specialist departments and suppliers. Incident Management is essential to the other ITIL processes as it provides valuable information about infrastructure errors.

Figure 4.1 below gives an example of Incident Management as a horizontal process in the organization that provides effective management and controls the incident workflow.

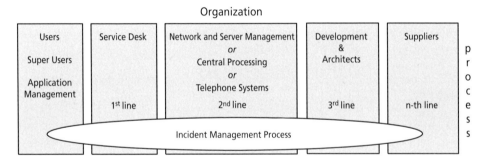

Figure 4.1 - Position of the Incident Management process in relation to the functions or departments of an IT organization

4.1.1 Terminology

Incident

The ITIL Service Support book defines an Incident as:

> *Incident - Any event which is not part of the standard operation of a service and which causes, or may cause, an interruption to, or a reduction in the quality of that service.*

In recognition of common practice, ITIL then goes on to broaden the interpretation of this definition of 'Incident', so that almost all calls to the Service Desk can be recorded and monitored as Incidents.

In this context, 'Incidents' include not only hardware and software errors, but also Service Requests - because both are handled in a similar way. That is, Incident Management handles their complete life cycles.

Service Requests can be made for 'standard services': that are agreed to be provided under SLA's; are delivered through agreed procedures which have appropriate checks and controls; and where records are maintained, e.g. on the CMDB.

Examples of Service Requests include:
■ Functional question or request for information.
■ Status inquiry.
■ Password reset.
■ Requests for batch jobs, restores and password authorizations.
■ Database extraction.
■ Request to provide new employee with appropriate IT functionality/services.

A Service Request may be for a Standard Change, which, as long as it is covered by a 'standard service', is handled under Incident Management and is not subject to the Request For Change process.

Service Request - *request from a user for support, delivery, information, advice or documentation, not being a failure in the IT infrastructure.*

If a Service is requested that is not for a defined 'standard service', and it alters the state of the infrastructure, then it triggers a Request For Change (RFC).

Request For Change - *formal part of the Change Management process, used to record details of a request for a change to any Configuration Item (CI) within an infrastructure, or to services, procedures and items associated with the infrastructure.*

An RFC is not handled by Incident Management but is dealt with formally by Change Management.

Impact, urgency and priority
When several incidents are being dealt with at the same time, priorities have to be set. These priorities are based on the seriousness of the error to the business and the user. In consultation with the user, and in accordance with the provisions of the SLA, the Service Desk assigns the priority, which determines the order in which incidents are dealt with. When incidents are escalated to second-line (tier two), third-line (tier three) or higher level support, their priority is maintained or may be adjusted in consultation with the Service Desk.

Of course, each user will think that their incident has the highest priority, but user requirements are often subjective. To make an objective assessment, the following criteria are discussed with the user:
■ **Impact of the incident** - extent of the deviation from the normal service level, in terms of the number of users or business processes affected. *Major Incidents* are those for which the degree of impact on the user community is extreme. Incidents for which the timescale of disruption - to even a relatively small percentage of users - becomes excessive should also be regarded as major.
■ **Urgency of the incident** - the acceptable delay, to the user or business process, in solving the incident.

The priority is determined primarily on the basis of urgency and impact. For incidents with the same priority, the effort required to solve them can determine the order in which they are dealt with. For example an incident with a low impact that can be resolved easily, may be dealt with before an incident with a higher impact and requiring a greater effort.

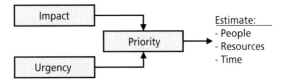

Figure 4.2 - Determining the impact, urgency and priority (source: itSMF)

Incident Management has options for reducing the impact or urgency, such as swapping hardware or assigning another print queue. The impact and urgency may also change during the life of an incident, for example when it affects more users or during critical periods.
Impact and urgency can be combined in a matrix, such as in Table 4.1.

I M P A C T

priority ╱ resolution time	high	medium	low
high	critical < 1 hour	high < 8 hours	medium < 24 hours
medium	high < 8 hours	medium < 24 hours	low < 48 hours
low	medium < 24 hours	low < 48 hours	planning planned

(left axis label: URGENCY)

Table 4.1 - Example of a priority coding system (source: itSMF)

Escalation
If an incident cannot be resolved by first-line support within the agreed time, then more expertise or authority will have to be involved. This is known as escalation and can take place at any time and at any support level (tier) in the resolution process.

We distinguish between functional and hierarchical escalation:
- **Functional escalation (horizontal)** - functional escalation means involving personnel with more specialist skills, time or access privileges (technical authority) to solve the incident. With this type of escalation departmental boundaries may be exceeded and may eventually include external suppliers.
- **Hierarchical escalation (vertical)** - hierarchical escalation means involving a higher level of organizational authority, when it appears that the current level of authority is insufficient to ensure that the incident will be resolved in time and/or satisfactorily.

The Incident Manager, who has overall responsibility for the Incident Management process, aims to have reserve capacity to cater for functional escalation of an incident, so that regular hierarchical escalation can be avoided.

First, second and Nth-line support
Incident routing, or functional escalation, was introduced above. The routing is determined by the required level of expertise, urgency and authority. First-line support (also known as tier 1 support) is normally provided by the Service Desk. Typically, second-line support is provided by the management departments, third-line by the software developers and architects, and the fourth-line by suppliers. The smaller the organization, the fewer escalation levels there are. In larger organizations, the Incident Manager may appoint Incident Coordinators in relevant departments to support him or her. For example, the Coordinators act as the interface between

the overall Incident Management process and the support line organization. They each coordinate their own support teams. Figure 4.3 illustrates the escalation process.

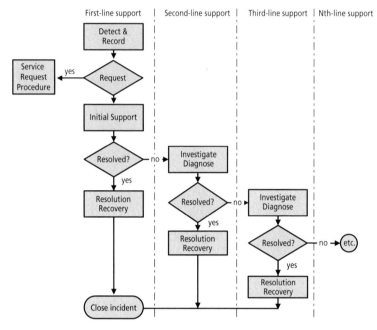

Figure 4.3 - Incident escalation. Note: 'Nth-line' is also known as 'Tier N'.

4.2 Objectives

The objective of Incident Management is to return to the normal service level, as defined in the SLA, as soon as possible, with the smallest possible impact on the business activity of the organization and the user. Incident Management needs to keep effective records of incidents so that it can measure and improve the process, provide appropriate information to other service management processes, and report on progress.

4.2.1 Benefits

- For the **business** as a whole:
  - More timely resolution of incidents resulting in reduced business impact.
  - Improved user productivity.
  - Independent, customer-focused incident monitoring.
  - Availability of SLA-focused business management information.
- For the **IT organization**:
  - Improved monitoring, allowing performance against SLA's to be more accurately measured.
  - Useful management and SLA reporting concerned with service quality
  - Better and more efficient use of personnel.
  - No lost or incorrectly registered incidents and service requests.
  - More accurate CMDB, as it is essentially being audited while incidents are registered in relation to CI's.
  - Improved user and customer satisfaction.

Failing to implement Incident Management may result in the following adverse effects:
- As nobody is responsible for monitoring and escalating incidents, incidents may become unnecessarily severe and reduce the level of service; users are referred repeatedly to other authorities, without the incident being resolved.
- Specialists are constantly interrupted by phone calls from users, which means they cannot do their work properly. Consequently, several people may be working on the same incident, may waste time unnecessarily, and may come up with conflicting solutions.
- A lack of management information about the user domain and services.
- Due to the above problems, the costs incurred by the customer and the IT organization will be higher than needed.

4.3 The process

4.3.1 Incident Management activities
Figure 4.4 shows the input and output of the process, and its activities.

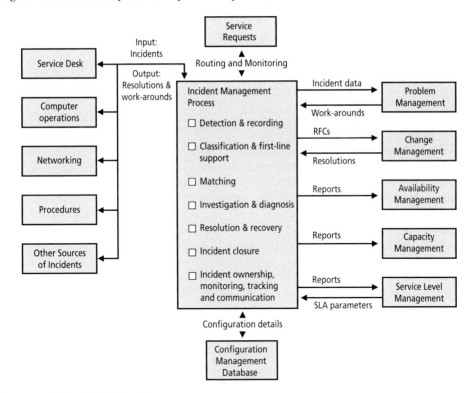

Figure 4.4 - Position of the Incident Management process

Incidents can arise from any part of the infrastructure and are often reported by users. Incidents may also be detected by other business or IT departments within the organization, and automatically through detection systems that have been set up to trap application and technical infrastructure events.

4.3.2 Relationships with other processes

Configuration Management
The Configuration Management Database (CMDB) plays an important part in Incident Management as it defines the relationships between resources, services, users and Service Levels. For example, Configuration Management shows who is responsible for an infrastructure component, so incidents related to a particular component can be routed more effectively. It also helps to decide on appropriate workarounds, such as diverting print queues and moving users to a different server. During incident registration, the configuration details are linked to the incident record to provide better information about the error. Where necessary, the status of the relevant components in the Configuration Management Database can be updated.

Problem Management
Problem Management has requirements for the quality of incident recording to facilitate the identification of any underlying errors. Problem Management assists Incident Management by providing information about problems, known errors, workarounds and temporary fixes.

Change Management
Incidents can be resolved by implementing changes, for example by replacing a monitor. Change Management provides Incident Management with information about scheduled changes and their status. Furthermore, changes can cause incidents if the changes are incorrectly implemented or contain errors. Incident Management will, in turn, provide information back to Change Management about these incidents.

Service Level Management
Service Level Management monitors the agreements with the customer about the support to be provided. Incident Management must be familiar with the Service Level Agreement (SLA) so that this information can be used when communicating with users. The incident records can be used to generate reports to determine if the agreed level of service is indeed being provided.

Availability Management
To measure aspects of the availability of services, Availability Management uses the incident records and the status monitoring provided by Configuration Management. A service can be assigned the status 'down', just like a CI in the CMDB. This information can be used to determine the actual availability of a service and the response time of the service provider. This capability requires time-stamping of actions taken in the progression of incidents, from their initial detection to their closure.

Capacity Management
Capacity Management is concerned with incidents that relate to its remit, such as incidents caused by a shortage of disk space or by slow response time. These incidents may be signaled to the Incident Management process by a business manager, by a system manager or by the system itself.

4.4 Activities
Figure 4.5 illustrates the steps included in the process:
- **Incident acceptance and Recording** - the incident is detected or reported and an incident record is created.
- **Classification and initial support** - the incident is coded by type, status, impact, urgency,

priority, SLA, etc. The user may be given suggestions to solve or work around the issue, even if only temporarily.

- If the call concerns a **Service Request** the relevant procedure is initiated.
- **Matching** - a check is made to see if the incident is known, and possibly related to an existing incident, problem or known error, and if there is a solution or a workaround.
- **Investigation and Diagnosis** - if there is no known solution then the incident is investigated.
- **Resolution and Recovery** - once the solution has been found, the issue can be resolved.
- **Closure** - the user is asked if they are satisfied with the solution and then the incident can be closed.
- **Progress monitoring and tracking** - the entire incident cycle is monitored, if it appears that an incident cannot be resolved in time or with the current level of expertise, then escalation will occur.

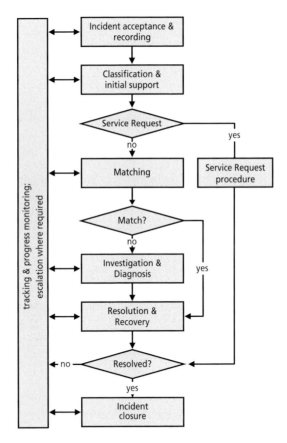

Figure 4.5 - Incident Management process

4.4.1 Acceptance and recording

In most cases incidents will be recorded by the Service Desk. All incidents should be recorded immediately, for the following reasons:

- Recording backlogs are rarely correctly caught up with.
- The progress of an incident can only be monitored if it is recorded.
- Recorded incidents assist with the diagnosis of new incidents.
- Problem Management can use recorded incidents to uncover the causes.

- It is easier to determine the impact if all calls have been recorded.
- Without recording, compliance with the agreed service levels cannot be monitored.
- Recording incidents immediately can prevent situations where either several people are working on the same problem, or nobody is doing anything to progress the incident to closure.

The place where the incident is detected determines who reports it. Incidents can be detected as follows:

- **By a user** - who reports the incident to the Service Desk.
- **By a system** - when an application or technical infrastructure event is trapped, such as when a critical threshold is exceeded, the event is logged as an incident in the incident recording system, and where necessary routed to a support group.
- **By a Service Desk agent** - who ensures that the incident is recorded.
- **By someone in another IT department** - who records the incident in the incident recording system or reports it to the Service Desk.

Recording the same incident twice must be avoided. Hence, when recording an incident a check needs to be made to see if there are similar open incidents:

- **If there are (and they concern the same incident)** - the incident information is updated or the incident is recorded separately and linked to the main incident record; the impact and priority can be amended if necessary and information about who or what detected the incident is added.
- **If there are not** - then a new incident is recorded.

In both cases the rest of the incident recording process is the same, although the first case is much simpler than the second:

- **Assigning an incident reference number** - in most cases the system automatically assigns a unique incident reference number. The user is usually informed of the number so they can refer to it in later communications.
- **Recording basic diagnostic information** - time, symptoms, user, person dealing with the issue, location and information about the affected service and/or hardware.
- **Supplementing incident information** - with other relevant information about the incident (e.g. from a script or interview procedure) or from the CMDB (generally on the basis of the relationship defined in the database).
- **Alerting** - if there is an incident with a high impact, such as failure of an important server, then the other users and management departments are warned.

4.4.2 Classification

Incident classification aims to determine the incident category to facilitate monitoring and reporting. The more extensive the classification options, the better. However, this also demands a higher level of commitment from personnel. Sometimes it is attempted to combine several classification aspects in a single list, such as type, support group and origin. This is often confusing. It is better to use several short lists.

This section addresses issues relevant to classification.

Category

First, incidents are assigned to a category and subcategory, for example on the basis of the suspected origin of the incident or relevant support group:

- **Central processing** - access, system, application.

- **Network** - router, segment, hub, and IP address.
- **Workstation** - monitor, network card, disk drive, keyboard.
- **Use and Functionality** - service, capacity, availability, back-up, manual.
- **Organization and Procedures** - order, request, support, communication.
- **Service Request** - request by the user to the Service Desk for support, delivery, information, advice or documentation. This may be covered by a separate procedure or dealt with in the same way as other incidents.

Priority

Next, the priority is assigned, to ensure that the support groups will pay the required attention to the incident. Priority is often indicated by a number based on the Urgency (How quickly does it need to be fixed?) and Impact (How much damage will there be, if not fixed soon?). Priority = Urgency * Impact.

Service

A list may be used to identify the service(s) related to the incident, with reference to the relevant SLA. This list will also supply the escalation times for the related service as determined by the SLA.

Support group

If the Service Desk cannot solve the incident within predefined timescales, it is determined which support group should deal with the incident. This routing, also described as functional escalation, is often based on the category to which the incident has been assigned. When defining the categories, the structure of the support groups may have to be considered.

Appropriate incident routing is essential for effective Incident Management. One of the Key Performance Indicators for quality of the Incident Management Process should therefore be 'the number of incidents routed correctly'.

Timelines

On the basis of the priority and the SLA, the affected user(s) will be informed about the estimated maximum time to resolve the incident (cycle time), and when updates on progress will be available. These timelines are recorded in the system.

Incident reference number

The user is informed of the incident reference number for future reference.

Workflow position (status)

The incident status indicates its position in the incident workflow. Examples of status include:
- New.
- Accepted.
- Planned.
- Assigned.
- Active.
- Suspended.
- Resolved.
- Closed.

4.4.3 Matching

After classification, checks are made to see if a similar incident has occurred previously and, if this is true, to see if there is a solution or workaround. If the incident has the same symptoms as a problem or a known error, then the incident can be linked to it.

4.4.4 Investigation and Diagnosis

The Service Desk routes incidents, for which no immediate solution is available or which go beyond their expertise, to a support group with more expertise and technical competence. This support group will then investigate and resolve the incident, or route it to another support group.

4.4.5 Resolution and Recovery

After successfully completing the analysis and solving the incident, the solving support group records the solution in the system. For some solutions, a Request For Change (RFC) will have to be submitted to Change Management. In the worst case, if no solution is found, the incident remains open.

4.4.6 Closure

Once a solution has been implemented, the support group routes the incident back to the Service Desk. The Service Desk contacts the person who reported the incident to verify that it has indeed been resolved. The incident can be closed if they confirm that it is solved correctly; otherwise the process is restarted at the appropriate place.

During closure, the incident record must be updated to show the incident's final category and priority, the affected service(s)/users/customers, and the component(s) (CI) identified as the cause of the incident.

4.4.7 Progress tracking and monitoring

The Service Desk, as the owner of all incidents, is responsible for progress monitoring and for informing the user about the status of their incident. User feedback may be appropriate after a status change, such as further routing or a change in the expected cycle time. During tracking and monitoring there may be functional escalation to other support groups, or hierarchical escalation to force decisions on the resolution.

4.5 Process control

Process control is based on the reports to the various target groups. The Incident Manager is responsible for these reports, and also for drawing up a distribution list and a reporting calendar. The reports may be highly detailed and customized for the following functions:
- **Incident Manager** - report required for:
  - dentifying missing links in the process.
  - Identifying conflicts with SLA's.
  - Keeping track of the process.
  - Identifying trends.
- **IT Line Management** - report for the support group management to facilitate control within each support group area. This requires information about:
  - Incident resolution progress.
  - Incident cycle time in the various support groups.

- **Service Level Management** - this report will primarily contain information about the quality of the services provided. The Service Level Manager will receive all information needed for Service Level reports to the customers. Reports to the customers should provide information about whether the agreements with respect to the Service Levels within the Incident Management process have been fulfilled.
- **Process managers of other Service Management processes** - the reports to the managers of other processes will primarily be informative. For example, Incident Management could provide the following information based on the incident records:
  - Number of reported and recorded incidents.
  - Number of resolved incidents, subdivided by resolution time.
  - Number of unresolved incidents and their status.
  - Incidents by period, customer group, support group and resolution in accordance with the SLA.
  - Incidents by category and priority, by support group.

4.5.1 Critical success factors

Successful Incident Management requires:

- An up-to-date CMDB to help estimate the impact and urgency of incidents. Alternatively this information can be obtained from the user, but it will be less complete, it might be highly subjective, and it will take more time to collect.
- A knowledge base, for example an up-to-date problem/known error database to assist with recognizing incidents, and what solutions and workarounds are available. This should also include supplier and other appropriate third-party databases.
- An adequate automated system for recording, tracking and monitoring incidents.
- Close ties with Service Level Management to ensure appropriate priorities and resolution times.

4.5.2 Performance indicators

Assessment of the process performance requires clearly defined objectives and measurable targets, which are often referred to as Performance Indicators. These are reported on regularly (e.g. weekly) by the Incident manager to produce historical data that can be used to identify trends. Examples of such parameters include:

- Total number of incidents.
- Average resolution time.
- Average resolution time, by priority.
- Percentage of incidents resolved within the SLA targets.
- Percentage of incidents resolved by first-line support (without routing).
- Average support cost per incident.
- Resolved incidents per Service Desk workstation or per Service Desk staff member.
- Incidents resolved without visiting the user.
- Number of incidents (or percentage) with initial correct classification.
- Number of incidents (or percentage) routed correctly.

4.5.3 Functions and roles

Processes span the hierarchy of the organization. This can only be successful if the responsibilities and authorities associated with the activities that have to be performed are clearly described. To provide flexibility it may be useful to use an approach based on roles. In smaller organizations, or to reduce costs, roles may be combined. For example, many organizations combine the Change Management and Configuration Management roles.

Incident Manager

In many organizations, the role of the Incident Manager is assigned to the Service Desk Manager. The Incident Manager is responsible for:

- Monitoring the effectiveness and efficiency of the process.
- Controlling the work of the support groups.
- Making recommendations for improvement.
- Developing and maintaining the Incident Management system.

Support group personnel

First-line support is responsible for recording, classifying, matching, routing, resolving (except those assigned to other support groups) and closing incidents.

The other support groups are primarily involved in investigation, diagnosis, and recovery, all within the set priorities.

4.6 Costs and possible problems

4.6.1 Costs

Costs associated with Incident Management include initial implementation costs such as defining and communicating the process and the procedures; training and instructing personnel (customers as well as support staff); and the selection and purchase of tools to support the process. Selecting the tools can be time-consuming. There are also running costs associated with the personnel and use of the tools. These costs depend greatly on the Incident Management structure, its scale of activities, its responsibilities, and the number of sites involved.

4.6.2 Possible problems

The introduction and implementation of Incident Management can be affected by the following problems:

- **Users and IT staff bypassing Incident Management procedures** - if users resolve errors by themselves, or directly contact specialist staff, without following the procedures, the information about incidents that is critical to successful Problem Management, Configuration Management, etc. will be incomplete. Additionally, the IT organization will not get information about the service levels and the number of errors, leading to management reports that do not adequately describe the situation.
- **Incident overload and backlog** - if there are an unexpectedly large number of incidents, there may be insufficient time for each incident to be recorded effectively, before the next incident is demanding attention. This can result in incidents that are not clearly described and a failure to correctly follow the procedures for allocating and routing incidents. Consequently, resolution becomes inefficient and the workload increases even more. It's necessary to have the right skills and competencies available as well as a supply of resources. Furthermore, addressing the front-end 'gateway' alone can cause downstream workflow problems.
- **Escalations** - incidents that are not resolved quickly enough or that require specialized resources will escalate. Too many escalations may have an adverse impact on the specialists by distracting them from their regular work.
- **Lack of a clear definitions and agreements** - if the services and products that are supported, and the levels of support, are not clearly defined in a Service Catalogue and agreed in Service Level Agreements, Operational Level Agreements and Underpinning Contracts, it is difficult for Incident Management to manage and to meet the expectations of customers and users.

- **Lack of commitment** - resolving incidents using a process-based approach requires a high level of commitment from management and staff. If the introduction of this approach within an organization requires a significant change to the current ways of working, there may be serious resistance within the organization.

5 PROBLEM MANAGEMENT

5.1 Introduction

As stated in the preceding chapter, Incident Management takes action if there is an incident, and ceases activities once service has been restored to the affected user(s). This means that the root cause of the incident is not always resolved, and the incident may recur.

Problem Management investigates the infrastructure and all available information, including the Incident Database, to identify the underlying cause of actual and potential failures in the provision of service. These investigations are needed because the infrastructure is complex and distributed, and the links between incidents may not be obvious. For example, several errors may lie at the cause of a problem, while several problems may be associated with the same error. First we have to identify a cause. Once the underlying cause has been identified and an acceptable workaround produced, the problem becomes a known error. Subsequently, once a permanent solution to the underlying cause can be produced a Request For Change (RFC) can be raised to eliminate the known error. Even after that, Problem Management continues to track and monitor known errors in the infrastructure. Therefore, information is recorded about all identified known errors, their symptoms, and the solutions available.

5.1.1 Definitions of 'problem' and 'known error'

Figure 5.1 shows the relationship between a problem, known error and RFC, and defines these terms.

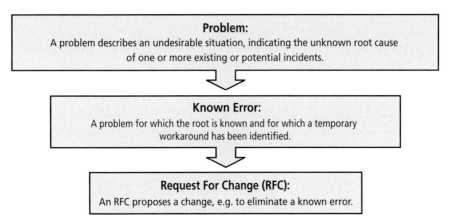

Figure 5.1 - Relationship between problems & known errors

In ITIL the term 'known error' is also used to indicate the status of an incident. In this Problem Management chapter we will use the term 'known error' for problems only: a known error is the status a problem gets when it has successfully been diagnosed and a workaround has been found.

5.1.2 Relationship with Incident Management

Problem Management supports Incident Management by providing workarounds and temporary fixes, but does not have responsibility for resolving the incident. Incident Management aims to resolve an incident quickly, by whatever means possible, including a workaround, while Problem Management takes the time to identify the root cause of incidents and problems and eliminate them. Problem records are created in addition to incident records. Thus, the investigation of a problem can lead to the resolution of a number of incidents if they are still open. Figure 5.2 shows the relationships between incidents, problems, known errors and changes.

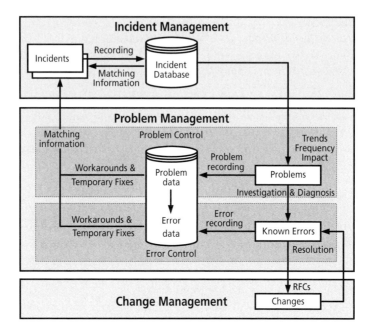

Figure 5.2 - Relationships between Incident Management, Problem Management and Change Management (source:itSMF)

5.2 Objectives

The objective of Problem Management is to resolve the underlying root cause of incidents and consequently prevent incidents from recurring. Problem Management includes proactive and reactive activities. Reactive Problem Management aims to identify the root cause of past incidents and presents proposals for improvement or rectification. Proactive Problem Management aims to prevent incidents from recurring by identifying weaknesses in the infrastructure and making proposals to eliminate them.

5.2.1 Benefits

Problem Management ensures that:
- Failures are identified, documented, tracked and resolved.
- Symptoms and permanent or temporary solutions for failures are documented.
- Requests For Change are raised to modify the infrastructure.
- Avoidable incidents are prevented.
- Reports are issued about the quality of the IT infrastructure and process.

Problem Management can improve the quality of service by significantly reducing the number of incidents and reducing the workload on the IT organization. Some of the benefits include:
- **Improved IT service quality and management** - as failures are documented and/or eliminated.
- **Increased user productivity** - by improving service quality.
- **Increased support personnel productivity** - as solutions are documented, Incident Management agents can resolve incidents more quickly and efficiently.

- **Improved IT service reputation** - because the stability of the services is increased, customers are more likely to entrust the IT organization with new business activities.
- **Enhanced management and operational knowledge and learning** - Problem Management stores historical information that can be used to identify trends, and which can then lead to measures to prevent avoidable new incidents. Historical information is also useful for investigation and diagnosis, and when preparing RFC's.
- **Improved incident recording** - Problem Management introduces standards for incident recording and classification to identify problems and their symptoms effectively. This also improves incident reporting.
- **Higher first-line resolution rate** - as Problem Management makes workarounds and solutions to incidents and problems available in a knowledge base, first-line support is more likely to be able to resolve incidents.

5.3 The process

5.3.1 Problem Management activities

The **inputs** to Problem Management are:
- Incident details, including workarounds.
- Configuration details from the Configuration Management Database (CMDB).
- Supplier details about the products used in the infrastructure, including technical details and the known errors within those products.
- The Service Catalogue and Service Level Agreements.
- Details about the infrastructure and the way in which it behaves, such as capacity records, performance measurements, Service Level reports, etc.

The major **activities** of Problem Management are:
- **Problem Control:** defining, investigating and diagnosing: problem control focuses on transforming problems into known errors.
- **Error Control:** monitoring and controlling known errors and raising RFC's: error control focuses on resolving known errors structurally through the Change Management process.
- **Proactive Problem Management:** preventing avoidable incidents by improving the infrastructure and raising RFC's.
- **Providing information:** reports on the results and major problems.

Outputs include:
- A known error database, which in fact is a subset of the problem database.
- Requests For Change (RFC).
- Up-to-date problem records (updated with information about known errors, solutions and/or workarounds).
- Closed problem records once the root cause has been eliminated.
- Management information.

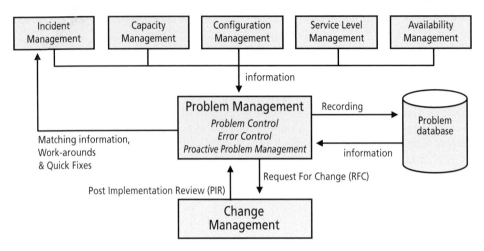

Figure 5.3 - Position of the Problem Management process (source:itSMF)

5.3.2 Relationship with other processes
The following processes are linked to Problem Management.

Incident Management
Incident Management is an important provider of information to Problem Management. Effective incident records are essential for successful Problem Management as this information is used to identify problems.

Problem Management supports the Incident Management process. Problem Management analyzes the problem, and - until a solution for the problem has been found - Problem Management can provide Incident Management with a workaround (found while studying the problem) to deal with the incident. Once the cause has been identified and a known error has been defined, it may be possible to provide a temporary fix that will prevent the occurrence of further incidents for the time being, or to reduce the impact of an incident. Ideally, Problem Management will provide an RFC that will lead to a permanent resolution.

Note: both Incident Management and Problem Management can provide workarounds.

Change Management
Change Management is responsible for the controlled implementation of changes, including the RFC's proposed by Problem Management to eliminate problems. Change Management is responsible for assessing the impact and required resources for the planning, coordination and evaluation of requested changes. It also informs Problem Management about the progress and completion of corrective changes. These corrective changes are evaluated in consultation with Problem Management. This results in a Post-Implementation Review (PIR), after which all associated incident and problem records (known errors) can be closed, provided the change has been successful.

Configuration Management
Configuration Management provides essential information about components of the infrastructure, blueprints, hardware and software configurations and services. The Configuration Management process also provides relationships between these components such as 'is connected to', 'uses', and 'forms part of'. These relationships are vitally important to the Problem

Management investigations as they define the interrelationships between the complete IT infrastructure.

Availability Management
Availability Management aims to plan and realize the agreed availability levels, and provides information to Problem Management. Problem Management supports Availability Management by identifying the causes of unavailability and remedying them. Availability Management addresses the design and architecture of the infrastructure and aims to prevent problems and incidents by optimizing availability design, planning and monitoring. Problem Management will often work with Availability Management in the analysis of service failures (Service Outage Analysis (SOA)).

Capacity Management
Capacity Management optimizes the utilization of the IT resources. Capacity Management provides essential information to Problem Management that can be used to define problems. Problem Management supports Capacity Management by identifying the causes of capacity-related problems and rectifying them.

Service Level Management
Service Level Management includes negotiating and agreeing quality targets for the delivery of IT services. Service Level Management provides information to Problem Management that is used to define problems. The Problem Management procedures should support the agreed service quality levels. Problem Management also fulfills this role for Financial Management and IT Service Continuity Management.

5.4 Activities

5.4.1 Problem Control
This activity is responsible for identifying problems and investigating their root cause. The imperative of Problem Control is to turn problems into known errors by identifying the underlying cause of the problem and identifying a workaround. Problem Control activities are shown in Figure 5.4.

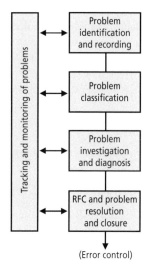

Figure 5.4 - Problem Control

Problem identification and recording
In principle, any incident with an unknown cause should be associated with a problem. However, this will normally only be worthwhile if the incident occurs repeatedly or is expected to recur, or if there is a single significant incident.

The activity of 'identifying problems' is often allocated to problem analysts. However, other personnel, such as Capacity Management personnel can also assist with the identification of problems.

Problem details are similar to incident details, but in this case there is no need to include information about the user, etc. However, the incidents associated with the problem should be identified and related to the problem.

Examples of instances when problems are identified:
- Analysis of an incident indicates that an incident recurs, and leads to a significant volume or trend.
- Analysis of the infrastructure identifies weak areas where new incidents may arise (also analyzed by Availability Management and Capacity Management).
- A serious incident occurs which requires a permanent solution, as further occurrences should be avoided.
- Service Levels are threatened (capacity, performance, costs, etc.).
- Recorded incidents cannot be linked to an existing problem or known error.

Trend analysis can uncover areas that need further attention. The additional efforts can be expressed in terms of the cost and benefits to the organization. For example, by identifying the areas that need more support and determining how relevant they are to the services provided.

This assessment can be based on severity, the 'pain factor' of incidents, which takes into account:
- Impact on business activities caused by the incidents.
- Number of incidents.
- Number of users and business processes affected.
- Time and cost of resolving the incidents.

Problem classification and allocation
Problems can be classified by area (category). Identification points to the lowest level CI's that affect the problem. The classification is accompanied by an impact analysis, which determines the seriousness of the problem and its effect on the services (urgency and impact). Next a priority is assigned, in the same way as in the Incident Management process. Personnel and resources are then allocated on the basis of the problem's classification, and time is made available to resolve the problem.

The classification includes:
- **Category** - identifying the relevant domain, for example hardware or software.
- **Impact** - on the business process.
- **Urgency** - extent to which deferral of the solution is acceptable.
- **Priority** - combination of urgency, impact, risk and required resources.
- **Status** - e.g. problem, known error, resolved, closed pending PIR.

The classification is not static, but may change during the life cycle of a problem. For example, the availability of a workaround or a temporary fix may reduce the urgency and impact of a problem, while new incidents may increase its impact and urgency.

Problem investigation and diagnosis

Investigation and diagnosis is an iterative phase - it is repeated several times, each time getting closer to the desired resolution. Often, it is attempted to reproduce the incident in a test environment. More expertise might be needed, i.e. specialists of a support group may assist with the analysis and diagnosis of the problem.

Problems are not only caused by hardware and software. They can be caused by a documentation error, human or procedural error, such as releasing the wrong software version. It is useful therefore to include procedures in the CMDB and subject them to version control. Most errors can be traced to infrastructure components.

Once the cause of the problem is known and the CI or combination of CI's responsible have been identified, a link can be established between the CI and the incident(s), then a known error can be defined, provided an acceptable workaround is produced. After that, Problem Management continues with the Error Control and Problem Control activities.

Temporary fixes

During the resolution process, it may be necessary to approve a temporary fix or emergency fix if the problem is causing serious incidents. If a temporary fix requires modification of the infrastructure then an RFC will have to be submitted first (before the root cause has been determined). If the matter is very serious and delay is unacceptable, the urgent RFC procedure may have to be followed.

5.4.2 Error Control

Error Control consists of monitoring and managing known errors until they are successfully resolved, where possible and appropriate. Error Control does this by raising a Request For Change to Change Management, and by evaluating the changes in a Post-Implementation Review (PIR). Error Control monitors all known errors from their identification through resolution. Error Control may involve many departments and covers both the production and development environments.

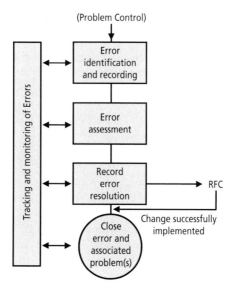

Figure 5.5 - Error Control

Error identification and recording

Once the cause of the problem has been identified and the relevant CI is known and a workaround has been produced, the problem is assigned the status of or linked with a 'known error' and the Error Control process starts. This can then be communicated to Incident Management if there are still open incidents. The known error and workaround can then also be used in the incident matching process for improved incident resolution.

Error assessment, investigating a solution

Personnel involved in Problem Management assess what is needed to resolve problems and - once the root cause has been determined - known errors. They compare different solutions, taking into consideration Service Level Agreements, costs and benefits and the impact and urgency of the RFC. All resolution activities should be recorded and there should be facilities for monitoring problems (known errors) and for determining their status.

Determining the selected solution, recording resolution

Problem Management needs to *determine* the most appropriate business solution to each problem. This involves determining whether a temporary fix is required or permanent resolution, or indeed both. Alternatively, it may be decided not to fix a problem e.g. because there may be no business justification for doing so. For example, a company that is experiencing failures with its in-house developed ERP system may have put a moratorium on any code fixes on the existing system, as the company has made the strategic decision to move to SAP by year-end. In this, and similar cases, the cost of making the fix may outweigh the benefits. In most cases, the cost of resolution is acceptable and the incident may be easily closed. In some cases it will be impossible to resolve the problems and their associated incidents without a disproportionate effort. Whatever the decision taken, the information concerning the known error should be recorded and made available to Incident Management.

Once an appropriate solution has been identified, sufficient information will be available to raise an RFC. Change Management then manages the implementation of the actual resolution through the RFC.

Failure sources in other environments

In most cases, failures are only identified in the production environment. However, products from the development environment (external supplier or internal developer) may also contain failures and known errors (faults). Note: For a development organization the software development environment is their production environment.

Normally, the development environment and suppliers should specify the failures contained in a specified version. Web sites and trade magazines often provide information about faults in popular products. Some vendors supply knowledge databases for their products that contain the known errors for these products.

If the known error in the supplied product is not too serious and the workaround is acceptable, or there is a business imperative to move forward with the release despite this shortcoming, it may be decided to use the developed item in the production environment, and then it is essential that the known errors, together with their workarounds are included within Error Control. A link is provided to Incident Management to ensure that incidents resulting from the implementation can be recognized quickly. Before starting the implementation, Change Management should decide if these known errors are acceptable. This decision is often taken under considerable pressure as the users are waiting for the new functionality.

Post-Implementation Review (PIR)

Once implemented, changes intended to resolve problems, known errors and their associated incidents have to be reviewed in a Post-Implementation Review (PIR) before the associated records can be closed. If the change was successful then all problem and known error records, together with their associated incident records can be closed. In the case of a problem record, its status is changed to 'resolved' in the Problem Database. Incident Management is informed so that incidents associated with the problem can also be closed. For major problems a separate Major Problem Review should also be undertaken to understand:

- What was done well.
- What was done badly.
- How can we do it better next time.
- How can we prevent recurrence of the failure.

Note: Many organizations implement the process so that the problem can only be closed after the associated incidents have been closed (and thus verified for closure by the customer), otherwise the problem would have to be reopened if the associated incidents could not be closed.

Tracking and monitoring

This activity monitors the progress of problems and known errors during all stages of their life cycle. These actions are performed within both Problem Control and Error Control. The objectives of this are:

- Determining if the impact or urgency of the problem changes, adjusting the assigned priority, where necessary.
- Monitoring the progress of diagnosing and implementing a solution, and monitoring the success of the RFC. For this reason Change Management regularly informs Problem Management about the progress of the RFC's it has submitted.

5.4.3 Proactive Problem Management

In general, Proactive Problem Management is concerned with the quality of the services and infrastructure. Proactive Problem Management (i.e. preventing problems) concentrates on trend analysis and identifying potential incidents before they occur. This is done by looking at components which are either weak or may be overloaded. If there are several domains, then attempts will be made to prevent failures occurring in one domain from also appearing in other domains. Weaknesses of infrastructure components can be identified and investigated.

5.4.4 Providing information

During the process, information about workarounds and temporary fixes is provided to Incident Management. Any impacted users can subsequently be quickly informed through the Service Desk. Problem Management uses the CMDB to decide what information should be provided and to whom. The SLA can also provide information about what has to be communicated and to whom.

5.5 Process control

5.5.1 Critical success factors

The basic requirements for successful Problem Management are:

- A well-defined process framework and set of process objectives, interfaces and resources.
- A set of comprehensive and well-documented procedures.

■ Good Incident Management data and effective cooperation between Incident Management and Problem Management. When allocating tasks and activities you should be aware of the conflict between fire fighting by Incident Management and identifying the root causes by Problem Management.

5.5.2 Management reports and Performance Indicators

The success of Problem Management is demonstrated by:
■ The reduction in the number of incidents, by managing and resolving problems.
■ The reduction of time needed to resolve problems.
■ A decrease in the cost associated with the resolution of failures.

Process parameters may also be reported for internal management purposes, to assess and control the efficiency of Problem Management.

Problem Management reports can be extensive and cover the following subjects:
■ **Time reporting** - divided into Problem Control, Error Control and Proactive Problem Management and by support group and supplier.
■ **Component quality** - incident, problem and known error details can be used to identify components affected by frequent failures, and to determine if suppliers meet their contractual obligations.
■ **Effectiveness of Problem Management** - details about the number of incidents, before and after solving a problem, recorded problems, recorded known errors and the number of RFC's raised and successfully implemented.
■ **Relationship between reactive and proactive Problem Management** - increasing proactive intervention instead of reacting to incidents shows an increasing maturity of the process.
■ **Quality of the services being developed** - services and components handed over from the development environment should be of a high quality; otherwise they will introduce new failures. Reports about new services and components and their known errors are relevant for quality monitoring.
■ **Status and Action Plans for open problems** - summary of what has been done so far, and what will be done next to reduce the impact of problems, including planned RFC's and required time and resources.
■ **Proposals to improve Problem Management** - if the information about the above factors indicates that the process does not comply with the objectives on the Problem Management process in the Service Quality Plan, then proposals may be made for process improvements and identification of the additional resources. Regular process audits may be carried out to review, plan and improve the process.

The reports depend on the scope of Problem Management. If the scope extends to components in the development environment, then known errors can be defined and monitored by Problem Management even while the software is being developed.

5.5.3 Functions and roles

Processes cut across the functions or departments of the organization and their hierarchy. Effective processes require that the responsibilities and authority associated with their implementation are clearly defined. To provide flexibility, it may be useful to take an approach based on roles. In small organizations, or for financial reasons, roles may be combined, for example Problem Management and Availability Management. The last bullet in 5.5.2 explains why many organizations avoid the combination of Service Desk / Incident Manager and Problem Manager.

Problem Manager
The Problem Manager is responsible for all Problem Management activities such as:
- Developing and maintaining Problem Control and Error Control procedures.
- Assessing the efficiency and effectiveness of Problem Control and Error Control.
- Providing management information and using it to proactively prevent the occurrence of incidents and problems.
- Managing Problem Management personnel.
- Obtaining the resources for the activities.
- Developing and improving Problem Control and Error Control systems.
- Conducting 'Post Mortems' or Major Problem Reviews.
- Analyzing and evaluating the effectiveness of Proactive Problem Management.

Problem support roles
The responsibilities of personnel with problem support roles include:
- **Reactive responsibilities:**
  - Identifying and recording problems by analyzing incident details.
  - Investigating and managing problems based on their priority.
  - Raising RFC's.
  - Monitoring the progress of known errors.
  - Advising Incident Management about workarounds and temporary fixes.
  - Conducting major problem reviews.
- **Proactive responsibilities:**
  - Identifying trends.
  - Raising RFC's.
  - Preventing problems spreading to other systems.

5.6 Costs and possible problems

5.6.1 Costs
In addition to the costs of support and diagnostic tools, there are also personnel costs that must be considered. In the past, time was rarely set aside for these activities. Apart from internal IT personnel involved in Problem Management, there are also the costs of hiring additional expertise from external suppliers and support organizations. However, the benefits of these activities should easily outweigh their costs.

5.6.2 Possible problems
Where possible the following issues should be avoided when implementing Problem Management:
- **Poor link between Incident Management and Problem Management** - if there is a poor interface between incident details and problem and known error details, then Incident Management will not be aware of the workarounds for the problems, and Problem Management will find it difficult to assess and monitor the impact of problems. There will also be less documented expertise about the IT infrastructure and less historical data. The success of Problem Management largely depends on creating this link between the two processes.
- **Poor communication of known errors from the development environment to the live production environment** - software and technical infrastructure transferred to the production environment should be accompanied by details of any known errors. Transferring the

knowledge of known errors at the time of the system deployment prevents wasting the time of the organization diagnosing errors that are already known. Thus, there should be effective data exchange between both record-keeping systems, or there should be a unified system.

■ **Lack of commitment** - if the previous approach was informal, there may be resistance to a formalized approach to Problem Management, particularly with respect to documentation and keeping time records. For this reason, personnel involved in Problem Management activities should be kept well-informed of the developments in the implementation of the process.

6 CONFIGURATION MANAGEMENT

6.1 Introduction

Every IT organization has information about its IT infrastructure. Such information is particularly likely to be available after major projects. However, the art is in keeping the information up-to-date. Configuration Management aims to provide reliable and up-to-date details about the IT infrastructure. Importantly, these details include not just details on specific items in the infrastructure (Configuration Items, or CI's), but how these CI's relate to one another. These relationships form the basis for impact assessment.

Configuration Management checks if changes in the IT infrastructure have been recorded correctly, including the relationships between CI's, and monitors the status of the IT components, to ensure that it has an accurate picture of the versions of Configuration Items (CI's) in existence.

If Configuration Management is effectively implemented, it can provide information about the following subjects:

- **Product policy:**
  - Which IT components are we currently using, how many of each model (version), and how long have we had them?
  - What are the trends in the various product groups?
  - Which IT components can be phased out and which require upgrading?
  - What licenses do we have and are they adequate?
  - Which maintenance contracts should be reviewed?
  - How standardized is our IT infrastructure?
- **Troubleshooting information and impact assessment:**
  - Which IT components will we need for a disaster recovery procedure?
  - Will the disaster recovery plan still be effective if the configurations are modified?
  - Which IT components are affected by a rollout?
  - Which network is equipment connected to?
  - Which software modules are included in each suite?
  - Which IT components are affected by a change?
  - Which RFC's are under consideration for specific IT components?
  - Which incidents and problems have occurred in the past and are currently relevant?
  - What IT components are responsible for known errors?
- **Provision of services and charging:**
  - Which IT component configurations are essential for certain services?
  - Which IT components are in use at a site and who are they used by?
  - What are the standard IT components that users can order that are supported?

6.1.1 Basic concepts

Configuration Items (CI's)

In the terminology of Configuration Management, IT components and the services provided with them are known as Configuration Items (CI's). As shown in Figure 6.1, CI's can include PC hardware, all kinds of software, active and passive network components, servers, central processors, documentation, procedures, services and all other IT components to be controlled by the IT organization.

If Configuration Management is applied to Information Systems rather than Information Technology alone, the CMDB may also be used to store and control details of IT users, IT staff and business units. Those CI's will have to be subject to Change Management as well, for example in staff introduction and exit processes.

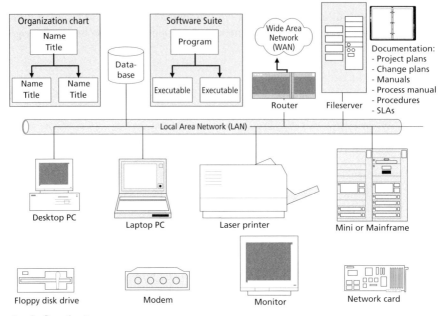

Figure 6.1 - Configuration Items

Configuration Management Database (CMDB)
All CI's are included in the Configuration Management Database (CMDB). The CMDB keeps track of all IT components, their versions and status and the relationships between them. In its most basic form, a CMDB could consist of paper forms or a set of spreadsheets.

Development departments often use something like a CMDB for version control of all program modules. A CMDB could consist of several physical databases that form a logical entity. It is advisable to optimize the integration.

Configuration Management should not be confused with Asset Management:
- **Asset Management** is an accounting process for monitoring assets whose purchase price exceeds a defined limit, which keeps records of the purchase price, depreciation, business unit and location. An effective Asset Management system can provide a basis for setting up a Configuration Management system.
- **Configuration Management** goes beyond Asset Management, by keeping technical information on CI's and details of the relationships between CI's and the standardization and authorization of CI's. Configuration Management also monitors feedback about current information such as the status of IT components, their location, and the changes that have been made to them.

6.2 Objectives
Configuration Management aims to assist with managing the economic value of the IT services (a combination of customer requirements, quality and costs) by maintaining a logical model of

the IT infrastructure and IT services, and providing information about them to other business processes. Configuration Management implements this by identifying, monitoring, controlling and providing information about Configuration Items and their versions.

The objectives of Configuration Management include:
- Keeping reliable records of details of IT components and services provided by the organization.
- Providing accurate information and documentation to support the other Service Management processes.

6.2.1 Benefits
Configuration Management contributes to the cost-effective provision of high quality IT services by:
- **Managing IT components** - the IT components are essential to the delivery of IT services. Each element of the IT services will include one or more CI's and Configuration Management checks what happens to them.
- **High quality IT services** - Configuration Management assists with processing changes, identifying and solving problems and supporting users. This reduces the number of errors and therefore also reduces costs by preventing duplication of effort.
- **Effective problem solving** - Configuration Management assists with localizing the affected CI's and manages the modification and replacement of the CI's. Configuration Management also provides information about trends as an input to Problem Management.
- **More rapid processing of changes** - Configuration Management facilitates rapid and accurate impact analysis so changes can be processed more quickly and more effectively.
- **Better control of software and hardware** - the rollout of packages can be combined, possibly also with hardware rollouts, such that the whole combination can be tested in advance. The CMDB and baselines (infrastructure snapshots, recorded positions) can be used to develop test and distribution plans for specific groups. The CMDB also contains details about reliable software versions for back-outs.
- **Improved security** - managing the versions used provides information about the authorized changes to CI's and the use of different software versions. Information from the CMDB can also assist with monitoring licenses.
- **Compliance with legal requirements** - illegal copies will be identified when audit results are compared with the CMDB. This can bring extra benefits because illegal software can contain viruses. In this way Configuration Management can prevent the introduction of viruses into the organization. The introduction of illegal and contaminated software by staff may not be easily avoidable for some organizations. However, the fact that staff *know* that they will be discovered due to the existence of Configuration Management, CMDB and audits, along with the knowledge that subsequent disciplinary action will be taken, can certainly discourage this practice. It is the thought that no-one will find out that will encourage staff to break the rules on illegal software.
- **More precise expenditure planning** - the CMDB can provide information about maintenance costs and contracts, licenses and expiration dates.
- **Better support for Availability Management and Capacity Management** - these processes depend on correct configuration details for analyzing and planning services.
- **A solid foundation for IT Service Continuity Management** - if there is a backup copy of the CMDB in a safe place, it can play an important part in restoring services after a disaster. The CMDB is also essential in identifying the CI's required for disaster recovery, including the relevant procedures and the manuals if they are included in the CMDB.

6.3 Process

6.3.1 Configuration Management activities

The following is a summary of the Configuration Management processes. The first two areas, Planning and Identification, deal with setting up the discipline whilst the others deal with running the discipline.

- **Planning** - determines the strategy, policy and objectives of the process, analysis of available information, identifying tools and resources, creating interfaces with other processes, projects, suppliers, etc.
- **Identification** - sets up the processes to keep the database up-to-date. The activities include developing a data model for recording all IT infrastructure components, the relationships between them and information about their owner or person responsible for them, status and available documentation. Procedures for new CI's and for changes to CI's must also be developed. As the demands for information are changing continuously, the identification of configuration data is also changing continuously.
- **Control** - ensures that the CMDB is always up-to-date by only admitting, recording and monitoring authorized and identified CI's. Control ensures that no CI is added, changed, replaced or removed without appropriate documentation, such as an approved RFC with an updated specification.
- **Status accounting** - stores current and historical details about the status of CI's during their life cycle. Status monitoring can be used to identify changes in the status such as 'under development', 'being tested', 'stock', 'live use', and 'phased out'.
- **Verification** - verifies the Configuration Management Database by audits of the IT infrastructure to confirm the existence of recorded CI's and to check the accuracy of the records.
- **Reporting** - provides information to other processes and reports about the trends and developments in the use of CI's.

6.3.2 Relationship with other processes

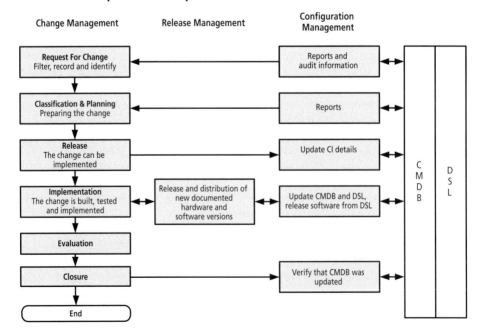

Figure 6.2 - Relationships between the CMDB and other processes

Configuration Management is heavily dependent on and has a high level of integration with Change and Release Management. It also supports a number of the other disciplines.

Incident Management

Incident Management needs information across the whole infrastructure. When recording incidents, Incident Management needs to access CI information, e.g. to determine the CI's location and owner, to determine if there is a problem or a known error with a workaround associated with the CI, which customers and which services are impacted, and the relevant SLA.

Problem Management

Problem Management needs information about the complexity of the infrastructure. Problem Management should be able to link problems and known errors to CI's and uses CMDB data to analyze incidents and problems. Verification of the actual configuration of the infrastructure against the authorized configuration in the CMDB can identify deviations or defects in the infrastructure.

Change Management

Change Management uses the CMDB to identify the impact of changes to be implemented. Change Management authorizes changes and associates changes with the relevant CI's. Change Management is responsible for recording RFC's. Thus, Change Management provides the major input for updating the CMDB.

Change Management is essential to the successful implementation of Configuration Management.

Release Management

Release Management provides information about release plans with versions and status of CI's covering major and minor releases. Release Management provides information about implemented changes. Before implementing a change it requests information about CI's such as the status, location and source code location in the DSL.

Service Level Management

Service Level Management (SLM) needs information about services along with the relationships between services and the underlying infrastructure CI's. SLM data can also be stored on the CMDB and related to the appropriate CI's. The Service Level (e.g. Gold, Silver, Bronze) can be recorded against the service CI, or the component hardware or software CI.

Financial Management

Financial Management needs information about the use of services and CI's, for example which department uses a processing service and who has a PC. It combines this with information from the SLA's to determine the prices to be charged. This process also monitors IT components and investments (Asset Management).

Availability Management

Availability Management uses the CMDB to identify the CI's, which contribute to a service and for Component Failure Impact Analysis (CFIA). It draws up plans for changes to address identified weaknesses. The availability of a service (chain of infrastructure components) is only as good as the weakest component (link in the chain). Configuration Management provides information about the composition of the chain, as well as about each of the elements.

IT Service Continuity Management

IT Service Continuity Management uses standard configurations from the CMDB (baselines) to specify disaster recovery requirements and checks that these configurations are available at the disaster recovery site.

Capacity Management

Capacity Management uses data from the CMDB to plan the optimization of the IT infrastructure, to allocate the workload and to develop a capacity plan.

6.4 Activities

6.4.1 Planning

The aim, objectives, scope and priorities of Configuration Management have to be defined within Service Management and should be aligned with the business objectives. The scope of Configuration Management is detailed in the Identification step. The relevant steps to implement Configuration Management are outside the scope of this book.

6.4.2 Identification

Identification relates to defining and maintaining naming conventions and version numbers of physical components of the IT infrastructure along with documentation, the relationships between them and the relevant attributes. Baseline configurations of current and future hardware are described in the form of CI clusters.

The general question about the identification of IT components is:

'What services and associated IT infrastructure components should be controlled by Service Management disciplines and what information do we need for that?'

When developing an identification system, decisions have to be taken about the scope and level of detail of the information to be recorded. An owner or stakeholder has to be identified for each property (characteristic) to be recorded. The more properties that are recorded, the more effort it will take to update the information. The general question above can be detailed to determine the information to be recorded. Examples of such questions are:

- What resources are available for collecting and updating the information?
- How mature are administrative and logistics processes?
- At what levels are components installed, replaced, developed and/or distributed by the organization, independently of the major component?
- What activities carried out by third parties should be measurable and under control?
- Which components will impact the services if they are affected by a fault and what information is relevant when diagnosing such faults?
- Which components should have their status and status history recorded?
- Which components are used in the organization in several versions or variants?
- Which components may affect the capacity and availability of the services after a change?
- Which high-cost components should be protected against theft or loss?
- What are the current and future information needs of the other processes?
- Which components should have information such as the serial number, purchase date, and supplier available, and what information does the accounting department require?
- What requirements are associated with the provisions of the SLA?

- What information do we need for charging purposes?
- Are our ambitions realistic or should some issues be deferred?

The answers to these questions provide information about a number of activities. A decision has to be made on the scope (breadth) of the CMDB, the level of breakdown (depth) and the level of detail (detail). The depth can be divided into: the number of levels, the relationships to be tracked, naming conventions, and attributes. These areas are discussed below.

Detailing the Scope (of CI Types)

When setting up a CMDB and when updating the data model of entities and relations, it has to be decided what part of the IT infrastructure should be controlled by Configuration Management. For example, should PDA's, networked copiers and fax machines, keyboards and IT staff, be included, or are they out of scope? The Configuration Management scope affects the scope of diagnoses by Problem Management, impact analysis by Change Management, the verifiability of SLA's, the analysis and planning by Availability Management and impact management.

Additionally, the IT services and their contribution to, or impact on the customers' business activities, can also be analyzed and recorded in the CMDB with the agreements made with the users about support and services.

The scope can be divided into areas with their own information requirements and approach to implementation. Examples of these areas are workstations, data communication, file, print and application services, central processing, databases, IT systems and telephone services. To develop each area, a separate project can be set up in the relevant management environment.

The scope of the CMDB can also include documentation, such as Service Level Agreements (SLA's), procedures, manuals, technical specifications, organization charts, people and project plans. Like other CI's, these documents will be physically present elsewhere, but are entered in the CMDB under their version number, date of publication, author and other information. Hence, these document characteristics can be controlled by Configuration Management, Change Management and Release Management.

Figure 6.3 shows the relationships between a service and CMDB components. Underneath this we find the other CI's required for the service. Keeping track of these relationships makes it easier to determine the impact of incidents on the services. It is also possible to generate a report of all components used for a service. This information can then be used to plan improvements to the service. The CI 'service' can also have relationships with other CI's such as agreements with the customer in the form of a Service Level Agreement. In the example, Service B is completely outside the scope of the CMDB, in which case not all CI's that contribute to 'Service A' are covered by the scope of the CMDB, which means that Service A cannot be fully supported.

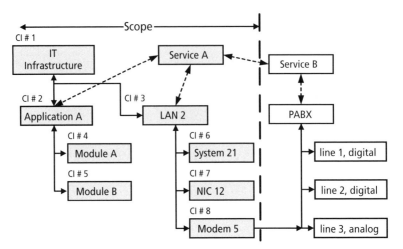

Figure 6.3 - CMDB scope

After determining the number of areas in the scope we can identify the CI life cycle elements to be included by the scope. Issues need to be resolved like: are CI's to be included in the CMDB while their status is 'under development' or 'on order', or are they only included once they have been incorporated in the infrastructure? The advantage of including products under development is that their specifications cannot be changed without consultation and that their transfer to the management environment will be smoother. The status monitoring activity of Configuration Management will be affected by this choice, but it may also broaden the scope of Configuration Management in terms of the product life cycle.

Level of detail (attributes)
Determining the level of detail of attributes held for each type of CI is an important aspect of setting up Configuration Management. One size definitely does not fit all. This determines the information available about individual CI's and the names and attributes to be covered.

When determining the detail to be covered, the requirements of change, incident, problem and other management disciplines, along with the associated workload and available resources needed to support Configuration Management, must be carefully balanced.

CI relationships
The relationships between CI's are useful for diagnosing errors and predicting the availability of services. Many different logical and physical relationships can be recorded:
■ **Physical relationships:**
  - *Forms part of:* this is the parent/child relationship of the CI, e.g. a floppy disk drive forms part of a PC, and a software module forms part of a program.
  - *Is connected to:* e.g. a PC connected to a LAN segment.
  - *Is needed for:* e.g. hardware needed to run an application.
■ **Logical relationships:**
  - *Is a copy of:* copy of a standard model, baseline or program.
  - *Relates to:* a procedure, manual, documentation, an SLA, or a customer area.
  - *Is used by:* e.g. a CI needed for providing a service, or a software module which is called by a number of programs.

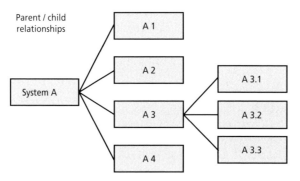

Figure 6.4 - CI parent/child relationships

Depth - Level of breakdown

When defining the depth of the CMDB, the levels of breakdown of a system or component, a hierarchy of components and elements is created. The parent CI's are selected and the number of CI levels of breakdown are defined. The highest level is formed as the overall IT infrastructure itself. The lowest level is the most detailed level at which control must be exercised. Incorporating a CI in the CMDB is only useful if the control of it and related information is beneficial to other ITIL processes.

Relevant considerations for depth are: the level at which the change is made, the significance of the component involved and the value of being able to perform impact assessments at that level. Taking the first point, if changes are made at a program level and not a module level then program level is sufficient, however, if they are made at a module level and modules are incorporated into a number of programs, then the lowest level should be the module. Taking the second and third points, recording the PC mouse in the CMDB is unlikely to be relevant in impact assessments and will not provide meaningful help in asset management.

Initial implementations usually start off at a high level and then selectively lower levels of breakdown are introduced especially where Release Management is implemented.

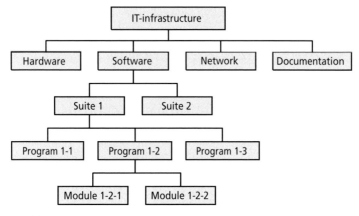

Figure 6.5 - CMDB breakdown

The following general considerations apply to the definition of the CMDB.

- The more levels, the more information must be handled. This increases the workload and results in a larger and more complex CMDB.
- The fewer levels, the less control and information there is about the IT infrastructure.

Handling Variants of a CI Type

If the CMDB has too little detail, the changes to underlying components cannot be monitored effectively. In that case, any change to the components of a parent CI will result in the creation of a variant of the parent CI. For example, a PC available with two types of hard disk could occur as Variant A and Variant B. If there are many changes to child components, the variant numbering will become complex and difficult to maintain. However, if there are more underlying levels then the variants can be maintained at the appropriate level. More attributes can also be recorded for the child components, and known errors can be associated with them, and during diagnosis questions can be asked such as: 'Which driver is needed for this hardware option?', 'Which segment is the network interface card connected to?' and 'Which programs use this library?'.

Handling Variants of a CI

Variants are also used if there are several forms of a CI that coexist; i.e. there is a parallel relationship. Versions exist, for example, if both an old and new version of a CI are used at the same time, i.e. there is a serial relationship. The effective use of these two concepts assists change planning. If each variant is then developed separately, separate version number systems should be introduced for each variant. This is undesirable as it makes the IT infrastructure more complex and increases the maintenance effort. In most cases it is advisable to continue to develop the source of all variants and where possible use the new version to create the required variants.

Naming conventions and labeling

Each CI should have a unique and systematic name to ensure it can be distinguished from other CI's. The most basic option is a simple numbering system, possibly divided into ranges for each area. New numbers can be generated when a new CI is created. If possible, the names should be meaningful, to support communication with users.

The naming conventions can also be used for physically labeling CI's, so that they are easily identifiable during audits, maintenance and incident recording. Some of the naming conventions recommended by ITIL include:

- Physical labels for hardware should be easily accessible and readable by users, and should be difficult to remove. It could be agreed with third party service providers that support contracts refer to the labels. A user should also be able to read out a label when reporting an incident.
- Controlled documents, such as SLA's, procedures, and organization charts should be marked with a CI number, version number and a version date.
- Copies of software should be stored in the DSL (Definitive Software Library), see the chapter on Release Management. All stored software should have a CI number, and where possible, installed software should also have a version number, and copy number.

Attributes

For each CI type the detailed development of the CMDB of its attributes and relationships need to be defined. Attributes are used to store information relevant to the CI type. The following attributes may be used when setting up infrastructure CI's in a CMDB.

ATTRIBUTE	DESCRIPTION
CI number/label or bar code number	Unique identification of the CI. This is frequently a record number allocated automatically by the database. Although not all CIs can be physically labeled, they all have a unique number.
Copy or serial number	Supplier's identification number in the form of a serial number or license number.
Audit tool identification number	Audit tools often use their own identifiers that may be different for each area. This attribute provides the link to this environment.
Model number/catalog reference	Unique identification used by the supplier in the catalog. Each version of a model has a different number, e.g. PAT-NL-C366-4000-T.
Model name	Full model name, which often includes a version identifier, e.g. 'PII MMX 400 MHz'.
Manufacturer	Manufacturer of the CI.
Category	Classification of the CI (e.g. hardware, software, documentation, etc.).
Type	Description of the CI-type, provides for the details about the category, e.g. hardware configuration, software package, or program module.
Warranty expiry date	Date when the warranty expires.
Version number	Version number of the CI.
Location	Location of the CI, e.g. the library or media where software CIs reside, or the site/room where hardware CIs are located.
Owner responsible	Name and/or designation of the owner or person responsible for the CI.
Responsibility date	Date the above person became responsible for the CI.
Source/supplier	The source of the CI, e.g. developed in-house, bought in from supplier X, etc.
License	License number or reference to the license agreement.
Supply date	Date on which the CI was supplied to the organization.
Accepted date	Date on which the CI was accepted and approved by the organization.
Status (current)	Current states of the CI, e.g. 'under test', 'live', 'phased out'.
Status (scheduled)	The next scheduled status of the CI, with the date and indication of the required action.
Cost	Cost of acquisition of the CI.
Residual value after depreciation	Current value of the CI after depreciation.
Comment	Text field for comments, e.g. to describe how one variant differs from another.

Table 6.1 - Examples of attributes

It depends on the Service Management tool how events like incidents are included in the CMDB: as a CI attribute or in another way. Generally, the numbers of the relevant CI's are included in the incident record, problem record and change record. Whatever approach is selected, relationships have to be maintained between the CI and the following records:

ATTRIBUTE	DESCRIPTION
RFC numbers	RFC number(s) currently or formerly open for the CI.
Change numbers	Change number(s) currently or formerly open for the CI.
Problem numbers	Problem number(s) currently or formerly open for the CI.
Incident numbers	Incident number(s) related to the CI.

Table 6.2 - Other records related to CI's

Maintaining the relationships between CI's is an important element of Configuration Management. Depending on the type of database, these relationships may be included as CI attributes, or in a separate table.

ATTRIBUTE	DESCRIPTION
Parent CI relationships	Key or CI number of the parent CIs.
Child CI relationships	Key or CI number of the child CIs.
Other relationships	Relationships between the CI and other CIs, apart from the parent and child relationships referred to above, e.g. this CI 'uses' or 'is connected to'.

Table 6.3 - Relationship attributes

Some databases have a method of providing a historical log of attributes and relationships. This can be useful for the 'Current status' fields to obtain information about downtime, repairs and maintenance. It can also be useful to track the ownership history.

It can be necessary to keep lists of attributes with technical information for each CI type. Each CI type will have different features. For example, for a PC: hard disk capacity, BIOS manufacturer and BIOS version, RAM, IP number, etc. Many System Management systems will record this information, in which case it is sufficient to provide a link to the CI type record to prevent duplication of the information. However, you should remember that these systems provide only the current information, without indicating if the results are from an approved change or an unauthorized situation.

Links should also be created to other reliable sources for information about: locations, users, departments, telephone numbers, budget holders and budget numbers. There are many options, but the workload and change control methods for maintaining these files must always be considered.

Baselines
A configuration baseline is a snapshot of a group of CI's taken at a specific point in time. A configuration baseline can be used as:
■ An authorized/supported product that may be incorporated in the IT infrastructure (these baselines are included in the product catalogue).
■ Standard CI's for recording cost information (cost items).
■ Starting points for the development and testing of new configurations.
■ A back-out if there are problems with new configurations after changes.
■ A standard for supplying configurations to users, e.g. a 'standard workstation'.
■ A starting point for supplying new software.

A standard workstation is a common example of a product baseline. By limiting the number of different standard workstations it becomes easier to estimate the impact and required resources for rolling out new functions and improvements, and to test them. The baselines can also be used to set a policy for combining and planning changes, e.g. for Packaged Releases. Baselines help to reduce management costs and facilitate project planning.

A product catalogue is another useful application of baselines. This catalogue lists the certified configurations which may be used in the IT infrastructure, and which users can request. In that case, a new CI is a copy from the catalogue, with a unique number and label.

Before a new model or product can be added to the infrastructure it has to be included in the product catalogue. This requires three decisions to be made to warrant the inclusion or exclusion of the new product:
- **Business** - does it serve the business interests of the user?
- **Finance** - are the support costs acceptable?
- **Impact** - is the impact on the service acceptable?

Setting up the CMDB
The CMDB can initially be populated with information from the financial records and existing IT infrastructure records, supplemented with technical data from suppliers. Only information with an identified stakeholder should be recorded, and the stakeholder must be committed to updating the information through Change Management processes.

6.4.3 Status accounting
The life cycle of a component can be divided into a number of stages with a status code assigned to each stage. This depends on the characteristics of the IT infrastructure that the organization wants to record. Keeping a record of the date of each status change can provide useful information about the life cycle of a product: order time, installation time and the maintenance and support it needs.

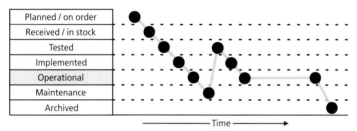

Figure 6.6 - Example of CI status monitoring

The status of a component can also determine what may be done with it. For example, if the status of non-operational spares is tracked, this hardware may not be deployed elsewhere without consultation, for example as part of a disaster recovery plan.
The following status classification could be used:
- **New CI's:**
  - In development/on order.
  - Tested.
  - Accepted.
- **Existing CI's:**
  - Received.
  - RFC open for the CI, new version has been requested.
  - The change has been approved and included in the plans, a new CI and documentation (which is also a CI) will be provided.
  - Undergoing maintenance.
  - Down.
- **Archived CI's:**
  - Phased out.
  - Deleted.
  - Removed.
  - Stolen.

- Sold or lease expired.
- In archival storage awaiting donation, sale, or destruction.
- Destroyed.

■ **All CI's:**
- In stock.
- Order has been received, or changed version available.
- Under test.
- Released for installation.
- Live (active), the CI is being used.
- Spare.

6.4.4 Control of CI's

The information must be managed effectively to keep the CMDB up-to-date. Whenever an activity changes the recorded characteristics of a CI, or the relationships between CI's, the change should be recorded in the CMDB. Note: changes to characteristics of CI's can only be made by a change authorized by Change Management; Incident Management can only change the *status* of an existing CI to reflect the reality of a situation e.g. system down.

Configuration Management controls all IT components received by the organization and ensures that they are recorded in the system. Hardware can be recorded when it is ordered or delivered, and software can be recorded when it is included in the Definitive Software Library (DSL).

One of the control tasks is ensuring that CI's are only recorded if they have been authorized and included in the product catalogue. For this reason, Configuration Management maintains close ties with suppliers, Incident Management, Problem Management and Change Management.

If changes coordinated by Change Management are made in the IT infrastructure then Configuration Management has to include this information in the CMDB. Configuration Management imposes requirements on the maturity of other processes in the organization, particularly Change Management and Release Management and the processes of the purchasing department.

To ensure that the actual situation reflects the authorized CMDB, the following actions are monitored by Configuration Management when a:
■ CI is added.
■ CI changes its status, e.g. 'up' or 'down' (useful for Availability Management).
■ CI changes owner.
■ CI changes in relationship to another CI.
■ CI is removed.
■ CI gets other relationships with a service, documentation or other CI's.
■ CI license is renewed or modified.
■ CI details are updated after an audit.

Where there are process problems then it is Configuration Management's responsibility to make sure they are resolved.

6.4.5 Verification and audits

Audits are used to verify if the current situation still reflects the details in the CMDB. For example, audit tools can automatically analyze workstations and report on the current situation and

status of the IT infrastructure. This information can be used to check and update the CMDB. Audits may be carried out in the following situations:
- After the implementation of the new CMDB.
- A period after implementation.
- Before and after major changes.
- After disaster recovery.
- At any other convenient time.

The following questions are asked during an audit:
- Are all RFC's, in all stages of implementation, recorded in the CMDB, and is this controlled by Configuration Management?
- Is the CMDB still up-to-date, and if not, why?
- What is the impact on Change Management (actual impact analysis of planned changes)?
- Does the naming of new CI's comply with the naming conventions?
- Are variants used correctly?
- Have the baseline configurations been recorded correctly, and are they immediately available?
- Do the contents of the Definitive Software Library (DSL) and the Definitive Hardware Store (DHS) correspond with the information in the CMDB? If not, why not?

Audits can also be carried out randomly or when the Configuration Manager thinks that the information may not be correct. If there is a link with the audit tools, then audits or delta reports can be generated almost daily for the relevant area.

Audit tools should not be allowed to automatically update the CMDB when discrepancies are found. All discrepancies indicate that Change Management processes have been bypassed and therefore must be investigated and dealt with retrospectively by Change Management.

6.5 Process control

Configuration Management should review and report on the effectiveness of, and the conformance with, the Configuration Management processes, and on the other processes that it depends on. It should also make sure the processes are operating in a manner that adds value without imposing unnecessary overheads.

6.5.1 Critical success factors

The critical factor for successful Configuration Management is that information in the database is up-to-date. This means that Change Management and Release Management must be strictly enforced and that there should always be a stakeholder for the information to be recorded.

When introducing Configuration Management, it is essential that the implementation is divided into stages correctly. Attempts to introduce extensive scopes of Configuration Management at once generally fail because the organization cannot cope with it. The records maintained before the introduction of the process should be phased out to prevent duplication. When introducing the process, it is important to promote some clear benefits of Configuration Management (Quick Wins). It is also important that the recording elements of the process are allocated to personnel who not only have the required skills but also the appropriate attitude.

6.5.2 Management reports and performance indicators

Configuration Management reports can include the following elements:

- Information about the quality of the process.
- Number of observed differences between the records and the situation found during an audit (deltas).
- Number of occasions on which a configuration was found to be unauthorized.
- Number of occasions on which a recorded configuration could not be located.
- Attribute level differences uncovered by audits.
- Time needed to process a request for recording information.
- List of CI's where more than a given number of incidents or changes were recorded.
- Statistical information about the structure and composition of the IT infrastructure.
- Growth data and other information about IT infrastructure developments.
- Summaries, reports and proposals for improvement, like recommendations for changes in the scope and level of CI's tracked by Configuration Management, due to business, technical, market price and other relevant changes.
- List of the personnel costs when implementing the process.

6.5.3 Functions and roles

Processes cut across the hierarchy of the organization. This is only possible if the responsibilities and authority associated with their implementation are clearly defined. To provide flexibility, it may be useful to take an approach based on roles and responsibilities. In small organizations, or for financial reasons, roles may be combined for example Change Management and Configuration Management. The tasks of the Configuration Manager could include:

- Proposing changes to the scope and level of detail of Configuration Management.
- Ensuring that the Configuration Management process is communicated throughout the organization.
- Providing personnel and training for the process.
- Developing the identification system and naming conventions.
- Developing the interfaces to other processes.
- Evaluating existing systems and implementing new systems.
- Planning and implementing the population of the CMDB.
- Creating reports on effectiveness, conformance and value.
- Organizing configuration audits.

6.6 Costs and possible problems

6.6.1 Costs

The costs of the introduction and implementation of Configuration Management largely depend on its scope and level of detail. These costs include the costs of hardware, software and personnel involved in setting up and then running Configuration Management. The costs of hardware and software depend on:

- Additional hardware required and its configuration.
- Additional software required and its configuration.
- License fees based on number of users.
- Application and database design, population, customization and implementation.
- Database development.
- Database maintenance.
- Additional personnel costs associated to the process.

The personnel costs depend primarily on the size of the organization and level of detail of the CMDB.

6.6.2 Possible problems

The IT organization should make a clear commitment to the characteristics of the IT infrastructure to be recorded, and it should provide the necessary resources for this form of management. The organization should also commit itself to the use of the CMDB and should incorporate any relevant data and data structures from any relevant databases used before the introduction of the CMDB into the CMDB. The CMDB should be looked upon as the core instrument of the IT organization and used as the prime source of information to everybody in IT.

The following problems may affect successful implementation:

- **Wrong CMDB scope or CI level of detail** - if the CMDB scope is too narrow, important parts of the infrastructure won't be easily checked, fixed, secured, or restored. If the CMDB scope is too wide, the cumbersome database will be an obstacle that slows down all service management processes. If there are too many levels, attributes, and relationships, it will take a great effort to maintain the CMDB. Too little detail can mean recording insufficient information about the CI's and related incidents, problems, known errors and RFC's.
- **Inadequate manual systems** - some organizations want to keep paper records for as long as possible and only purchase automated tools when this becomes unfeasible. This can introduce delays, confusion, and a shortage of personnel and resources. It is better to select a tool earlier on the basis of the functional requirements.
- **Affect of urgent changes** - there will always be situations where changes have to be implemented quickly. This often happens outside normal office hours. If the CMDB is also relevant in this situation, it is advisable to immediately record the change in the CMDB, but the person responsible may not be present. If this can wait till the next working day then the change records and the CMDB should be updated as soon as possible through the proper Change Management process.
- **Overambitious schedules** - if the schedule for the changes (RFC's) does not allow time for implementing Configuration Management, then the work will be delayed and Configuration Management will appear to be the bottleneck. Realistic schedules should be drawn up on the basis of past experience.
- **Management acceptance** - people may be hesitant to accept Configuration Management because it is a relatively new process that is not always clearly visible. There must be sufficient commitment for its successful implementation. Hence, the Configuration Manager must promote the process and inform the rest of the organization about it. Experience shows that the process costs will be much lower if Configuration Management is introduced as a separate discipline with dedicated staff and a manager responsible for the process.
- **Bypassing the process** - personnel in a hurry will try to bypass Configuration Management. If this situation still exists, even after providing all the information about the resulting risks of bypassing the process, disciplinary measures may have to be taken.

7 CHANGE MANAGEMENT

7.1 Introduction

The rapid development of IT technology and the business market means that change is now a matter of course. Business needs to change to improve their services and reduce their costs and need IT to support and be part of the continuing business change process.

However, experience shows that IT incidents affecting the business are often related to changes. The causes for such incidents are numerous: they may be caused by carelessness, a lack of resources, insufficient preparation, poor impact analysis, inadequate testing, or teething problems. If the incidents related to changes are not brought under control, the IT service provider, and consequently the business itself, can spiral out of control. The number of incidents rises, with each incident requiring fire fighting, which in turn may easily lead to the introduction of new errors causing new incidents. The daily planning of change often fails to take the increasing pressure of work into account so that change is poorly managed. This in turn has an impact on the routine operation and maintenance of IT services.

Change Management aims to manage the process of change and consequently limit the introduction of errors and so incidents related to changes. The motto of Change Management is:

Not every change is an improvement, but every improvement is a change.

Figure 7.1 shows the cycle of changes as a process supplied with proposals for new developments and improvements (Service Delivery and Problem Management), changes (requests made to Change Management) and solutions (Problem Management):

- **Innovation and improvement** - the introduction of new services and new technical capability in the IT infrastructure will be responsible for some of the new, long-term errors in the IT infrastructure.
- **Changes** - anything from a minor installation of a PC to the relocation of a mainframe; if done carelessly, changes will introduce errors into the IT infrastructure.
- **Corrective measures** - aim to correct errors.

Change Management operates like a thermostatic control between **flexibility** (allowing changes which may lead to errors) and **stability** (allowing changes to remedy errors). Corrective measures reduce the number of incidents, as a result of which the pressure of work will also fall.

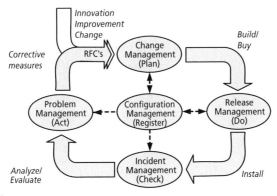

Figure 7.1 - Inputs to the change process

7.1.1 Basic terms
Change authorities
There are two authorities in Change Management:

- **The Change Manager** - the person responsible for filtering, accepting and classifying all Requests For Change (RFC). In a large organization, the Change Manager may be supported by Change Coordinators who represent him or her by liaising with the various areas of the organization. Change Management is also responsible for obtaining the required authorization. To some extent, the process already has the authorization by declaration, but it may be necessary to approach the IT Management (e.g. Steering Committee or Executive Committee) for some of the changes. The Change Manager is also responsible for planning and coordinating the implementation of the changes.

- **The Change Advisory Board (CAB)** - this consultative body meets regularly to assess, prioritize and plan changes. Normally, only the more significant changes are presented to the CAB. A CAB/EC (Emergency Committee) should be appointed with the authority to make emergency decisions. The Board's membership is flexible and includes representatives from all major IT sections:
  - Change Manager (chair).
  - Service (Level) Manager.
  - Representatives of the Service Desk and Problem Management.
  - IT Line Managers.
  - Business Managers (or their representatives) from the customer environment.
  - User group representatives.
  - Application development representatives.
  - Software and Systems managers.
  - Supplier Representatives.

Process scope
The scope of the Change Management process is determined alongside the scope of the Configuration Management and Release Management processes. Configuration Management provides the information to assess the impact of changes. After implementing the change, Configuration Management will update the CMDB. If the CMDB keeps track of mice and keyboards, then replacing a keyboard counts as a change. Determining the scope is a dynamic activity, as the scope can change and therefore the need for information from the CMDB will also change. Hence, the scope should be reviewed regularly and the CMDB data model should be updated correspondingly.

To ensure that Change Management and Configuration Management cooperate effectively, the changes and related information for the CMDB have to be recorded. It could be assumed that a number of routine management tasks, which are clearly defined and covered by procedures need not be controlled by Change Management. These are called Standard Changes and are developed using Change Models, which act as procedure design templates that are defined by Change Management. Examples of such routine activities include: creating user IDs, changing network connections and installing PCs. In the case of Standard Changes, the activities are not performed under the full Change Management process as changes, but can be classified as Service Requests under Incident Management. A careful assessment of routine operations can be useful to prevent Change Management becoming overloaded and too bureaucratic.

For example, if there are fourteen steps that are usually followed when a new employee is hired (establish an account, set up his or her workstation, set up e-mail, etc.), this type of routine occurrence does not require the scrutiny that significant changes to the infrastructure do. As a result, these kinds of standard changes become repeatable and once the Standard Change procedure is approved by Change Management they can be treated as Service Requests and are outside of the control of Change Management.

Change Models are also used to provide variants to the RFC process for different types of change (e.g. project created infrastructure change or network configuration change) to steer such changes through specific assessment, planning and approval threads. In these cases the RFC process is the backbone of these Change Models but using a repeatable template of work activities still involving Change Management and appearing on change schedules.

7.2 Objectives

The objective of Change Management is to ensure that standard methods and procedures are used, such that changes can be dealt with quickly, with the lowest possible impact on service quality. All changes should be traceable, in other words, one can answer the question, 'what changed'?

7.2.1 Benefits

To be able to provide IT services effectively, the organization should be able to deal with a large number of changes smoothly and responsibly.
Specific benefits of Change Management include:
■ Reduced adverse impact of changes on the quality of IT services.
■ Better estimates of the costs of proposed changes.
■ Fewer changes are reversed, and any back-outs that are implemented proceed more smoothly.
■ Enhanced management information is obtained about changes, which enables a better diagnosis of problem areas.
■ Improved user productivity through more stable and better IT services.
■ Improved IT personnel productivity, as they are not distracted from their planned work by urgent changes or back-out procedures.
■ Increased ability to accommodate frequent changes without creating an unstable IT environment.

7.3 The process

7.3.1 Change Management activities

The Change Management process approves or rejects each RFC. The process is facilitated by the Change Manager, but the actual decisions about more significant changes are taken by the Change Advisory Board (CAB). The CAB has members from many parts of the organization, as well as customers and suppliers. Configuration Management is responsible for providing information about the potential impact of the proposed change.

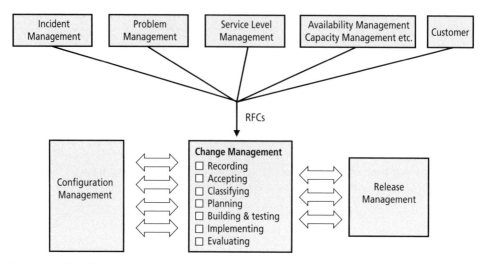

Figure 7.2 - Position of Change Management (source: itSMF)

Inputs for Change Management include:
- RFC's.
- CMDB information (specifically the impact analysis for changes).
- Information from other processes (Capacity Database, budget information, etc.).
- Change planning (Forward Schedule of Change: FSC).

Process **outputs** include:
- Updated change planning (Forward Schedule of Change: FSC).
- Triggers for Configuration Management and Release Management.
- CAB agenda, minutes and action items.
- Change Management reports.

7.3.2 Relationship with other processes

Change Management has the following relationships with other processes.

Incident Management

Incident Management has a two-sided relationship with Change Management. On the one hand, Change Management puts through changes requested by Incident Management to take away the effect of an incident. On the other hand, despite the many precautions, the implementation of changes can still lead to errors and so incidents. These may be related to poor implementation or to users who were not adequately prepared for the change. Relevant personnel in Incident Management must be informed of the implementation of changes, so that they can quickly identify and remedy any related incidents.

Configuration Management

Change Management and Configuration Management are tightly coupled processes, so much so that the two processes can effectively be integrated, a step which is recommended in the ITIL Service Support guidance.

Changes are recorded under the control of Configuration Management and impact analysis of changes is also done by Configuration Management. Configuration Management identifies the relationships between the CI (in the change being addressed) and other CI's, to show what is affected by the change.

Problem Management

The relationship between Change Management and Problem Management is much like that between Change Management and Incident Management. On the one hand changes are often requested to correct errors and so solve problems. On the other hand, if the implementation of changes is not adequately controlled, the changes can introduce new errors and so problems.

Release Management

Changes often result in the development and distribution of a new set of applications or technical infrastructure, which are subject to Release Management disciplines. Also many changes affecting the same area of IT applications or infrastructure are packaged together into a release that is subject to Release Management. This usually provides the benefit of more thorough testing and communication. The rollout of the new releases is controlled by Change Management.

Service Level Management

Service Level Management is involved in determining the impact of the changes on services and business processes. Depending on the situation, Service Level Management may be represented on the CAB. If a change has a major impact or high risk, its implementation and the timeframe will always have to be discussed with the customer. Change Management reports to Service Level Management in the form of a Projected Service Availability (PSA) report. In this report, Change Management lists the changes to the agreed SLA's and the impact of the Forward Schedule of Changes (FSC) on the service availability.

Availability Management

Availability Management initiates changes that aim to improve service availability. It also verifies if the intended improvement is actually obtained. Availability Management will often be involved in estimating the potential impact of changes, as such an impact could affect the availability of the service.

Capacity Management

The Capacity Manager should primarily be concerned with the cumulative effect of changes over an extended period, such as an increase in response time and the need for more processing, network or storage capacity. On the basis of the Capacity Plan, Capacity Management will regularly propose enhancements and changes in the form of RFC's to improve use of existing capacity as well as to extend it.

IT Service Continuity Management

Prevention measures and recovery plans that ensure the continuity of the services have to be monitored at all times, as infrastructure changes could make a plan unworkable or superfluous. Change Management works closely together with IT Service Continuity Management to ensure that IT Service Continuity Management is aware of all changes that could affect recovery plans and can take steps to ensure recovery can be completed.

7.4 Activities

Change Management uses the following activities to process changes:

- **Recording** - Change Management is responsible for ensuring that all sources of changes can submit RFC's and that they are adequately recorded.
- **Acceptance** - filtering the RFC's and accepting them for further consideration.
- **Classification** - sorting the RFC's by category and priority.
- **Planning and Approval** - consolidating changes; planning and approving their development and implementation; ensuring the required resources are available; and involving CAB where necessary to achieve the above.
- **Coordination** - coordinating the building, testing and implementation of the change.
- **Evaluation** - determining if each change was successful and learning lessons to improve the process.

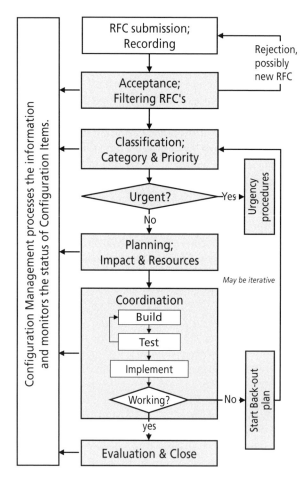

Figure 7.3 - Change Management activities

7.4.1 Recording

Firstly, all RFC's have to be recorded or logged. When an RFC is submitted to solve a problem, then the number of the known error must also be recorded.

What constitutes an RFC?

Not every request for a modification is treated as a change: some routine management tasks that are clearly defined and covered by procedures (standard changes) but do involve change to the infrastructure can be dealt with in the same way as Service Requests. This results in the following classification of changes:

■ **Standard Changes - as Service Requests** - where there are fully defined and approved change models, which are individually recorded, but not individually assessed by Change Management. These changes are made routinely. (Note: not all Service Requests are changes.)

■ **Non-standard changes** - all other modifications of the managed infrastructure that are not Standard Changes.

Where do RFC's originate?

RFC's may concern all aspects of the infrastructure within the scope of the ITIL processes. Anyone working with the infrastructure can submit an RFC. We can identify several sources of RFC's, such as:

■ **Problem Management** - proposes solutions to eliminate errors to stabilize the provision of services.

■ **Customers** - may request more, fewer or other services. These requests may be submitted directly as RFC's, or channeled through the Service Desk, Service Level Management or IT Customer Relations Management.

■ **Legislation** - if new regulatory changes are imposed on business activities, or if new requirements are introduced for IT security, Business Continuity and license management. The relevant processes control this.

■ **Suppliers** - suppliers issue new releases and upgrades of their products and identify the errors remedied by them. They may also communicate that they no longer support certain versions, or that the performance of a version cannot be guaranteed. This may initiate the submission of an RFC by Problem Management or Availability Management.

■ **Projects** - a project will often lead to a number of changes. Project management will have to coordinate this effectively with Change Management through the relevant processes, such as Service Level Management, Capacity Management, etc.

■ **All other IT personnel** - in principle, anyone can submit proposals to improve the services. Specifically, IT personnel can contribute to the improvement of procedures and manuals.

RFC recording

Here are examples of the information that could be included in an RFC:

■ Identification number of the RFC.
■ Associated problem/known error number (where relevant).
■ Description and identification of relevant CI's.
■ Reason for the change including justification and business benefit.
■ Current and new version of the CI's to be changed.
■ Name, location and telephone number of the person submitting the RFC.
■ Submission date.
■ Estimated resources and timeframes.

7.4.2 Acceptance

After recording the RFC, Change Management will make an initial assessment to check if any of the RFC's are unclear, illogical, impractical or unnecessary. Such requests are rejected, stating the reasons. The person who submitted the request should always be given an opportunity to defend his or her request.

A change leads to modification of the data in the CMDB, for example:
- A change in the status of an existing CI.
- A change in the relationship between the CI and other CI's.
- A new CI, or variation of an existing CI.
- A new owner or location of the CI.

If the RFC is accepted, the information required for the further processing of the change is included in a change record. Later, the following information will be added to the record:
- Assigned priority.
- Assessment of the impact and required costs.
- Category.
- Recommendations by the Change Manager.
- Date and time of authorization.
- Planned implementation date of the change.
- Backup plans.
- Support requirements.
- Implementation plan.
- Information about the builder and implementers.
- Actual date and time of the change.
- Date of the evaluation.
- Test results and observed problems.
- Reasons for rejection of the request (where relevant).
- Scenario and evaluation information.

7.4.3 Classification
Once an RFC has been accepted, its priority and category are specified:
- The **priority** indicates how important a change is relative to other RFC's, and it is derived from the urgency time scale and the business need for the change. If a change concerns the correction of a known error, then Problem Management may already have assigned the priority code. However, Change Management allocates the final priority code, after consideration of other RFC's being processed.
- Change Management determines the **category** on the basis of the impact of the change on the risk to services and the availability of resources. If the RFC has a high risk/impact of failure and there are insufficient resources available then Change Management should be cautious about pushing the change.

Determining the priority
Here is an example of a priority code system:
- **Low priority** - a change is desirable, but can wait until a convenient time (e.g. the next release, or scheduled maintenance).
- **Normal priority** - no great urgency or major impact, but the change should not be deferred. In the CAB meeting it is given a normal priority when allocating resources.
- **High priority** - a serious error affecting a number of users, or an inconvenient error affecting a large group of users, or related to other urgent matters. This change is given the highest priority in the next meeting of the CAB.
- **Highest priority** - the RFC concerns a problem that seriously affects the use of essential services by users, or it concerns an urgent IT change (e.g. new function for business reasons, an emergency legislation or a temporary fix that cannot wait). Changes with this priority are classified as 'urgent changes'. Urgent changes do not follow the normal procedures, if the required

resources are immediately made available. An emergency meeting of the CAB or the IT Steering Committee may be required. Especially for this purpose, a CAB/EC (Emergency Committee) should be installed, with the authority to make emergency decisions. All plans made earlier may be delayed or interrupted.

The codes could be associated with numbers, e.g. low=1/highest=4.

Determining the category

Categories are determined by Change Management, where necessary in consultation with the CAB, which indicates the impact of the change and the demand it makes on the IT organization. Some examples of categories:

- **Minor impact** - a change requiring little work with little risk of it causing significant service problems. The Change Manager can approve these changes without submitting them to the CAB.
- **Substantial impact** - a change that will require significant efforts and which will have a substantial impact on the services. These changes are discussed at a CAB meeting to determine the required efforts and potential impact. Before the meeting, the relevant documentation is circulated among the CAB members and possibly to specialists and developers.
- **Major impact** - a change that will require very large amounts of effort and could impact a major part of the organization. The Change Manager requires prior authorization from the IT management or IT Steering Committee, after which the change must be submitted to the CAB.

The codes could be associated with numbers, e.g. minor=1/major=3.

Most changes fall into the first two categories. In addition to the classification, the groups working on the solution and the services affected by the change must also be specified.

7.4.4 Planning and Approval

Change Management plans the changes using a change calendar, or Forward Schedule of Change (FSC). The FSC contains details of all approved changes and their planned implementation dates. Members of the CAB advise on the planning of significant changes, the availability of personnel, resources, costs, affected service aspects, and ensure that the customers are involved. The CAB acts as an advisory committee. Change Management has a delegated authority, as it acts on behalf of the IT management. Major changes may have to be approved by the IT management, before being presented to the CAB. This change approval can consist of three aspects:

- **Financial approval** - cost/benefit analysis and budget.
- **Technical approval** - impact, necessity and feasibility.
- **Business approval** - approval by the customers requiring the change and those functions impacted by the change.

For effective planning, Change Management has to maintain contact with the project offices and all others in the organization who build and implement the changes. Moreover, careful consideration must be given to communicating the change plan effectively, possibly in the form of a Forward Schedule of Changes (FSC).

Change policy

RFC's can be combined into a single release. In that case, a single back out plan will suffice if something goes wrong. Such a bundled release should itself be considered as a change, even if it comprises several changes, which should each be approved separately. Releases can be planned with a functional objective for the business typically as maintenance releases of given applications. They can cover hardware and software and are implemented by Release Management. It is advisable to define a policy for this area and to communicate it to the IT organization and the customers (see also Release Management). The policy should aim to avoid unnecessary disruption to the user ('digging up the road every week').

In consultation with the affected IT departments, the CAB can specify regular time windows for implementing changes at a time which minimizes the impact on service. Suitable times could be at the weekend or outside regular office hours. Similarly, periods can be established during which few or no changes are allowed, such as during office hours or the end of the financial year when all user departments are closing their books.

CAB meetings

Information about the planning of a change should be distributed before the CAB meeting. Relevant documents and information about the points on the agenda should also be circulated in advance of the meeting.

The CAB should have a number of fixed items on the agenda of its meetings, including:
- Unauthorized changes.
- Authorized changes that have not been submitted to the CAB.
- RFC's which must be assessed by the members of the CAB.
- Open and closed changes.
- Evaluations of past changes.

Estimating the impact and resources

When estimating the required resources and impact of the change, the members of the CAB, the Change Manager and all others involved (identified by the CAB) should consider the following aspects:
- Capacity and performance of the affected service(s).
- Reliability and recoverability.
- IT Services Continuity Management plans.
- Back-out plans.
- Security.
- Impact of the change on other services.
- Recording and approval.
- Required resources and costs (support and maintenance).
- Number and availability of required specialists.
- Required cycle time of the change.
- New resources to be purchased and tested.
- Impact on operations.
- Any conflicts with other changes.

CAB members can also advise on the priority.

7.4.5 Coordination

Approved changes are communicated to the relevant product specialists who can then build and integrate the changes. The changes are tested before being implemented. Release Management can play an important role in building, testing and implementing approved changes. Appropriate attention should be given to communication of the planned changes.

Building

Not all changes have a specific building phase. For example, standard changes such as relocating a PC can be planned and implemented immediately.

Building may include the creation of a new software version, with new documentation, manuals, installation procedures, a back-out plan, and hardware changes. Change Management provides control and coordination. It is supported by Release Management and line management, which should work to ensure that there are appropriate resources allocated to implement the plans.

A back-out procedure will have to be written as part of the delivery of a change to reverse the change if it does not provide the required result. Change Management should not approve the change if there is no back-out procedure. If the change impacts the user environment then a communication plan will have to be written. An implementation plan is also drawn up during the building phase.

Testing

The back-out procedure, change implementation, and envisaged result of the change should all be thoroughly tested. Consideration should be given to the criteria defined earlier by the CAB. In most cases, a separate test environment or test laboratory will be needed for testing. Early stages of testing can be carried out by the builders, but the change should not be implemented without some independent testing. This usually takes two forms - user acceptance testing where the business community (usually the customer of the change) tests the functionality of the change, and operational acceptance testing where those having to support and maintain the changed infrastructure perform an independent test. This will include technical support areas and the Service Desk. They will test support documentation, back-up and restore procedures etc. Clear instructions are also required for monitoring the quality of the test and for documenting the test results.

Implementing

Anyone in the relevant department who is responsible for the management of the IT infrastructure may be asked to implement a change to that infrastructure. Change Management ensures that the change is on schedule. There must be a clear communication plan indicating who has to be informed of the change, for example the users, Service Desk, Network Management, etc. If a change cannot be adequately tested, it may be possible to apply the change to a small pilot group of users and to evaluate the results before implementing it on a larger scale.

7.4.6 Evaluation

With the possible exception of standard changes, implemented changes should be evaluated. Where necessary, the CAB decides if any follow-up is needed. The following matters should be considered:

- Did the change lead to the required objective?
- Are the users satisfied with the result?
- Were there any side effects?
- Were the estimated costs and efforts exceeded?

If the change was successful, the RFC can be closed. The results are included in the Post-Implementation Review (PIR) or change evaluation. If the change was not successful, then the process is restarted where it went wrong, using a modified approach. Usually it is best to back-out the change and to create a new RFC based on the original RFC. Continuing with an unsuccessful change often makes matters worse.

Evaluation procedures with a specified time limit can help to ensure that change evaluations are not neglected. Depending on the nature of the change, an evaluation can be carried out after a few days, or after a few months. For example, a change to a PC that is used every day can be evaluated after a few days, while a change to a system, which is only used once every week can only be evaluated after three months.

7.4.7 Implementing urgent changes

However good the planning is, there may be changes that demand absolute priority. Urgent changes are very important and have to be carried out as soon as possible. In most cases, resources devoted to other activities have to be diverted to these changes. Urgent changes can have a serious impact on the planned work. Hence, the objective is that the number of urgent or unexpected changes (priority 'highest') should be minimized. Some preventive measures include:

■ Ensuring that changes are requested in time, before they become urgent.
■ When remedying errors due to a poorly prepared change, the situation should not be rolled back beyond a previous version, the Previous Trusted State. Afterwards, an improved implementation of the change should be prepared carefully.

Despite the above measures, urgent changes may still occur, and they require procedures to deal with them quickly, without Change Management losing control of the process. If there is time, the Change Manager can organize an emergency meeting of the CAB/EC. Such a meeting should only be of the specific members needed to evaluate, authorize and resource it. If there is no time or if the request is made outside office hours, then there must be an alternative method for obtaining authorization. The CAB/EC process doesn't have to be a face-to-face meeting, but could be a telephone conference call instead.

An example is mentioned in the Incident Management process, where an emergency fix can be applied to solve a serious incident. If the matter is very serious and delay is unacceptable, the urgent RFC procedure may have to be followed.

There may also be insufficient time for the normal tests to be performed before the change is made but afterwards, all the required stages of the normal process must be completed to ensure that any tests that were skipped are still carried out, and that the files are updated (change records and the CMDB), to ensure that 'what changed?' is traceable.

7.5 Process control

7.5.1 Management reports

Change Management aims to strike a balance between flexibility and stability. Reports can be provided on the following issues to show the current situation of the organization:

■ Number of changes implemented in a period (overall and per CI-category).
■ List of the causes of changes and RFC's.

■ Number of successfully implemented changes.
■ Number of back outs and their reasons.
■ Number of incidents related to implemented changes.
■ Graphs and trend analysis for relevant periods.

7.5.2 Performance Indicators

Performance indicators show to what extent the Change Management process is successful in effectively and efficiently dealing with changes, with the smallest possible adverse impact on the agreed service level. These indicators cover issues such as:
■ The number of changes completed per time unit, by category.
■ Rate at which changes are implemented.
■ Number of rejected changes.
■ Number of incidents resulting from changes.
■ Number of back outs related to changes.
■ Cost of the implemented changes.
■ The number of changes within resource and time estimation.

7.6 Costs and possible problems

7.6.1 Costs

Costs include:
■ **Personnel costs** - In most cases, there are already personnel coordinating the changes. Still, additional personnel costs may be incurred in fulfilling the Change Manager task and setting up the Change Advisory Board. However, to some extent these costs will be offset by the coordination effort already provided within the organization in handling change. In many cases, Change Management is introduced to improve the service quality, and the additional costs incurred are classified as quality costs. After a successful introduction the change coordination costs are offset by a reduction in the cost of solving incidents and problems.
■ **Tool costs** - The costs of hardware and software have to be determined in advance. Often, when introducing several processes, an integrated tool is purchased for Change Management, Problem Management, Configuration Management and Incident Management. When dealing with complex IT environments, it becomes almost impossible to control these management processes without such tools.

7.6.2 Possible problems

The following problems may be encountered when introducing Change Management:
■ Paper-based systems are too difficult to use and will present too many problems.
■ There may be resistance against an umbrella Change Management authority that monitors all aspects of the IT infrastructure. In that case, IT personnel will have to be trained to become aware that all components of the IT infrastructure can have a significant impact on each other and that changes applied to configurations require overall coordination.
■ There may be attempts to implement changes without going through the agreed procedures. It is absolutely essential that there be an organizational reaction to such attempts. The integrity of the Change Management process depends on full compliance. Staff member complaints about and suggestions for improving the Change Management processes are to be tolerated and welcomed, respectively, but non-compliance must be dealt with decisively, or the entire process will be undermined.
■ Other means of ensuring compliance with Change Management procedures include:

- Undertaking regular audits, possibly by an independent auditor, to assess compliance with the Change Management procedures.
- Management supervision of internal and external support staff and developers.
- Ensuring control of all CI's and versions by protecting the CMDB and arranging for Configuration Management to undertake regular Configuration Audits.
- Ensuring that Incident Management reports if users have access to hardware and software that is not included in the CMDB.
- Incorporating the conditions and procedures in contracts with external suppliers.
- Appointing a highly experienced Change Manager with a broad experience and sufficient business (this aspect is often underestimated) and technical knowledge.
- Getting the right person in the role is crucial and should not be overlooked as is often the case.

Some problems can be addressed by implementing the following suggestions:
- Ensure that each change follows the complete procedure.
- Communicate with all IT personnel and all suppliers to ensure that they accept Change Management, and do not try to implement changes without coordination.
- Ensure that changes are evaluated and that standard changes are handled by effective change models that reduce the workload through the full RFC process.
- Work with Configuration Management to ensure that CI changes are entered in the CMDB.

8 RELEASE MANAGEMENT

8.1 Introduction

As organizations become increasingly dependent on IT processes, the effective monitoring and protection of these processes also becomes more important. As the rate of change also keeps increasing, there is a growing need for controlling the process of change.

Changes to the IT infrastructure occur in a complex, distributed environment. In modern client-server applications this often affects both the clients and the servers. The release and implementation of hardware and software demands careful planning in these cases. A release is a set of new and/or changed Configuration Items, which are tested and introduced into the live environment together. A release is defined by the RFC's that it implements. Release Management takes a planned project style approach to implementing changes in IT services, which addresses all technical and non-technical aspects of the changes.

Release Management aims to ensure the quality of the production environment by using formal procedures and checks when implementing new versions. Release Management is concerned with implementation, unlike Change Management, which is concerned with the complete change process and focuses on risk. Release Management works closely with Configuration Management and Change Management to ensure that the common CMDB is updated with every release. Release Management also ensures that the contents of releases are updated in the Definitive Software Library (DSL). The CMDB also keeps track of hardware specifications, installation instructions, and network configurations. Stocks of hardware, particularly standard-ized basic configurations, are stored in the Definitive Hardware Store (DHS). However, in gen-eral, Release Management is primarily concerned with software.

In large projects in particular, Release Management should be part of the overall project plan to ensure effective implementation and to provide funding for ongoing Release Management capa-bilities after the project. An annual fixed budget can be allocated to facilitate ongoing Release Management and in particular the provision of adequate testing capabilities to handle routine activities such as minor changes. Although costs will be incurred when setting up the process, these are minor compared to the potential costs associated with poor planning and control of software and hardware, such as:

- Major interruptions due to poorly planned software releases.
- Duplication of work because there are copies of different versions.
- Inefficient use of resources because nobody knows where the resources are.
- Loss of source files, which means that software has to be purchased again.
- No virus protection, which means that entire networks need decontamination.

8.1.1 Basic concepts

Releases

Releases comprise one or more authorized changes. The first subdivision is based on the release level. Releases are often divided into:

- **Major releases** - major rollout of new hardware and software, generally with significantly increased functionality. These releases often eliminate a number of known errors, including workarounds and temporary fixes.
- **Minor software releases and hardware upgrades** - these generally include a number of minor improvements and fixes of known errors. Some may have been implemented as emer-

gency fixes earlier but are now comprehensively dealt with in the release. Such a release also ensures that the 'Previous Trusted State', the starting point for all tests, is updated.

■ **Emergency fixes** - normally implemented as a temporary fix for a problem or known error.

Release Units

'Release Unit' describes the portion of the IT infrastructure that is normally released together for control and effectiveness of the changes made. For example, software changes can be made at the system, suite, program or module level. Release management policy must decide whether only changed components should be released at that level or whether all related components at that level should be included in the Release Unit. A good example is a DLL (Dynamic Link Library) in the Windows environment, which is often used by several programs. Sometimes, a new DLL version is provided with a package, which may require retesting and reinstallation of all other software packages. This process also develops policies on the minimum content of a release.

Release identification

Release policy defines how copies of software items can be distributed from the DSL to the relevant environments:

■ **Development environment** - the development of a new version can be based on an earlier version from the DSL. The version number is incremented with each new version. Software may only be changed in the development environment.

■ **Test environment** - the environment for testing versions. Often divided into technical test areas by developers, functional test areas by users, implementation test areas by release builders, and possibly a final acceptance test area by users and the management organization.

■ **Production environment** - the live environment where information systems are made available to users.

■ **Archive** - holds older versions of software items that are no longer used but may be reapplied to production should a back out be necessary.

As several releases may be available, they are given unique identifiers. The release identification should refer to the relevant CI and include a version number of two or more digits, for example:

■ **Major releases** - Payroll system v.1, v.2, v.3, etc.
■ **Minor releases** - Payroll system v.1.1, v.1.2, v.1.3, etc.
■ **Emergency fix releases** - Payroll system v.1.1.1, v.1.1.2, v.1.1.3, etc.

Figure 8.1 shows the testing and possible modification of each new version before its release. As part of the release, the old version is archived should a back out be necessary.

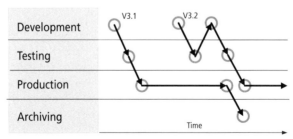

Figure 8.1 - Release management version release

Figure 8.2 illustrates a back out being applied.

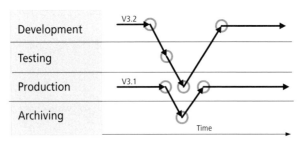

Figure 8.2 - Release management back out

Release types

The number of changes that can be developed, tested and implemented within a given period should be estimated. The benefits of scale and thoroughness of building and testing a number of changes together in a release must be balanced against the risk of a release becoming too complex for safe implementation.

The rapid development of new hardware and software versions in the market means that a release may be outdated before it can be released. On the other hand, frequent changes can adversely impact the service.

Change Management has to decide about the number of changes that can be included in a release, along with how the rollout will be implemented. Change Management can select one of the following options for releasing each change:

■ **Delta Release** - a Delta Release is a partial release, which only includes changed hardware and software components. This often relates to an emergency fix or a temporary fix. The disadvantage of this type of release is that it is not always possible to test all links with the rest of the environment and those modules that are no longer called by the software are not deleted. A Delta Release is appropriate if the software can be isolated from the rest of the IT environment. The advantage of a Delta Release is that setting up the test environment takes less work.

■ **Full Release** - a Full Release means that all the components of the release unit are built, tested and distributed in its entirety, including components that were not changed. This approach is particularly advisable when it is not entirely clear what has been changed. The software and hardware will be tested more thoroughly and there will be fewer incidents after implementation. When preparing a Full Release it is easier to judge if the expected performance criteria will be met. The advantage of a Full Release is that a number of changes can be implemented simultaneously. The preparation will be easier as standard installation scripts can be used. During installation, the program environment can also be cleaned up. However, a Full Release requires more preparation and resources than a Delta Release.

■ **Package Release** - a Package Release is a bundle of Full and/or Delta Releases of related applications and infrastructure that are released at longer time intervals. It provides longer periods of stability for the users by fixing minor software errors, which the users can live with, along with incorporating new functions are activities that can often be combined effectively. Similarly, scheduled upgrades, for example to third party software such as systems software and office applications are appropriate for Package Releases.

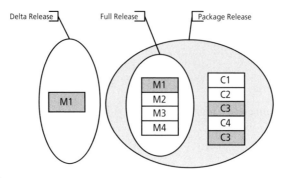

Figure 8.3 - Release types

Definitive Software Library (DSL)

The Definitive Software Library (DSL) is a secure repository that holds the definitive authorized versions (master copies) of all software CI's. The DSL may be physically in many locations and comprise of a number of secure media vaults and fireproof safes. Release Management covers the life cycle of software from the time it is incorporated in the DSL. Releases are configured with the known good software secured in the DSL. Installation scripts are then developed and CDs may be burned at decentralized environments.

The DSL may include several versions of the same software, including archived versions, documentation and source code. Hence, the DSL should be backed up regularly, as it not only contains the current version, but also the back-out versions. If there are several sites with local management, then each site will have a copy of the DSL for rolling out software.

Definitive Hardware Store (DHS)

The Definitive Hardware Store contains spares and stocks of hardware. These are spare components and assemblies that are maintained at the same level as their counterparts in the live environment. The hardware in the DHS is used to replace or repair similar configurations in the IT infrastructure. Details of the composition of these configurations should be included in the CMDB.

Configuration Management Database (CMDB)

During all Release Management activities, it is advisable to check information about CI's in the CMDB. As software versions are incorporated in the DSL and hardware versions are incorporated in the DHS, the CMDB details are also updated. To support Release Management, the CMDB should contain details about:
- Contents of planned releases, including hardware and software CI's with reference to the original RFC.
- Hardware and software CI's which may be impacted by a release.
- Details of the physical location of hardware covered by the release.

8.2 Objectives

Release Management manages and distributes software and hardware versions used for production, which are supported by the IT department to provide the required service level.
The objectives of Release Management include:
- Planning, coordinating and implementing (or arranging the implementation) of software and hardware.

- Designing and implementing efficient procedures for the distribution and installation of changes to IT systems.
- Ensuring that the hardware and software related to changes are traceable, secure and that only correct, authorized and tested versions are installed.
- Communicating with users and considering their expectations during the planning and roll-out of new releases.
- Determining the composition and planning of a rollout, together with Change Management.
- Implementing new software releases and hardware in the operational infrastructure, under control of Change Management and supported by Configuration Management. A release may include any number of related CI's, not only hardware and software, but also documentation such as reports, plans and user and support manuals.
- Ensuring that the original copies of software are securely stored in the Definitive Software Library (DSL) and that the CMDB is updated. The same applies with respect to the hardware in the DHS.

8.2.1 Benefits

Together with effective Configuration Management and Change Management, Release Management helps to ensure that:

- The software and hardware in live use are of high quality because they are developed and tested under quality control before being released.
- The risk of errors in software and hardware combinations or release of an incorrect version is minimized.
- The business carefully handles its software investments, which it largely depends on.
- There are fewer separate implementations and each implementation is thoroughly tested.
- The risk of incidents and known errors occurring is reduced by testing and controlling implementation.
- The users are more involved in the testing of a release.
- A release calendar is published in advance so that user expectations are more in-line with the releases.
- The business has a central software and hardware design and build, or procurement facility, followed by the distribution to the site.
- The business can standardize software and hardware versions between sites to facilitate support.
- The risk of illegal software is reduced, along with the risk of incidents and problems due to the wrong or infected software or hardware versions being introduced into the live environment.
- Unauthorized copies and incorrect versions are more easily detected.

8.3 The process

8.3.1 Release Management activities

The Release Management process includes the following activities:

- Release policy and planning.
- Release design, building and configuration.
- Testing and release acceptance.
- Rollout planning.
- Communication, preparation and training.
- Release distribution and installation.

These activities are not really chronological. Release policy and planning may be undertaken each 6 months or year, while other activities are typically performed daily.

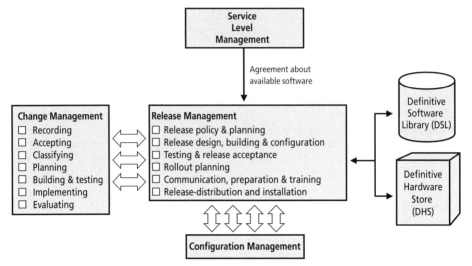

Figure 8.4 - Release Management (source: itSMF)

Successful Release Management depends upon the input from and cooperation with the other ITIL processes (Figure 8.4). The major interfaces are with the following processes.

8.3.2 Relationship with other processes

Configuration Management

Configuration Management is responsible for recording the available software and hardware versions in the CMDB as basic configurations. The software added to the DSL and the hardware for the DHS is recorded in the CMDB at an agreed level of detail. The status monitoring provided by Configuration Management indicates the status of each CI, for example 'live use', 'in development', 'being tested', 'in stock' or 'archived'.

Change Management

Change Management is responsible for ensuring that there is adequate testing of the release. Change Management also decides how many changes may be combined in a release. Change Management describes the procedures to ensure that changes are authorized, including the impact analysis and analysis of the required resources. In most cases, the Release Manager is responsible for implementing software and hardware changes and generally sits on the Change Advisory Board.

Service Level Management

An IT service generally consists of providing infrastructure hardware together with standard software or software developed in-house. Release Management is responsible for making hardware and software available and for managing it.

8.4 Activities

8.4.1 Planning & Implementing Release Management

Planning and implementing the Release Management discipline is heavily dependent upon implementing Configuration Management and Change Management. It should involve the initial planning and implementation of Release Management capabilities and then the ongoing review and improvement of:

- Release policies covering release levels, types, units, identification, frequency and phasing, the scope of controlled deliverables and necessary documentation.
- Release procedures covering all release management activities outlined below.
- Roles and responsibilities of all staff especially Release Management staff.
- Tools including: Change Management tools to manage the progress of changes and releases, CMDB tools that holds details on CI's at different points in their life cycle, Software Configuration Management tools that manage different versions of software code, Build Management tools to automate the build process, Software distribution tools, Software and Hardware auditing tools along with Desktop and Server management tools.

8.4.2 Release Management Activities

Figure 8.5 shows the Release Management activities and their position in the life cycle of a Change.

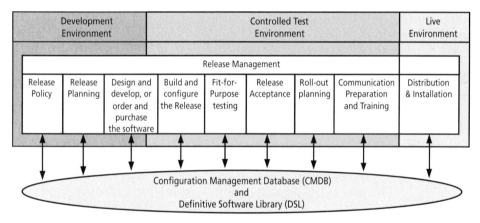

Figure 8.5 - Release Management activities

Release policy and planning

For each system, the Release Manager should develop a release policy defining how and when releases are configured. Major releases can be planned ahead together with the release identification or version number, so that the addition of changes can be considered at appropriate times.

The Release Manager also specifies at what level CI's can be distributed independently of each other (release units). This depends on the nature of the system under release control:

- The potential impact of the release on other components.
- The number of person-hours and cycle time to build and test isolated changes compared with the effort associated with collecting them and implementing them simultaneously.
- The difficulty of the installation at the user sites. It may be easier to install a full program because standard techniques are available for that.
- The complexity of the dependencies between the new software, hardware, and the rest of the IT infrastructure - the easier it is to isolate software or hardware, the easier it is to test it.

Before a release can be planned, information has to be collected about the product life cycle, products to be handed over, description of the relevant IT service and service levels along with the authorization of the relevant RFC's.

The following issues are considered when planning a release:
- Coordinating the content of the release.
- Agreeing the schedule, sites and organizational units.
- Drawing up the release schedule.
- Drawing up a communication plan.
- Site visits to determine the hardware and software actually in use.
- Agreeing on roles and responsibilities.
- Obtaining detailed quotes and negotiating with suppliers about new hardware, software and installation services.
- Drawing up back-out plans.
- Drawing up a quality plan for the release.
- Planning the acceptance of the release by the management organization and users.

The results of this activity are part of the plan for the change, and include plans for the release, test plans and acceptance criteria.

Design, building and configuration
It is advisable to develop standard procedures for designing, building and configuring releases. A release may be based on sets of components (CI's) developed in-house or purchased from third parties and configured. Installation instructions and instructions for configuring releases should also be treated as part of the release and should be included as CI's under the control of Change Management and Configuration Management.

It is advisable to set up and test all hardware and software in a 'laboratory' before installation on site. The software and hardware components of a release should be carefully configured and recorded such that they are reproducible. Operating instructions should be drawn up to ensure that the same set of components is combined every time. Often, standardized hardware is reserved which is only used for compiling or creating images. Preferably this part of the process should be automated to make it more reliable. In software development environments, this activity is known as Build Management, which comes under responsibility of Release Management.

Back-out plan
A back-out plan at the level of the entire release defines the activities needed to recover the service if something goes wrong with the release. Change Management is responsible for making sure that back-out plans are created, however Release Management should help to ensure that the back-out plans are practical. Particularly when implementing a Package Release combining several RFC's, it can be necessary to coordinate the different back-out plans for the release. If something goes wrong with a Full Release or a Delta Release, then it is advisable to roll the release back completely to the Previous Trusted State. If a release cannot be rolled back fully, then contingency measures need to be taken to restore as much of the IT service as possible.

It is advisable to fulfill the requirements of the back-out plan in advance, such as making backups and providing a spare server. To address the case where the implementation could take longer than expected, and where that delay would endanger the normal provision of services, the back-out plan should also include deadlines to show when a back-out should be started to restore the service in time (for example before Monday morning, 7:00 AM). A back-out plan should be included in the risk analysis of the change, and the users must have accepted the plan.

The actual building of the release can include compiling and linking software modules, or filling databases with test data or data such as postcode tables, tax rates, time zones and currency tables, as well as user information. This is often handled by automated installation scripts, which are stored in the DSL together with the back-out plans. Complete releases should be identified in the CMDB as standard configurations to facilitate their configuration in future. Test plans cover the testing and acceptance of the quality of the software, hardware, procedures, operating instructions and rollout scripts before the release, and possibly also the evaluation test after the release. The installation scripts should also be tested. The information needed for this activity includes:
- Definition of the release.
- Release schedule.
- Instructions for configuring and building the release.
- Description of items to be purchased or licensed.
- Automated installation scripts and test plans.
- Source copies of the software for incorporation in the DSL.
- Back-out plans and procedures.

Testing and release acceptance
The most common cause of unsatisfactory changes and releases is inadequate testing. To avert this, before implementation, the release should undergo a functional test by representatives of the users and an operational test by IT management personnel who will consider the technical operation, functions, operational aspect, performance, and integration with the rest of the infra-structure. The tests should also cover the installation scripts, back-out procedures, and any changes to the management procedures. A formal acceptance of each step should be submitted to Change Management. The last step is approving the release for implementation.

Change Management must arrange the formal acceptance by the users and sign-off by the developers, before Release Management can start the rollout.

Releases should be accepted in a controlled test environment that can be reinstated to a known configuration state. This baseline state for the release should be detailed in the release definition, which should be recorded in the CMDB. If the release is not accepted then it is sent back to Change Management as failed Changes.

The results of this activity include:
- Tested installation procedures.
- Tested release components.
- Known errors and shortcomings in the release.
- Test results.
- Management and support documentation.
- List of affected systems.
- Operating instructions and diagnostic tools.
- Contingency plans and tested back-out plans.
- Training program for personnel, managers and users.
- Signed acceptance documents.
- Change authorization for the release.

Rollout planning

The release plan drawn up during the preceding stages is now supplemented with information about the exact implementation activities and schedule.

Rollout planning includes:
- Drawing up a schedule and list of tasks and required human resources.
- Making a list of the CI's to be installed and to be phased out along with the way in which they are phased out.
- Drawing up an activity plan for each implementation site, considering the available release times along with the time zones for an international organization.
- Mailing release memos and other communications to relevant parties.
- Drawing up plans for the purchase of hardware and software.
- Purchasing, securing storage, identifying and recording all new CI's in the CMDB for the release.
- Scheduling update/review meetings with management, management departments, Change Management and user representatives.

There are several ways to implement a rollout:
- The release can be **rolled out in full** - the Big Bang approach.
- The release can be **rolled out in stages**, combining several options:
  - Functional increments, where all users get new functions at the same time.
  - Site increments, where groups of users are dealt with.
  - Evolutionary, where the functions are expanded in stages.

Communication, preparation and training

Personnel who communicate with customers (Service Desk and Customer Relations Management), operational personnel and representatives of the user organization should be aware of the plans and how they can affect routine activities. This can be implemented through joint training sessions, cooperation and joint involvement in release acceptance. Responsibilities should be communicated and it should be verified that everyone is aware of them. If the release is rolled out in stages, then users should be made aware of that by informing them about the plans and when they can expect the new functions.

Changes to the Service Level Agreements (SLA), Operational Level Agreements (OLA) and Underpinning Contracts (UC) should be communicated in advance to all relevant personnel. Distribution and installation

Distribution and installation

Release Management monitors the logistics processes for purchase, storage, transport, delivery, and hand-over of software and hardware. The process is supported by procedures, records, and accompanying documents such as packing slips, so that it can provide reliable information to Configuration Management. The hardware and software storage facility should be secure and accessible only to authorized personnel.

It is advisable to use automated tools for software distribution and installation where possible. This will reduce the time required for distribution and increase the quality, while requiring fewer resources. Often, these tools will also facilitate verification of a successful installation. Before undertaking any installation, it is advisable to check if the environment where the release will be made fulfills the conditions, such as sufficient disk space, security, environmental controls or limitations like air conditioning, floor space, UPS/power, etc.

After installation, the information in the CMDB should be updated to facilitate verification of any license agreements.

8.5 Costs and possible problems

8.5.1 Costs
Release Management costs include:
- Personnel costs.
- Storage costs for the DSL and DHS, building, testing and distribution environments.
- Costs of software tools and required hardware.

8.5.2 Possible problems
The following problems may be encountered:
- **Resistance to change** - initially, some resistance may occur among personnel used to the old familiar methods. For example they may find it difficult to accept that for some activities they will receive instructions from another area. To address their concerns, they will need to be informed about the benefits of the ITIL approach.
- **Bypassing Release Management** - unauthorized software may introduce viruses in the organization, adversely affect services, and make support more difficult. Firm action should therefore be taken against personnel and users, particularly in the PC environment, who attempt to use unauthorized software.
- **Urgent fixes** - Release Management should not be bypassed, even if an urgent change is needed.
- **Distribution** - if software is to be released at several sites, then it should be ensured that this is synchronized, to prevent version differences between sites.
- **Testing** - without an adequate test environment it may be difficult to assess new versions or new software properly before the release.

9 SERVICE DESK

9.1 Introduction

The Service Desk plays an important role in user support. A full-blown Service Desk serves as the front office for the other IT departments, and can deal with many customer queries without needing to contact specialist personnel. For the user, the Service Desk provides the single point of contact with the IT organization, which ensures that they find the right person to help them with their issue or request. In other words, the users need not endlessly look for somebody who can solve their problems. Often, the Service Desk also follows up on calls originating from within the IT organization. For example incidents that are detected within the department (automatically or by personnel), and calls for service that come from within the IT organization.

This chapter is different from the rest of the book in that here we focus on a function, organizational unit, or a department, while the rest of the book deals with processes. The subject is included here because the Service Desk plays an essential role in IT Service Management. To indicate the broader activities, we speak of a Service Desk instead of a Help Desk, as we used to. A Help Desk was normally involved in the incident process only, whereas the Service Desk covers a broader range of support activities.

The Service Desk handles activities related to a number of basic ITIL processes:
- The primary process is **Incident Management** as many incidents are recorded (logged) and monitored by the Service Desk, and many Service Desk calls are related to incidents. This includes coordinating third-party activities involved in incident handling.
- The Service Desk may be charged with installing software and hardware and may therefore have a role in **Release Management** or **Change Management**.
- If, when recording an incident, the Service Desk verifies the details of the caller and their IT resources, then the Service Desk plays a role in **Configuration Management**.
- The Service Desk may undertake activities concerning standard requests, such as installing LAN connections and relocating workstations in which case it will contribute to the evaluation of changes and be involved in **Change Management**.
- The Service Desk can inform users about the supported products and services they are entitled to. If the Service Desk is not authorized to meet a request then it should politely inform the user of this and notify **Service Level Management** of the request.

Figure 9.1 - Service Desk processes

The Service Desk handles activities related to a number of other ITIL processes as well, e.g. Infrastructure Management (Operations). The Service Desk maintains the contacts with customers through promotion of, and providing information about, the services. The Service Desk is an excellent tool for the daily contacts with users to monitor customer satisfaction.

9.2 Objectives

The objective of the Service Desk is to support the provision of the services that have been agreed by guaranteeing access to the IT organization and undertaking a range of support activities (from various processes).

By serving as an initial point of contact, the Service Desk reduces the workload on other IT departments by intercepting irrelevant questions and questions which are easily answered. The Service Desk acts as a filter that only lets calls through to second and third-line support where this is actually necessary. As an initial point of contact it always acts professionally when dealing with users and ensures that they do not have to search endlessly for a solution.

9.3 Structure

9.3.1 Accessibility

One of the major tasks of the Service Desk is ensuring the accessibility of the IT organization. Users should be encouraged to call the Service Desk if they have any questions or need any support. The manner in which calls are processed can be monitored with reports produced by the telephone system (PABX).

To make a reliable impression, the Service Desk should be consistent and efficient in all customer contacts. This can be supported by the use of procedures based on questionnaires and standard responses, for example using scripts.

A number of different media can be used to improve accessibility, although telephone and e-mail contacts are the most common. Voice mail, fax, Internet gateways, and automatically generated messages (e.g. text messages to mobile phones or pagers) can also be used.

9.3.2 Business support

Calls to the Service Desk can be divided into incidents concerning the technical infrastructure, incidents and questions about the use of an application, questions about the status of the services (incident progress), standard changes, and other requests. Depending on the type of Service Desk and the scope of the service organization, the Service Desk may deal with all calls or only with technical problems and requests while the ('pay the bills') customer organization deals with application support themselves. In the latter case, the customer department using the application has an application contact, a business operations support desk. This will try to answer questions from users and only route technical questions to the Service Desk of the IT organization. That way, the Service Desk will not be overloaded with questions related to the use of applications.

9.3.3 Structural options

There are several options for the structure of the Service Desk. Common approaches include:
- **Centralized Service Desk** as a single point of contact for all users, possibly with a separate Service Desk close to the users for business applications (split function Service Desk).

- **Local (distributed) Service Desks** across a number of sites. Normally, dividing the Service Desk across a number of sites will make it more difficult to manage.
- **Virtual Service Desk** where the location is immaterial due to the use of communications technology.

Centralized Service Desk

Figure 9.2 shows a split function Centralized Service Desk. If the IT organization is responsible both for providing the service (the Information System) and supporting the use of the Information System then it is best if the user can approach the Service Desk as a single point of contact. In that case, the IT Service Desk is responsible for call acceptance and recording, progress monitoring and escalation. Here, the business operations support function is part of the IT Service Desk or it is the responsibility of a support team managed by the Service Desk. This requires a common incident recording system.

If the IT organization is not responsible for business operations support, then the business operations support desk will represent the users when the IT service provider's support is required.

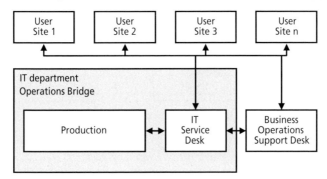

Figure 9.2 - Split function Service Desk

This approach can be combined with an operations bridge (a physical concentration of operational management activities, e.g. a Service Desk in combination with an Operations department) to provide direct communication between the Service Desk and operational management (Production, Operations), where Production includes Network Management, Computer Operations, etc. This direct communication facilitates a rapid response if there are errors that cannot be resolved immediately by the Service Desk. Ideally, the departments should be located in close proximity to each other.

Distributed Service Desk

Distributed Service Desks are split across a number of sites, in different buildings or even in different countries. Figure 9.3 shows an example of the structure of a distributed Service Desk. There is a further choice between:
- **A central point of contact** - routes calls through to local support. The central Service Desk can serve as the initial point of contact for users and specialize in incident recording. Modern call routing software increases the effectiveness of the Service Desk in resolving incidents.
- **Local points of contact** - with a central Service Desk to track and monitor incidents. This approach is often used if the local organization has its own language and culture. It is also used when the organization has a substantial number of custom applications in each line of business. For example, a chemical company has over three hundred categories of custom applications, and a thousand applications overall. With this level of customization, the only practical

solution is to distribute the Service Desk function out to each line of business, as knowledge 'on the ground' is required to resolve many incidents. Local responsibility for support costs can also motivate this structure.

■ **A call center** - this option is becoming increasingly popular and is often used by suppliers. A central telephone number, usually toll-free, provides access to a voice response menu where the user can select the subject about whom they need assistance, such as e-mail or Office applications. The call is then routed to a specialist support team. These support teams may be in different geographical areas, but the user will not be aware of this.

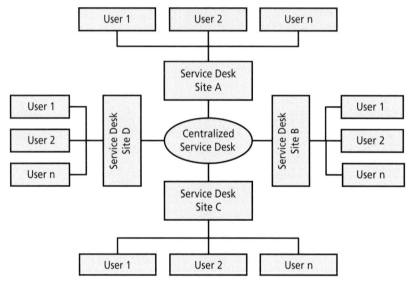

Figure 9.3 - Distributed Service Desk with central control

Virtual Service Desk

A modern, specialized version of the distributed Service Desk is the virtual Service Desk. This consists of a number of local Service Desks, which appear to form one unit as modern telecommunication technology and networks make the location immaterial. The Service Desk and support can now be located anywhere. Using a number of sites in different time zones around the world ('follow the sun support') support can be provided around the clock. The disadvantage of a virtual Service Desk is that it is more difficult to provide on-site support.

Lately, we have seen 'self-help' as a form of providing 'automated' Service Desk functionality. Self-help in the form of, for instance, web access to the knowledge database (look for known errors) and incident records (check status, etc.) is an important option to reduce cost and empower the end user community.

9.3.4 Service Desk personnel

Service Desk personnel requirements are determined by the mission and structure of the Service Desk. Here are some examples of missions and the associated human resource requirements:

■ **Call Center** - this type of support unit records calls only and does not provide a solution. The calls are routed to specialist departments that deal with them. In some cases, the recording and routing of calls can be automated using voice response systems.

■ **Unskilled or call recording Service Desk** - calls are recorded, described in general terms, and the majority of them immediately routed. The Service Desk is largely a dispatching function, and for the calls it is expected to handle itself, it needs extensive standardized procedures, scripts for dealing with calls, discipline, and an experienced manager. The advantage of this approach is that incident recording is standardized and incidents are monitored and managed on behalf of the user. The disadvantage is that the response time is longer and first-call resolution rates are much lower than with a skilled Service Desk.

■ **Skilled Service Desk** - this type of Service Desk has greater skills and experience than the previous type. Using documented solutions it can resolve many incidents, while some incidents are routed to support teams. First call resolution rates are generally much higher than with an unskilled Service Desk.

■ **Expert Service Desk** - this type of Service Desk has specialist knowledge of the full IT infrastructure and the expertise to resolve most incidents independently.

9.3.5 Service Desk technology

There are many technical options for setting up a Service Desk. Apart from an effective Service Management tool, they include:

■ Integrating service management tools with systems management tools.
■ Communication technology such as Computer Telephony Integration (CTI) or Voice Over Internet Protocol (VOIP).
■ Interactive Voice Response systems (IVR).
■ E-mail.
■ Fax servers (fax via e-mail or the Internet).
■ Forwarding calls to pagers, mobile phones, laptop and palmtop computers.
■ Knowledge, search and diagnostic tools (knowledge base, case based reasoning).
■ Automated systems management and network tools.
■ Intranet and Internet self-service platforms.

9.4 Activities

9.4.1 Responding to calls

A call is a user contact to the Service Desk. All calls should be logged to facilitate progress monitoring and provide metrics for process control.

There are two call categories:

■ **Incidents** - in essence all calls, except those relating to standard changes:
  - *Error reports* - true faults and complaints about the service.
  - *Service Requests* - Service Requests are classified in ITIL as incidents, but do not involve a failure in the IT infrastructure. Service Requests also do not fall into the Change Management category. Examples include, 'How do I?' questions, requests for information, e.g. status inquiries, documentation or advice, requests for password resets, batch job runs, file restores or database extracts, requests for consumables (including replacement of a mouse, keyboard, etc., if these are not CI's), supply of documentation e.g. user manuals, etc. Service Requests can also be *standard changes*. A standard change is in fact a routine change to the infrastructure that follows an established path, is the accepted solution to a specific requirement or set of requirements, *and is not handled in the Change Management process*. Examples include an upgrade of a PC in preparation for the use of specific software, setting up PC, software and network connections for new starters, straightforward standard installations and standard orders for workstations, peripherals and local applications. Standard

changes are changes, so they will involve a change to the recorded IT infrastructure.
■ **Changes** - these are non-standard changes, which are not handled as Service Requests. A request for such a change will follow the standard process of Change Management, requiring a formal Request for Change (RFC).

Note: ITIL considers both incident call types (error reports and Service Requests) to be 'incidents', since these calls are treated similarly. On the other hand, ITIL allows for isolated procedures for Service Requests, separated from the Incident Management process.

9.4.2 Providing information
The Service Desk should serve as the main source of information to users. This can be done passively (e.g. by providing a bulletin board), or actively (e-mails, on-screen log-in messages, or screen saver messages). All efforts should be made to inform users about current or expected errors, preferably before they are affected. The Service Desk should also provide information about new and existing services, provisions of the Service Level Agreements (SLA's) and order procedures and costs.

9.4.3 Supplier liaison
The Service Desk is often responsible for contacts with maintenance suppliers, including the repair and replacement of printers, workstations and, in some cases, telecommunications equipment. This type of maintenance may include the handling of incidents in the pure sense (disturbances) as well as changes and service requests.

9.4.4 Operational management tasks
Making back-ups and restores, providing LAN connections, disk space management on local servers, creating accounts, authorizing and resetting passwords may also be the responsibility of the Service Desk.

9.4.5 Infrastructure monitoring
The Service Desk may have access to tools, which can be used to estimate the impact of faults affecting essential equipment, such as routers, servers and gateways, mission-critical systems, applications, and databases. Often, these tools can detect faults and inform Incident Management automatically when a fault has occurred or is threatening. Formally, using these tools is a primary task of Operations, who should feed the information to the Service Desk.

9.5 Effectiveness
The satisfaction of the customer or user is the major indicator of Service Desk effectiveness. Some common Key Performance Indicators are:
■ Is the telephone answered quickly (e.g. 90% of the calls answered within X seconds)?
■ Are calls routed to second level support within X minutes (if they cannot be resolved at the Service Desk)?
■ Is the service restored within an acceptable time and in accordance with the SLA?
■ Are users advised in time about current and future changes and errors?

Some performance indicators can only be measured by means of a customer survey, e.g.:
■ Is the telephone answered courteously?
■ Are users given good advice on how to prevent incidents?

9.5.1 Management reports

The Service Desk should regularly (monthly as a minimum) verify if it meets the defined standards. Appropriate metrics include:

- Percentage of incidents closed without resorting to other levels such as second or third-line support or suppliers.
- The number of calls handled per workstation/user and the total for the Service Desk.
- Average incident resolution time, by impact, or time to realize a service request. Both the elapsed time and the time actually spent on the call should be specified.
- PABX reports on the average answer time, number of calls abandoned by users, average call duration, and relative metrics per Service Desk agent.

Standards can be set for these metrics, which are then used to monitor improvement or deterioration of the service. The Service Desk effectiveness can also be measured through regular surveys in the customer.

9.5.2 Critical success factors

If it is difficult to reach the Service Desk, the users will not contact it and instead try to resolve errors themselves, or find someone in the organization who can help them. Thus, Service Desk performance should be brought to the required level before running a publicity campaign.

If users try to contact specialists directly they should always be referred to the Service Desk.

There should be good SLA's and OLA's and a service catalogue in place to ensure that the support provided by the Service Desk has a clear focus.

10 SERVICE LEVEL MANAGEMENT

10.1 Introduction

Service Level Management is the process of negotiating, defining, measuring, managing and improving the quality of IT services at an acceptable cost. All of this must take place in an environment of rapidly changing business needs and rapid changes in technology. Service Level Management aims to find the right balance between quality supply and demand, customer-friendliness, and cost of IT services. It is important that both the provider and the customer realize that a service is being provided and being received. Service Level Management includes designing, agreeing, and maintaining the following:

- Service Level Agreements (SLA's).
- Operational Level Agreements (OLA's).
- Underpinning Contracts (UC's).
- Service Quality Plans.

10.1.1 Basic concepts

IT Service Providers and Customers

In theory, anyone who obtains IT services is a customer. In most cases, the IT organization will be the provider. As the IT organization itself generally also obtains IT services, and the IT organization is therefore a customer of IT Service Providers at the same time, there can be a complex web of relationships.

In the context of Service Level Management we use the following definitions of customer and provider:

- The **customer** is the representative of an organization who is authorized to make agreements on behalf of that organization about obtaining IT services. Hence, they are not the same as the end user of the IT services.
- The **provider** is the representative of an organization who is authorized to make agreements on behalf of that organization about the provision of IT services.

Service Level Requirements (SLR)

Service Level Requirements cover the detailed definitions of customer needs, and are used to develop, modify and initiate services. Service Level Requirements can serve as a blueprint for designing a service and its associated SLA(s), and may also be used as a design assessment.

Service Specification Sheets (Spec Sheets)

Service Spec Sheets describe the relationship between functionality (as agreed with the customer, therefore customer-focused) and technology (as implemented within the IT organization, therefore IT-focused) and provide a detailed specification of the service. The Spec Sheets translate Service Level Requirements (external specifications) into technical definitions needed to provide the service (internal specifications). The Spec Sheets also describe any links between the SLA's, any UC's and any OLA's. The Spec Sheets are an important tool to monitor correspondence between the internal and external specifications.

Service Catalogue

Developing a Service Catalogue can help the IT organization to profile itself and to present itself as an IT Service Provider as opposed to a mere implementer and maintainer of technology. The Service Catalogue provides a detailed description of the operational services in the customer's language, along with a summary of the associated service levels that the IT organization can provide to its customers. As such, it is an important communications tool. The Service Catalogue can help steer customer expectations, and in this way facilitate the alignment process between service customers and service providers. This document is derived from the external specifications in the Spec Sheets and should therefore be written in the customer's language, and not in the form of technical specifications.

Service Level Agreement (SLA)

A Service Level Agreement is an agreement between the IT organization and the customer, which details the service or services to be provided. The SLA describes the services in non-technical terms, in line with the perception of the customer, and during the term of the agreement it serves as the standard for measuring and adjusting the IT services. SLA's normally have a hierarchical structure, for example general services such as network and Service Desk services are defined for the organization as a whole and approved by management. More specific services, associated with the business activities, are agreed at a lower level in the organization, for example with the business unit management, budget holder or customer representative.

Service Improvement Program (SIP)

The Service Improvement Program, often implemented as a project, defines the activities, phases and milestones associated with improving an IT service.

Service Quality Plan (SQP)

The Service Quality Plan is an important document as it contains all management information needed to manage the IT organization. The Service Quality Plan defines the process parameters of the Service Management processes and operational management. The SLA is about what we deliver and the SQP is about how we deliver. It includes targets for each process, in the form of Performance Indicators. For example, for Incident Management it may contain the resolution times for various impact levels, and for Change Management it may contain the cycle times and costs of standard changes such as a relocation. Reports and reporting intervals are defined for all processes. The Performance Indicators are derived from the Service Level Requirements and are documented in the Spec sheets. If external providers contribute to the provision of services, for example when the Service Desk or PC maintenance are outsourced, then the Performance Indicators are also defined in the Underpinning Contracts.

Operational Level Agreement (OLA)

An Operational Level Agreement is an agreement with an internal IT department detailing the provision of certain elements of a service. For example, if the SLA contains targets for restoring a high priority incident, then the OLA's should include targets for each of the elements in the support chain (target for the Service Desk to answer calls, escalate, etc., targets for Network Support to start to investigate and to resolve network related errors assigned to them, etc.). OLA's support the IT organization providing the services.

Underpinning Contract (UC)

An Underpinning Contract is a contract with an external provider defining the provision of certain elements of a service; for example troubleshooting workstations, or leasing a communications line. This is similar to the external implementation of an OLA. In many organizations, an internal IT department provides the IT services. SLA's and OLA's are often descriptions of what was agreed between internal departments, rather than legal contracts. However, a UC with an external provider will normally be in the form of a formal contract.

10.2 Objectives

Service Level Management ensures that the IT services required by the customer are continuously maintained and improved. This is achieved by agreeing, monitoring and reporting about the performance of the IT organization; in addition creating an effective business relationship between the IT organization and its customers.

Effective Service Level Management improves the performance of the customer's business and results in greater customer satisfaction. Because the IT organization is more aware of what is expected from it and what it provides, it will be better able to plan, budget and manage its services.

10.2.1 Benefits

In general, the introduction of Service Level Management will have the following benefits:
- IT services are designed to meet the expectations, as defined in the Service Level Requirements.
- Service performance can be measured, which means that it can be managed and reported on.
- If the IT organization charges customers for the use of IT services, the customer can draw a balance between the required quality of service and the corresponding costs.
- As the IT organization can specify the services and components required, it can take more control of resource management and costs could be reduced over the long term.
- Improved customer relationships and customer satisfaction.
- Both the customer and the IT organization are aware of their responsibilities and roles, so there will be fewer misunderstandings or omissions.

10.3 The Process

Service Level Management is a process that links the IT service provider and the customer for those services. The Service Level Management process has several objectives:
- To integrate the elements required for the provision of IT services.
- To create documents that clearly describe the services by the various elements.
- To describe the service provided to the customer in a terminology that they understand and can relate to.
- To align IT strategy with the business needs.
- To improve IT Service Delivery in a controlled manner.

Service Level Management has a central role in IT Service Management processes, and has close links with the other Support and Delivery processes. Service Level Management forms a bridge with the customer, as it provides an opportunity to discuss the business needs of the customer without getting bogged down in technical details. The IT organization then translates these business needs into technical specifications and activities within the organization. The extent to which the customer need not be concerned about technology is a good measure of the success of Service Level Management.

Service Level Management demands effective and productive cooperation with customers, as the definition of appropriate service levels requires the contribution and effort of the customer. If the customer (the business) is not familiar with the subjects at hand, then this will have to be addressed first. Figure 10.1 shows the Service Level Management process workflow. It shows two component processes, which are largely parallel: the upper one is about making agreements, and the lower one is about ensuring that these agreements are fulfilled.

10.3.1 Service Level Management activities

Service Level Management includes the following activities:

- **Identifying** - identifying the customer's needs (relationship management) and promoting the IT organization. Understanding the business processes and needs of the customer.
- **Defining** - defining the services to be provided to meet the needs and requirements of the customer. These services are defined in Service Level Requirements and Service Spec Sheets. A Service Quality Plan will be created as a result of this activity.
- **Finalizing** - finalizing the contract, i.e. negotiating with the customer about the required service level, in relation to costs involved, and defining it in Service Level Agreements (SLA). Underpinning the SLA's with Operational Level Agreements (OLA) and Underpinning Contracts (UC). Writing or revising the Service Catalogue specifying the services available to the customer.
- **Monitoring** - monitoring the service levels.
- **Reporting** - drawing up Service Level Reports. Regularly reporting to the customer and the IT organization about the actual service levels, compared with the Service Level Achievements.
- **Reviewing** - reviewing the service together with the customer to determine opportunities for improvements. A Service Improvement Program may be initiated, if necessary. Frequent communication with the customer about their experience and ideas about the service provided. This may result in new or revised SLA's.

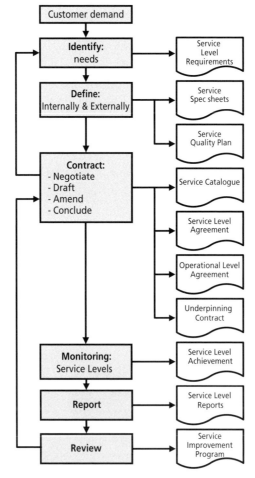

Figure 10.1 - Service Level Management process

Fully effective Service Level Management requires the introduction of the other Service Support and Service Delivery processes. All the processes contribute to some extent to Service Level Management. When defining a service and the associated service levels, the extent to which the required support processes are introduced should be considered. The relationships between Service Level Management and the other processes are outlined below.

10.3.2 Relationship with other processes

Service Desk

Although the Service Desk is a function, not a process, the relationship between the Service Desk function and the Service Level Management process is a particularly important one. The Service Desk is the initial point of contact for users and, through Incident Management, it aims to recover the agreed service levels as soon as possible in the event of an error. Because of its direct contact with the users of the IT services, the Service Desk can often provide valuable information about the quality perception (user satisfaction) of Service Level Management by the users. Normally, there will be a strong relationship between user satisfaction and customer satisfaction. The Service Desk also plays an important role in assisting with the definition of the response and solution times that will come into effect in the event of service interruption.

Availability Management

Availability Management is responsible for realizing and optimizing the availability of the services. Service Level Management provides Availability Management with input about the required availability of the IT services, while Availability Management provides information about the actual availability to Service Level Management.

Capacity Management

Capacity Management is responsible for managing the capacity of the IT infrastructure. There is a Capacity Plan with details of the current infrastructure usage and forecasts of future requirements. Capacity Management supports Service Level Management by providing information about the impact of a new service or extension of an existing service on the overall capacity. Capacity Management also indicates if the use made of a service is within the agreed limits.
Service Level Management provides information to Capacity Management about the expected current and future use, which Service Level Management has agreed, or is about to agree, with the customer.

Incident & Problem Management

Incident Management and Problem Management are good indicators of the effective implementation of the SLA agreements. Incident Management in particular has an important role in restoring the services as soon as possible after an error.

Problem Management aims to optimize the stability of the services by taking permanent measures to ensure that the errors do not recur.

Resolving incidents and problems is essential to providing a high-quality service. Service Level Management uses information from reports provided by these processes when reporting to the customer.

Change Management

The SLA can define the changes that can be requested by the customer organization, and the agreements for responding to these changes (whom to address the changes to, cycle time, costs, informing the organization, etc.). A change may also affect the service levels that have been agreed. Any changes to a service and the associated SLA are controlled by Change Management.

Release Management
Many IT services amount to the provision of infrastructure hardware together with custom-made or off-the-shelf software. Release Management monitors the agreements made by Service Level Management regarding the provision of hardware and software. Service Level Management reports on the quality of the IT service on the basis of information from Release Management reports.

IT Service Continuity Management
IT Service Continuity Management is concerned with the rapid recovery of IT services in the event of a disaster, and monitors the appropriate measures and procedures. The agreements about this with the customer are made within the Service Level Management process. The measures and costs are then included in the SLA. It may be agreed that in the event of a disaster, certain service levels no longer apply or are temporarily reduced.

Changes to the service and the SLA may require modification of the defined continuity measures and procedures.

Security Management
The security measures associated with the IT service can also be essential to effective Service Level Management. Both the IT organization and the customer will have certain security requirements. The corresponding agreements are defined in the SLA. Security Management ensures that the agreed security measures are implemented, monitored, and reported to Service Level Management.

Configuration Management
Configuration Management is responsible for entering details of the components and documentation related to a service in the CMDB, and providing information from this database. Hence, the creation or modification of a service or SLA will affect the CMDB. The Service Desk uses the CMDB to determine the impact of an error on the services, and to check the agreements about the response and solution times. The CMDB is also used to report about the quality of the CI's, so as to enable Service Level Management to report about the quality of the service provided.

Financial Management for IT Services
If the customer is charged for services provided by the IT organization, then this is also included in the SLA. These may be one-time charges, or charges for special or additional services. Financial Management provides Service Level Management with information about the costs associated with providing a service. It also provides information about charging methods and the rate the customer may be charged to recover the costs of a service.

10.4 Activities

The process steps are described in detail below, including the process workflow and the activities.

10.4.1 Identification

As businesses become more dependent on their IT services, the demand for higher quality IT services is also increasing. The perceived quality of a service depends on the expectations of the customer, the ongoing management of customer perceptions, the stability of the service, and the acceptability of the costs. As such, the best way to provide the appropriate quality is to first discuss the issue with the customer.

Past experiences show that customers are often not clear about their expectations themselves. Sometimes they simply assume that certain aspects of the service will be provided without having any clear agreements. These assumed (implicit) aspects of the IT services are often the cause of much confusion. This once again underlines the need for Service Level Managers to know their customers well, and to help their customers clarify their thinking about what services and service levels they really need, and at what cost.

The requirements of the customer must be expressed in measurable values so that they can contribute to the design and monitoring of IT services. If metrics have not been agreed with the customer, it is difficult to verify whether or not the IT service has fulfilled any of the agreements. Service Level Management plays a key part in understanding and defining what the customer needs.

The first step in concluding SLA's about the IT services provided today or in the future should be to identify and define the customer needs in the Service Level Requirements. Besides doing so once within the course of the process, this activity should also be carried out regularly, initiated by reports and reviews, at the request of the customer or for the benefit of the IT organization. This activity may cover either new or existing services.

10.4.2 Definition

Defining the scope and depth of the customer's requirements is considered as a design process within Service Level Management. According to the ISO 9001 model for quality assurance, a design process should include the following steps: design, development, production and installation and maintenance. The design process should be managed to ensure that the results at the end of the process correspond with the requirements of the customer. During the design process, the term 'external' refers to communication with customers, and 'internal' to the technical underpinning within the IT organization. The design process includes a number of steps, from detailing the customer's requirements and defining them in clear standards, to developing the technical requirements to provide the service.

Defining external standards

The first step of quantifying new or existing IT services is defining or redefining the customer's expectations about the service in general terms. These expectations are formalized in documented Service Level Requirements (SLR's). This should involve the whole customer organization. This step is generally considered as the most difficult part of Service Level Management.

At the beginning of this stage, the Service Level Manager must prepare for the meeting with the customer organization. The first questions to be asked are: 'What is required of the IT service and what elements should this service consist of?' A service could entail the use of a limited infrastructure, such as a Wide Area Network (WAN). Such a service can contribute to a composi service, such as access to a full information system, including the full underlying infrastructure (WAN, LAN, workstations, applications, etc.)

During these meetings, the users must be divided into groups. The Service Level Manager draws up a list of the user groups, and their requirements and authority. The following information is needed to define the Service Level Requirements:
- A description, from the customer's perspective, of functions to be provided by the service.
- Times and days on which the service must be available.
- Service continuity requirements.
- IT functions needed to provide the service.
- References to the current operational methods or quality standards to be considered when defining the service.
- A reference to the SLA to be modified or replaced, where relevant.

The design stage will produce a Service Level Requirements document, which is signed by the Service Level Manager and the customer. The Service Level Requirements can still be modified while the department is working on the design, procurement and implementation. Such changes may relate to the practicability of the envisaged functions or costs. Both parties must approve any such changes.

Translation to internal standards
During the specification phase, the Service Level Requirements are developed in detail. This stage aims to provide the following information:
- Unambiguous and detailed description of the IT services and required components.
- Specification of the way in which the service will be implemented and provided.
- Specification of the required quality control procedure.

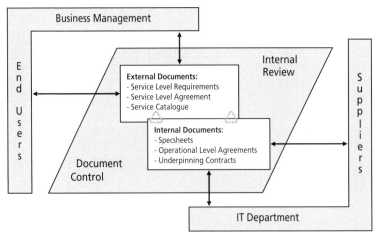

Figure 10.2 - Specification stage

n the specification phase it is recommended to distinguish between elements of the documen-
tion for internal use and those for external use (Figure 10.2). Specifications for external use
late to objectives agreed with the customers, and the design process is controlled by these
bjectives. These specifications are drawn up in cooperation with the customer organization, and
rm the input for the specifications for internal use.

Specifications for internal use refer to the internal objectives of the IT organization, which have to be fulfilled to meet customer demands. A separation between internal and external specifications can be most useful once the Service Level Management process is under way. This ensures that the IT organization does not bother its customers with technical details. From that time on, managing the service levels relates to keeping the internal and external specifications aligned. Document Control and Internal Reviews contribute to this by keeping records of related documents, managing versions and organizing regular audits.

Spec sheets (service specifications) describe in detail what the customer wants (external element) and how this will impact the IT organization (internal element). Spec Sheets need not be signed by both parties, however they are subject to Document Control. The Service Catalogue can be drawn up on the basis of the service specifications; hence, changes in the service levels can be included immediately in the Spec Sheets and Service Catalogue. The SLA is then revised in line with the revised Spec Sheets.

Service Quality Plan

It is recommended to include all management information (key performance indicators) and specifications for internal and external providers in a single document to provide comprehensive information about the contributions made to the IT services by each Service Management process.

10.4.3 Contract

Once the specification phase has been completed, the IT organization has effectively translated the business needs into IT resources and configurations. This information is then used to draw up or modify the following documents.

Service Level Agreement

When developing the SLA structure, it is recommended to first define the general aspects, such as network services for the whole company and develop a general service-based SLA model, before the negotiations begin. The SLA's could have a hierarchical structure, like that of the customer organization, in the form of a framework agreement with a number of tiers. Each tier has its own level of detail. The top tiers include agreements about general services to be provided to the organization. The lower tiers contain information relevant to specific customers.

The structure of a SLA depends on a number of the variables such as:
- **Physical aspects of the organization:**
  - Scale.
  - Complexity.
  - Geographical distribution.
- **Cultural aspects:**
  - Language(s) of the document (for international organizations).
  - Relationship between the IT organization and the customer.
  - Charging policy.
  - Uniformity of the business activities.
  - Profit or non-profit organization.
- **Nature of the business activities:**
  - General terms and conditions.
  - Business hours - 5 x 8 hours or 7 x 24 hours.

Underpinning Contracts and Operational Level Agreements

Any existing UC's or OLA's must be revised during the design process. Everyone involved should be aware of any UC's or OLA's that apply to the provision of a specific service. Configuration Management can help clarify the links to the Spec sheets.

Service Catalogue

The following tips can be helpful when writing a Service Catalogue:

■ Use your customer's language. Avoid technical jargon, and use terminology corresponding to the relevant business.
■ Try to look at things from the customer's point of view and use that approach to identify relevant information.
■ Provide an attractive layout as the IT organization uses this document to present itself to its customers.
■ Ensure that the document is available to the largest number of potential stakeholders, for example by publishing it on an Intranet site or on CD-ROM.

10.4.4 Monitoring

Service Level Management can only be monitored if the service levels are clearly defined in advance and correspond with the externally agreed objectives. The service levels must be measured from the customer's perspective. Monitoring should not be limited to technical aspects, but should also include procedural matters. For example, until the user has been informed that the service has been restored, they will assume that it is unavailable.

Availability Management and Capacity Management generally provide the information about the implementation of the technical objectives associated with the service levels. In some cases, information will also be provided from the Service Support processes, especially Incident Management. However, measuring internal parameters is insufficient, as this does not relate to the user's perception. Parameters such as response time, escalation time and support must also be measurable. A complete view is only obtained by combining management information from both the systems and Service Management.

10.4.5 Reports

Customer reports (Service Reports) must be provided at the intervals agreed in the SLA. These reports compare the agreed service levels and the service levels that were actually measured. Examples include reports about:

■ Availability and downtime during a specified period.
■ Average response times during peak periods.
■ Transaction rates during peak periods.
■ Number of functional errors in the IT service.
■ Frequency and duration of service degradation.
■ Average number of users during peak periods.
■ Number of successful and unsuccessful attempts to circumvent security
■ Proportion of service capacity used.
■ Number of completed and open changes.
■ Cost of the service provided.

10.4.6 Review
Service levels must be reviewed at regular intervals. The following aspects should be considered:
- Service level agreements since the previous review.
- Problems related to the services.
- Identification of service trends.
- Changes to services within the agreed service levels.
- Changes to procedures and estimates of the cost of additional resources.
- Consequences of failure to provide the agreed service levels.

If the IT services fail to meet the agreed service levels, actions may be agreed for improvement, such as:
- Developing a Service Improvement Program.
- Allocating additional personnel and resources.
- Modifying the service levels defined in the SLA.
- Modifying the procedures.
- Modifying Operational Level Agreements and Underpinning Contracts.

In many organizations where Service Level Management is being introduced, there are discussions about whether or not to associate sanctions with the failure to meet SLA agreements. This is a difficult issue as Service Level Management is based on the interaction between the IT department and the users of IT services, often within the same organization. In such a situation, where both the IT department and users work towards the same corporate objectives, it is doubtful if sanctions and especially financial penalties contribute to the corporate interests. It would be much better to make agreements based on a common interest about measures to be taken to prevent failure to meet the service levels. However, sanctions may be relevant if the IT service provider obtains a service from an external IT provider. However, in that case there is more likely to be a legally binding contract (UC) than a SLA.

10.5 Process control
A number of critical success factors have to be identified to optimize the process and its control. Performance indicators are also needed to measure and improve the process.

10.5.1 Critical success factors and key performance indicators
The success of Service Level Management depends on the following factors:
- A capable Service Level Manager with both IT and business expertise, and a supporting organization when necessary.
- Clear process mission and objectives.
- Awareness campaign to provide people with information about the process, develop understanding and gain support.
- Clearly defined tasks, authorities and responsibilities within the process, distinguishing between process control and operational tasks (customer contacts).

The following key performance indicators can be used to determine the effectiveness and efficiency of the Service Level Management process:
- Service elements included in SLA's.
- Elements of the SLA supported by OLA and UC's.
- Elements of the SLA's which are monitored, and where shortcomings are reported.
- Elements of the SLA's, which are regularly reviewed.

- Elements of the SLA's where the agreed service levels are fulfilled.
- Shortcomings, which are identified and covered by an improvement plan.
- Actions, which are taken to eliminate these shortcomings.
- Trends identified with respect to the actual service levels.

10.5.2 Management reports

Management reports, in contrast to service level reports, are not provided for the customer, but to control or manage the internal process. They may contain metrics about actual service levels supported, and trends such as:
- Number of SLA's concluded.
- Number of times an SLA was not fulfilled.
- Cost of measuring and monitoring the SLA's.
- Customer satisfaction, based on survey complaints.
- Statistics about incidents, problems and changes.
- Progress of improvement actions.

10.5.3 Functions and roles

Roles

Service Level Management needs to be controlled by a process manager. This manager should ensure that the process is effective and provides the envisaged benefits. This does not necessarily mean that one person fulfills this role. Many organizations have several Service Level Managers, each being responsible for one or more services or customer groups.

Responsibilities

The Service Level Manager is responsible for:
- Creating and updating the Service Catalogue.
- Defining and maintaining an effective Service Level Management process for the IT organization, including:
  - SLA structure.
  - OLA's with internal providers.
  - UC's with external providers.
- Updating the existing Service Improvement Program.
- Negotiating, concluding and maintaining SLA's, OLA's and UC's.
- Reviewing the performance of the IT organization and improving it where necessary.

10.6 Costs and possible problems

10.6.1 Costs

The costs of implementing Service Level Management can be divided into the following categories:
- Personnel costs (Service Level Manager and project team).
- Training costs.
- Documentation costs.
- Costs of accommodation, hardware and software.
- Costs of operational activities related to updating the Service Quality Plan, the Service Level Agreements and the Service Catalogue.

10.6.2 Possible problems

The following problems may be encountered:

- Service Level Management results in a businesslike relationship with the customer and requires that all IT personnel adhere to the agreements. This may require a culture change in the organization.
- Customers may need help specifying the Service Level Requirements.
- It can be quite difficult to express expectations of the customer in terms of measurable standards and associated costs.
- The Service Level Manager should be wary of overambitious agreements whilst the planning, measuring and monitoring tools, procedures, Service Quality Plan, and the Underpinning Contracts have not been developed. It is better to use a strategy of gradual improvement.
- The overhead costs associated with monitoring and measuring the service levels are easily underestimated. In a large organization this may require several dedicated staff.
- In practice, many IT organizations start by drafting Service Level Agreements and skip the analysis of the requirements of the customer, the design stage and the development of the Service Quality Plan. This can result in a process which is difficult to manage and which does not provide clear, measurable standards.
- The Service Level Management documents and process could end up becoming ends in themselves, instead of a means to a better relationship between the IT service provider and the customer.

11 FINANCIAL MANAGEMENT FOR IT SERVICES

11.1 Introduction

Most people view IT services as an important contributor to the support of routine business activities, but too few people realize that these services cost money. As the number of users grows the IT budget will grow. Customers become more concerned about IT spending as the budget grows, and less able, without assistance, to map this spending to the business. If charging for IT services is necessary, then without assistance the customer will find it difficult to map actual costs of IT services to business benefits.

ITIL was developed to structure the management of the IT infrastructure to promote the efficient and economic use of IT resources. One of the objectives was to stimulate cost awareness of customers to promote the wise use of IT resources in the perspective of business goals. Providing IT services to users at a reasonable cost depends on three factors:

- **Quality** - in operational terms of:
  - Capacity.
  - Availability.
  - Performance.
  - Disaster recovery.
  - Support.
- **Cost** - in terms of:
  - Expenditure.
  - Investment.
- **Customer requirements** - the cost and quality must be in-line with the users' business needs.

The first two factors are often in conflict as improving quality normally means increasing costs, while reducing costs normally means decreasing quality. However, these two factors can be balanced by focusing on the customer's needs.

An awareness of the costs associated with providing IT services and applying a realistic charging system for those services, puts the provision of IT services on a solid business footing. Customers will become more aware of the costs and feel that they are being charged a reasonable price, and are therefore less likely to squander IT resources.

11.1.1 Basic concepts

Budgeting

Budgeting involves predicting costs and controlling expenditure. This often starts by preparing a plan with the anticipated customer demand for the services and the related costs.

A forecast can be developed on the basis of historical data, while making allowances for current trends in the business and relying on personal expertise. If there is no historical data available, it may be possible to use similar services as a model.

Accounting

Accounting means monitoring how the IT organization spends its money. It is particularly important to be able to determine costs for each customer, service, activity, etc. Here, understanding the issues is more important than being able to determine the cost to the penny.

Charging

Charging refers to all the activities needed to bill the customer for the services provided to them. Charging includes determining the objective(s) of charging, as well as the methods for calculating charges. This requires an effective accounting system that fulfills the need for detail at the different accounting levels: analysis, turning, reporting.

Cost categories

Effective cost control requires an understanding of the nature of the costs. Costs can be classified in several ways.

For each product or service you could determine the costs that contribute to it directly and those that do not:

- **Direct costs** - costs related specifically and exclusively to an IT service. For example activities and materials directly and uniquely associated with a specific service (telephone line rental for Internet access).
- **Indirect costs** - costs that are not specifically and uniquely associated with an IT service. Examples include facilities (e.g. a desk), support services (e.g. network management), and administrative costs (including time).

One option for charging the indirect costs is simply to apportion them between services or customers.

Another option is to use Activity Based Costing (ABC). This method starts with collecting all the overhead costs in an organization and then allocating the costs of activities to the products and services that necessitated these activities.

In essence costs are charged on the basis of criteria other than direct costs. ABC can be a useful charging method if many costs are not directly related to the service volume. Instead of allocating indirect costs arbitrarily, ABC allocates them on the basis of activities carried out for products and services.

Another way to understand costs is to divide them into fixed and variable costs.

- **Fixed costs** - independent of the production volume; they include investments in hardware, software and buildings. In most cases, the monthly or yearly depreciation and interest are considered, rather than the purchase price. Fixed costs continue even if the production (service) volume is reduced or interrupted.
- **Variable costs** - costs whose levels change in line with changes in the production volume. Examples include external personnel, printer cartridges, paper, heating and electricity. These costs are linked with the services provided; as the production volume increases, the costs will also rise.

We distinguish capital and operational costs:

- **Capital costs** - concern the purchase of assets intended for long-term use within the organization. The costs are depreciated over a number of years. Thus, the costs amount to the depreciation, rather than the purchase price.
- **Operational costs** - day-to-day costs not associated with tangible production resources. Examples include hardware and software maintenance contracts, license costs, insurance premiums, etc.

Cost types

Once the cost accounting structure has been defined (for example by a department, service or customer), cost types can be set up for posting cost items in the accounts. The number of cost types will depend on the size of the organization. Cost types should have a clear and recognizable description and structure so that costs are easily allocated.

The cost types then are subdivided into **cost elements**. The charging methods for each cost element can be defined at a later stage. There are six main cost types, some for direct costs and some for indirect costs.

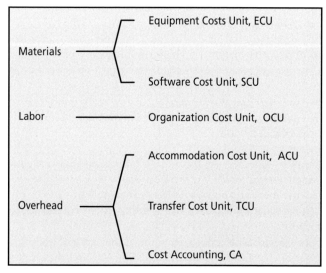

Figure 11.1 - Cost types and cost elements

Examples of these cost types include:
- **Equipment Cost Unit (ECU)** - all IT hardware such as:
  - Servers.
  - Disk storage.
  - Communications and networks.
  - Printers.
- **Software Cost Unit (SCU)** - direct and indirect costs to keep the system operating, including:
  - System software.
  - Transaction processing software.
  - Database management systems.
  - System management systems.
  - Application development systems.
  - Applications.
- **Organization Cost Unit (OCU)** - direct and indirect personnel costs, which may be fixed or variable, such as:
  - Salaries.
  - Training.
  - Travel costs.
- **Accommodation Cost Unit (ACU)** - all direct and indirect costs related to housing, such as:
  - Computer rooms.
  - Offices.
  - Other facilities such as test rooms, training rooms, air conditioning, etc.

■ **Transfer Cost Unit (TCU)** - costs associated with goods and services provided by another department. That is, internal charges between departments of an organization.
■ **Cost Accounting (CA)** - costs associated with the financial management activities themselves.

II.2 Objectives

Financial Management aims to assist the internal IT organization with the cost-effective management of the IT resources required for the provision of IT services. For this reason, the process aims to break down the IT service costs, and associate them with the various IT services provided. In this way, it aims to support management decisions with respect to IT investment and encourages the cost aware use of IT facilities.

It may be decided to base the charging methods on full cost recovery, recovery with financial support (budgets), or recovery with the objective of making a predefined profit.

II.2.1 Benefits

Once the IT organization has introduced Financial Management, it will be able to:
■ Determine the costs of IT services.
■ Identify and classify the cost structure.
■ Fairly allocate the costs to IT services provided to internal and external customers.
■ Introduce charging methods for the use of IT services, where appropriate.
■ Operate the IT department as a business unit, where required.
■ Recover all costs including capital costs (investment, repayment, depreciation and interest) from the customer.
■ Check the charges at regular intervals to determine if they are still realistic and acceptable.
■ Shape the behavior of customers and users by building cost awareness and tying costs directly to services.

Because of the diverse nature of the benefits, we make a distinction between Budgeting and Accounting (which are involved with Costing) and Charging.

The main advantage of **Budgeting and Accounting** is that it provides management with better information about the costs of providing IT services. This information enables the IT management to balance costs and quality to provide a financially justifiable service.

Budgeting and Accounting helps the IT Services Manager to:
■ Make decisions for each service, based on cost effectiveness.
■ Take a businesslike approach to decisions on IT services and the related investments.
■ Provide more information to support expenditure, for example by showing the costs of avoiding strategic expenditure.
■ Develop budgets and plans on the basis of reliable information.

The main advantage of **Charging** is promoting a businesslike relationship with the customer. A paying customer has rights and can make demands, but will also use resources more carefully if they are aware of the link between the demands they make and the invoice they receive.

Charging enables IT Services Management to:
■ Review IT services in a businesslike manner and make investment plans based on cost recovery.
■ Recover IT costs by linking them to the use made of the services.
■ Influence customer behavior, for example by charging higher rates during peak times, or sim-

ply by providing information on the cost and utilization of services upon which management can take action.

The introduction of charging should aim to influence customer behavior and not lead to a situation where the customer gets anything they want for payment. For example, it may not be possible to meet the requirements of all individual users at individual rates, even if these users are prepared to pay the price. Charging provides a businesslike environment for negotiation. Customers will become more aware of the costs associated with using IT facilities.

11.3 The process

The role of IT in industry has expanded greatly in recent years. Thus, the IT organization is faced with ensuring higher quality and cost-effective IT services. The developments related to the Internet mean that IT organizations also increasingly have to deal with customers and users outside the business. Bookshops, for example, put their catalogues on the Internet and serve customers throughout the world. This increases the scale of the operation and it often becomes necessary to get better information about the costs. Cost-effectiveness also requires agreements about the services to be provided and the reasonable costs to be charged for those services. IT organizations have to become more businesslike, and putting an effective cost control system in place is a part of doing just that.

An effective cost control system should fulfill the following criteria:
- Support the development of an investment strategy that allows for the flexibility provided by modern technology.
- Identify priorities in the use of resources.
- Cover the costs of all IT resources used in the organization, including updating relevant information.
- Support management with day-to-day decisions so that long-term decisions can be taken with the lowest possible financial risk.
- Be flexible and able to respond quickly to changes in the business activities.

11.3.1 Financial Management activities

Financial Management supports a business in planning and realizing its business objectives. It must be used consistently throughout the business, with a minimum of conflict, to optimize its efficiency. In an IT organization, Financial Management is implemented through three major processes: Budgeting, Accounting and Charging. This cycle is illustrated in Figure 11.2.

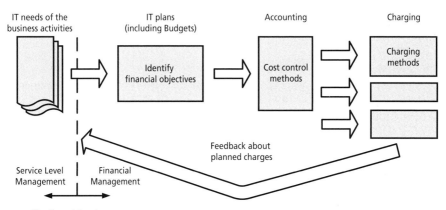

Figure 11.2 - The financial cycle

Financial Management for IT Services interacts with almost all the other IT Service Management processes, but has particular dependencies and responsibilities with respect to the processes discussed below.

11.3.2 Relationship with other processes

Business processes

Service Level Management is important in terms of defining the vision, strategy and planning in line with the business processes (Figure 11.3). Although these activities fall outside the scope of Financial Management, they make an important contribution to this area. This is because the business has a vision of the future, which is used to define measurable objectives which affect all business units and which can also be used to set measurable objectives for the IT organization.

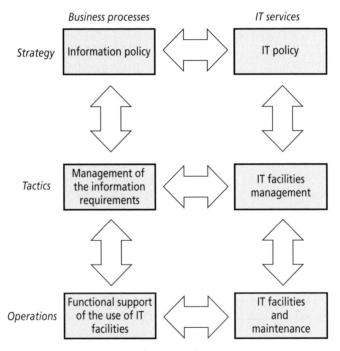

Figure 11.3 - Relationship with the business processes (source: itSMF)

Hence, the IT strategy should be based on the business objectives. As the IT organization becomes more familiar with the business, opportunities will be created for the cost effective use of new IT technology. The IT costs of implementation and operation have to be compared with the business benefits in terms of reduced operating costs and increased turnover.

Service Level Management

The SLA defines the expectations of the customer and obligations of the IT management organization. The costs incurred to fulfill the customer's requirements have a major impact on the form and scale of services agreed with the customer. The Financial Manager of the IT organization confers with the Service Level Manager about issues such as the costs of meeting current and future business requirements, the charging policy of the organization and its effect on customers, and how the policy affects customer behavior.

The more a SLA allows different service levels for different customers, the more important and the greater the potential benefits of charging for IT services. This will also increase the overhead resulting from the Budgeting, Accounting and Charging processes.

Capacity Management
The provision of capacity and availability will be influenced by cost information. It may be necessary to discuss the cost of provision of increased capacity and improved availability with the customer or the business as a whole. Information on the cost versus business benefit may influence the decision on whether to purchase additional capacity or improve availability.

Configuration Management
Configuration Management specifies, identifies, and records all changes to all infrastructure components. The use of information, including cost information in the CMDB facilitates the collection of historical cost data. Configuration Management can also be used to reconcile asset data with data from financial systems.

II.4 Activities

11.4.1 Budgeting
The objective of Budgeting is planning and controlling the activities of an organization. Corporate and strategic planning concerns the long-term objectives of a business. Budgets define the financial plans for the objectives during the period covered by the budget. These periods normally range from one to five years.

Budgeting methods
One of the following methods is selected, depending on the financial policy of the business:
- **Incremental budgeting** - last year's figures are used as the basis for the new budget. This is then adjusted to reflect the expected changes.
- **Zero-Base budgeting** - this method starts with a blank piece of paper: the Zero Base. Past experience is ignored. This requires managers to justify all their resource needs in terms of costs in their budget. This means that every expense has to be evaluated and decided if it should be made, as well as what the cost should be. Obviously, this method is much more time-consuming, and it is therefore normally only used every few years. The incremental method is used for the years in between.

Budgeting process
Budgeting starts by identifying the key factors that limit the growth of the company. In many businesses this is the sales volume; however, it could also be a lack of space or materials. Often, financial constraints determine the budget. This process includes defining the following secondary budgets (we will ignore the approval processes used in every business):
- **Sales and marketing budget** - if the sales volume determines the budget, then the marketing department is responsible for a large part of the process. An accurate assessment and analysis of the customers, markets, sales regions, products, etc. is essential for drawing up a good budget.
- **Production budget** - the production budget provides detailed information about the services to be provided: quantities, delivery times, person-hours required, materials required, etc.
- **Administrative budgets** - based on the service to be provided, you have to determine the overhead budgets for the relevant departments such as production, sales and distribution, research and development, etc.

■ **Cost and investment budgets** - the cost budget results from the plans in the above budgets. The investment budget identifies the expenditure associated with the replacement and purchase of the means of production. Investment projects initiated in the preceding year may also affect the investment budget.

Budget period

The financial (fiscal) year would be an obvious choice for the budget period. For a regular comparison between the actual and budget figures, the budget period is then divided into months or another regular period, such as four-week windows.

Some businesses not only draw up a detailed one-year budget, but also a general forecast for a three or five-year period. This informs senior management about the expectations over a longer period.

11.4.2 Accounting

To be able to run an IT organization as a business, it is essential that all the costs that IT is responsible for are identified and understood. Costs have to be determined, even if they will not be charged to customers. Costs can only be controlled if they are clearly understood. This is not so much about identifying minor costs, but primarily about the different ways in which costs can be structured. This increases the understanding of the way in which money is spent.

One of the primary accounting activities is defining the cost elements. This structure is fixed for one year, after which it can be modified. In most cases, a cost accounting method will have been selected when introducing a cost element structure to the business. Thus, the cost element structure should be compatible with the methods adopted by the business. In many cases, costs are recorded for each department, customer or product. However, ideally the structure should reflect the services provided. Even when the process is not used for charging, it is often useful to base the cost type structure on a service structure, such as that used in a service catalogue.

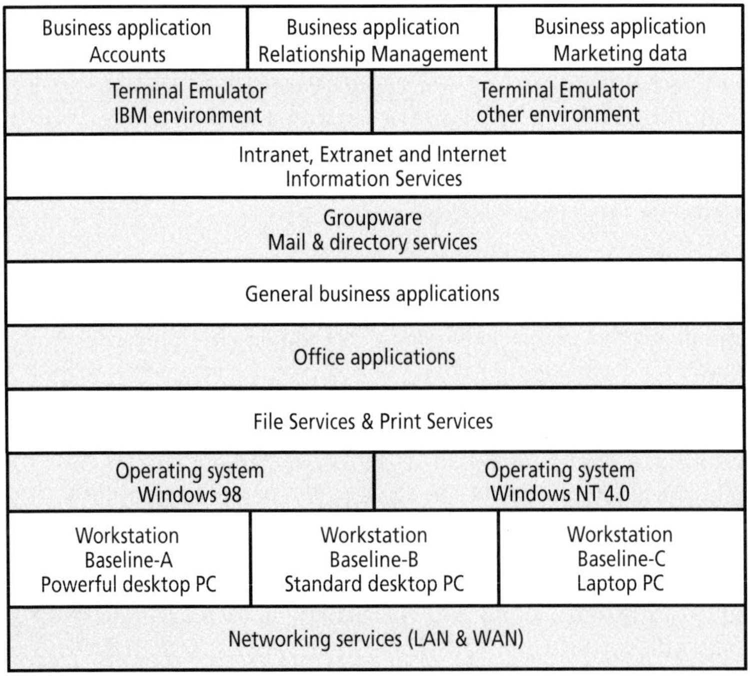

Business application Accounts	Business application Relationship Management	Business application Marketing data
Terminal Emulator IBM environment		Terminal Emulator other environment
Intranet, Extranet and Internet Information Services		
Groupware Mail & directory services		
General business applications		
Office applications		
File Services & Print Services		
Operating system Windows 98		Operating system Windows NT 4.0
Workstation Baseline-A Powerful desktop PC	Workstation Baseline-B Standard desktop PC	Workstation Baseline-C Laptop PC
Networking services (LAN & WAN)		

Figure 11.4 - Example of a service structure

In the example of Figure 11.4 there is a hierarchical structure of the service elements created by the IT organization to provide the services. In this structure, the lower-level service elements support the higher-level service elements. The higher the position of an element in this structure, the more relevant its function is to the business.

After defining the service elements, cost elements have to be defined which are then subdivided into cost units for personnel, hardware, software and overheads.

The advantage of structuring cost elements in-line with service elements is that expenditure on the hardware, software and support of the service becomes clearly visible. In addition to a structure based on direct costs as shown in Figure 11.4, it may also be decided how to allocate indirect costs to the services. The more detailed the service structure, the easier it will be to understand the costs. Alternatively, a less detailed catalogue could only list three standard workstations that include everything. In this case, the diagram would only have three columns and far fewer cost elements. This may be clearer, but it would also provide less detailed information. For example, there would be no clear cost element that network support should be allocated to and it would therefore be impossible to determine the support required for the network.

Budgets for the coming year are then drawn up for each service and cost element, on the basis of past experience and estimates of growth for the coming year. These budgets are monitored every month to identify any new developments such as unexpected growth, and to respond in accordance with the business policy where appropriate.

11.4.3 Charging

Keeping cost records is obviously not a new concept, but it is becoming increasingly important. Charging for internal costs is a relatively new development. Internal charging is an effective tool to encourage users to use the IT resources more carefully. However, charging for IT services is not that useful if the budget holders in the customer organizations are not charged for other services, such as the telephone, accommodation, mailroom, catering and personnel administration. In other words, charging should be compatible with the financial policies of the organization. If charging is found to be appropriate, then budget holders can address operational costs, which they can pass on in the price of their products and services.

Normally, charging is introduced to recover all the costs incurred. In that case, the IT organization operates as a business unit. This is only feasible if the actual operating costs of the IT services are known.

Charging Policy

It is useful to address charging policies before setting a rate.

There are a number of charging policies. The appropriate method can be selected depending on the objectives of Financial Management. Alternatively, when introducing charging in stages, a different policy might be used for each stage. The charging policies are:
- **Communication of Information** - customer managers are informed about the charges to make them aware of the costs of the use of IT services by their departments. There are two options for this:
  - Calculating the costs associated with each business unit and informing the managers concerned.
  - As above, but including the charges to be passed on, based on a specific charging method.
- **Pricing Flexibility** - rates are determined and charged on an annual basis. If the service

provider takes the initiative to invest in a service because it is used more frequently, the contract can include a clause for charging the additional costs. The alternative is to offer excess capacity to other potential customers.

■ **Notional Charging** - the costs are invoiced, but need not be paid. This method enables the IT organization to gain experience with the process and correct any mistakes in the charging system. It also gives the customer an opportunity to get used to charging. However, this charging method is only useful if eventually the costs will indeed be recovered, otherwise cost awareness will fall.

Rates
It is often difficult to set a rate for a service. Setting rates include the following activities:
■ Deciding on the objective of charging.
■ Determining direct and indirect costs.
■ Determining market rates.
■ Analyzing the demand for services.
■ Analyzing the number of customers and the competition.

To determine the rate for a service, the organization should first determine the objective and the intended benefit for customers and IT personnel.

Price is one of the four Ps in marketing: Product, Price, Promotion and Place. The price is not only relevant in terms of recovering the costs incurred, but also affects the demand for the product. A flexible pricing strategy can be used to promote products or to phase them out. The revenue from other services could subsidize a new service with few customers. The costs of a service must be clearly identified before the pricing strategy can be selected.

There is a wide range of pricing policies, such as:
■ **Cost Plus** - exists in several forms, all of which are based on charging the costs incurred plus a profit margin (cost + % mark-up). The costs and profit margin can be defined in a number of ways, such as:
  - Full costs including a profit margin.
  - Marginal costs plus a margin (sufficient to cover the average fixed costs, costs per item, and return on capital). For example, if the availability of the LAN/WAN is included in the charges for a network connection, then this element need not be included in other LAN services.
  - One of the above methods, with a margin of 0%.
■ **Going Rate** - for services where there are already price agreements.
■ **Target Return** - services whose price was determined in advance.
■ **Market rate** - (what the market will bear) - prices that match those charged by external suppliers.
■ **Negotiated Contract Price** - these prices are discussed with the customer. If the customer requests a new service then it is negotiated whether they have to bear all the investment costs, or only a proportion.

Volume discounts can be granted for services that can be provided at a lower price if the volume increases. To spread the demand on the systems, peak and off-peak rates can be used.

11.4.4 Reporting
Depending on the charging policy, the actual use of IT services is either invoiced or communicated to the customer. The costs are addressed in the regular meetings with the customer under

the Service Level Management process. Hence, Service Level Management is provided with the following information:
- IT services expenditure per customer.
- Difference between the actual and estimated charges.
- Charging and accounting methods used.
- Any disputes about charges, with the causes and solutions.

11.5 Process control

Accounting forms part of the overall IT Service Management structure and should be managed by a Financial Manager. This manager is responsible for the implementation and day-to-day management of the accounting and charging system and reports to IT management. The Financial Manager need not be part of the IT organization. Critical success factors, reports and performance indicators can be used to optimize Financial Management.

11.5.1 Critical success factors and performance indicators

Before introducing Financial Management, the users, personnel, and IT management must be informed of the objective of its introduction, and the costs, benefits and potential problems associated with the introduction.

Critical success factors for the introduction of an effective charging system include:
- Users must be aware of which services they are charged for.
- Users must be aware of the charging methods so that they can control their costs (for example through agreements or reports in terms of quantifiable performance units).
- The cost monitoring system must provide details and justification of expenditure.
- IT Service Management must provide balanced systems offering effective IT services at reasonable costs.
- IT management must be fully aware of the impact and costs of the introduction of Financial Management and be fully committed to it.
- Configuration Management must provide relevant information about the structure of the services to set up an appropriate accounting system.

The following performance indicators can help to control the process:
- Accurate cost-benefit analysis of the services provided.
- Customers consider the charging methods reasonable.
- The IT organization meets its financial targets.
- The use of the services by the customer changes.
- Timely reporting to Service Level Management.

11.5.2 Management reports

The Financial Management process must provide regular reports to the IT management about issues such as:
- Overall costs and benefits of the IT services.
- Cost analysis for each IT department, platform, or other relevant unit.
- Costs associated with the Financial Management system.
- Planning of future investments.
- Opportunities for cost reduction.

11.5.3 Functions and roles

Some IT organizations have their own Financial Managers, while other organizations have agreements with the financial department, which cooperates closely with IT management. Like any other process, Financial Management must have a process owner responsible for the development and maintenance of the financial system.

The IT Financial Manager who is responsible for the process must work on equal terms with the management of the other processes and the financial department to draw up guidelines for the budgeting, accounting and charging systems.

11.6 Costs and possible problems

11.6.1 Costs

The costs of this process can be divided into two categories:

- Administrative and organizational costs associated with planning, introducing and carrying out the process.
- Costs of the necessary tools, such as an application with hardware and a database.

11.6.2 Possible problems

The following problems may be encountered:

- The activities required for recording and monitoring costs are often not familiar for IT personnel.
- Monitoring, calculating and charging costs often requires information about the planning of non-IT services, such as buildings for which it is often impossible to obtain planning details.
- It is difficult to find personnel who are familiar with both IT and accounting.
- If the corporate strategy and objectives for the development of Information Systems have not been clearly formulated and documented then it becomes difficult to consider the necessary investments.
- The opportunities provided by the process are often insufficiently understood, resulting in insufficient cooperation.
- Lack of management commitment can mean that the process is not taken seriously by the organization.

12 CAPACITY MANAGEMENT

12.1 Introduction

Capacity Management aims to provide the required capacity for data processing and storage, at the right time and in a cost effective way. It is a balancing act. Good capacity management eliminates panic buying at the last minute, or buying the biggest box possible and crossing your fingers. Both of these situations are costly. Many data centers, for example, perpetually run at or below 20% average utilization (used capacity), over the business day (not making any allowance for system types, but including file & print servers, etc.). This isn't so bad when you have a handful of servers. But when you have thousands of servers, as many enterprise IT organizations do, these percentages mean vast sums of money are being wasted.

Capacity Management addresses the following issues:
- Can the purchase cost of processing capacity be justified in the light of business requirements, and is the processing capacity used in the most efficient way (cost versus capacity)?
- Does the current processing capacity adequately fulfill both current and future demands of the customer (supply versus demand)?
- Is the available processing capacity performing at peak efficiency (performance tuning)?
- Precisely when should additional capacity be made available?
- Do we know what future IT capacity is needed and when?

To implement its objective, Capacity Management needs a close relationship with business and IT strategy processes. Hence, this process is both reactive (measuring and improving) and proactive (analyzing and forecasting).

12.1.1 Basic concepts

Important concepts in Capacity Management include:
- **Performance Management** - measuring, monitoring and tuning the performance of IT infrastructure components for optimum performance.
- **Application Sizing** - determining the hardware or network capacity needed to support new or modified services and the predicted future workload.
- **Modeling** - using analytical, simulation or trending models to determine the capacity requirements of services and determining the best capacity solutions. Modeling allows various scenarios to be analyzed and the 'what-if' questions addressed.
- **Workload management** - dealing with understanding what the various business drivers are doing, and what resources they require - a foundational component of modeling, but also stands alone.
- **Capacity Planning** - developing a Capacity Plan, based on a Capacity Management Database, analyzing the current situation and predicting the future use of the IT infrastructure and the resources needed to meet the expected demand for IT services (preferably using scenarios).

12.2 Objectives

Capacity Management aims to consistently provide the required IT resources at the right time (when they are needed), and at the right cost, aligned with the current and future requirements of the business.

Thus, Capacity Management needs to understand both the expected business developments affecting customers, as well as anticipating technical developments. The Capacity Management process has an important role in determining returns on investment and cost justifications.

12.2.1 Benefits

The benefits of Capacity Management are:

- Reduced risks associated with existing services as the resources are effectively managed, and the performance of the equipment is monitored continuously.
- Reduced risks associated with new or modified services as Application Sizing means that the impact of new or modified services on existing systems is known.
- Reduced costs, as investments are made at the appropriate time, neither too early nor too late, which means that the purchasing process does not have to deal with last-minute purchases or overpurchases of capacity too far in advance of need.
- Reduced business disruption through close involvement with Change Management when determining the impact on IT capacity. Preventing urgent changes resulting from inadequate or incorrect capacity estimates.
- More reliable forecasts providing quicker and more accurate response to customer requests.
- Greater efficiency as demand and supply are balanced at an early stage.
- Managed, or even reduced, capacity-related expenditure as capacity is used more efficiently.

These benefits will improve the relationship with customers. Capacity Management confers with customers at an early stage, and anticipates the requirements. The relationships with suppliers will also be improved. Purchasing, delivery, installation and maintenance agreements can also be planned more effectively.

12.3 The process

Like many of the ITIL processes, Capacity Management goes back to the days of mainframe computers. Unfortunately, this means that some people think Capacity Management is therefore only relevant in mainframe environments. This is reinforced by the reduction in hardware costs in recent years. This has resulted in some organizations simply buying hardware with excess capacity, without considering the Capacity Management issues. The danger here is that the largest source of costs, risks, and possible problems in IT is not the hardware itself, but the proliferation of hardware creates additional management problems that are more expensive than the hardware itself.

Implementing Capacity Management will help prevent unnecessary investments and ad hoc capacity changes, as the latter aspect in particular can adversely impact the provision of services. These days the cost of IT does not so much come from the investments in capacity, as from managing it. For example, an excessive increase in storage capacity will impact tape back-up operations and it will take longer to find files stored on the network. This example illustrates an important aspect of Capacity Management: good Capacity Management is perhaps the most important ingredient in changing the perception (and reality) of an IT organization from an overhead group to a service provider. With good Capacity Management in place, the IT service provider could see, for example, that the eighteen strategic initiatives that are stated for IT this year will render the current backup solution obsolete. With this knowledge in mind, the Capacity Manager can ensure that the true cost of these initiatives is seen, i.e. that the cost of the new backup solution is apportioned across the eighteen initiatives. This is proactive. If, instead, there is no Capacity Management, the IT organization reacts only when the backup window is being exceeded. In this case, the customer sees the IT organization as an overhead, coming 'begging for money', simply because IT was not proactive in setting expectations and assigning costs up front.

Capacity Management aims to prevent surprises and rushed purchases by making better use of the available resources, and to increase capacity at the right time, or control the use of the resources. Capacity Management can also help coordinate the capacities of different aspects of a service to ensure that costly investments in certain components are used efficiently.

Today's IT infrastructures are extremely complex. This increases the capacity dependencies between components. Thus, the service levels agreed with the customer are becoming increasingly demanding to meet. A professional IT organization should therefore take an integrated approach to Capacity Management.

12.3.1 Capacity Management activities
Figure 12.1 shows the main Capacity Management activities.

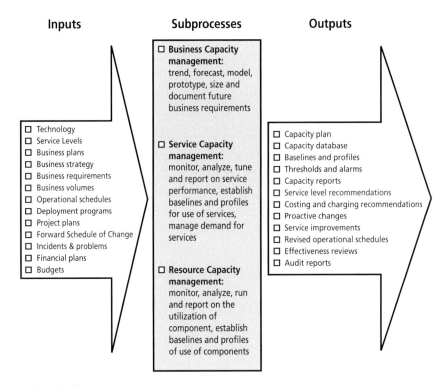

Figure 12.1 - Capacity Management process

Capacity Management has three subprocesses, or levels of analysis where capacity can be considered:

■ **Business Capacity Management** - the objective of this subprocess is to understand the current and future needs of the business. This can be done by obtaining information from the customer, e.g. from strategic plans, marketing plans or by undertaking trend analysis. This subprocess is primarily proactive.

■ **Service Capacity Management** - the objective of this subprocess is to determine and understand the use of IT services (products and services provided to customers). The performance and peak loads need to be understood in order to ensure that appropriate service agreements can be made and delivered. This subprocess has strong links with Service Level Management in terms of the definition and negotiation of service agreements.

■ **Resource Capacity Management** - the objective of this subprocess is to determine and understand the use of the IT infrastructure and components. Examples of resources include network bandwidth, processing capacity, and disk capacity. Potential problems have to be detected early to manage these resources effectively. The organization also needs to be kept abreast of technical developments. Actively monitoring trends is also an important activity within this subprocess.

As Capacity Management and the business's needs are related, Capacity Management is an essential element of the planning process. However, the support it provides to operational processes should not be underestimated. The links with the other Service Management processes are discussed below.

12.3.2 Relationship with other processes

Incident Management
Incident Management informs Capacity Management about incidents logged due to capacity or performance issues. Capacity Management can provide scripts for Incident Management to assist with the diagnosis or resolution of capacity problems.

Problem Management
Capacity Management supports Problem Management in both its reactive and proactive roles. Capacity Management tools, information, knowledge and expertise can be used to assist Problem Management with various activities.

Change Management
Capacity Management should be part of the CAB. Capacity Management can provide information about the need for capacity and the potential impact of a change on the provision of service. The information about the changes also provides valuable input to the Capacity Plan. Capacity Management can also submit RFC's during the implementation of the plan.

Release Management
Capacity Management supports distribution planning when the network and distribution servers are used for automatic or manual distribution, ensuring that sufficient capacity is available in all the required areas.

Configuration Management
There is a close connection between the Capacity Database (CDB) and the CMDB. The CDB may form part of the CMDB. The information provided by Configuration Management is essential for developing an effective CDB.

Service Level Management
Capacity Management advises Service Level Management about the feasibility of service levels (for example response times and Service Level Requirements, SLR's). Capacity Management measures and monitors performance levels and provides information for checking and where necessary changing the agreed service levels and associated reports.

Financial Management for IT Services

Capacity Management supports investment budgeting, cost/benefit analysis, and investment decisions. Capacity Management also provides essential information for charging capacity-related services, such as the usage of network capacity. It is essential that the Capacity Plan is consistent with all aspects of financial planning and plans.

IT Service Continuity Management

Capacity Management specifies the minimum capacity needed to continue or recover service provision in the event of a disaster. The capacity needs of IT Service Continuity Management should be constantly reviewed to ensure that they reflect day-to-day changes in the operating environment.

Availability Management

Capacity Management and Availability Management are closely connected. Performance and capacity problems can result in poor quality IT services. In fact, the customer may consider poor service performance to be equivalent to service unavailability. Because of the many dependencies, the two processes need to be coordinated effectively. They both use many of the same tools and techniques such as Component Failure Impact Analysis (CFIA) and Fault Tree Analysis (FTA).

12.4 Activities

The following Capacity Management activities are described below and are performed to a lesser or greater degree for each of the sub-processes of Business, Service and Resource Capacity Management.

Some core activities within this area are illustrated in Figure 12.2.

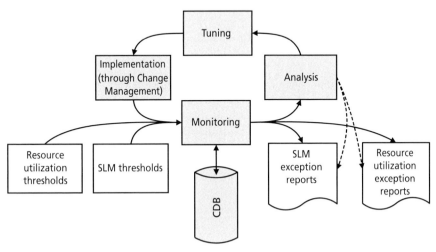

Figure 12.2 - Iterative activities of Capacity Management

12.4.1 Developing the Capacity Plan

The Capacity Plan describes the current and future requirements for capacity of the IT infrastructure and the expected changes in the demand for IT services, replacement of outdated components, and the technical developments. The Capacity Plan also defines the changes needed to provide the service levels agreed in the SLA's at an acceptable cost, together with the future needs of Service Level Requirements (SLR's). The Capacity Plan therefore describes not only the expected changes, but also the associated costs. A revised version of the plan should be produced each year, and it should be reviewed every quarter to confirm its validity.

In a way, the Capacity Plan is the most important output of Capacity Management. The outputs often include an annual plan that is synchronized with the budget or financial plans, long-term plans, and quarterly plans with details of the scheduled capacity changes. This provides a coherent set of plans, where the level of detail increases as the planning horizon approaches.

A Capacity Plan should contain performance expectations, upgrade points, expected costs for infrastructure upgrades (capital, recurring, operational, personnel), etc. These figures should be upgraded regularly for dynamic environments.

12.4.2 Modeling
Modeling is a powerful Capacity Management tool and is used to forecast the behavior of the infrastructure.

The tools available to Capacity Management range from measuring and estimating tools to extensive prototyping and testing tools. The former are cheap and often adequate for routine activities. The latter are usually only appropriate for large-scale implementation projects.

Between these two extremes, there are a number of techniques that are more accurate than an estimating, and cheaper than an extensive piloting. In order of increasing cost they include:
- Rule of thumb.
- Linear projection (Trend Analysis).
- Analytical modeling.
- Simulation.
- Baseline assessment (benchmark) (most accurate).
- Actual system.

Trend analysis can be used to obtain loading information and can also be used to predict approximate response times. Analytical modeling and simulation have their own benefits and costs. For example, simulation can be used to accurately predict the performance of a host, possibly as an element of Application Sizing. However, it is a time-consuming and resource-hungry method. Analytical mathematical models usually take less time, but the outcome is less reliable. The accuracy difference between analytical modeling and simulation is a function of the tool and the skill of the analyst/modeler and assumptions/boundary condition. A baseline means that an actual operating environment is created, for example at the supplier's computer center. This environment fulfills the performance requirements and is used for 'what if' or change simulations, such as 'what happens when an application component is transferred to another computer system?' or 'what happens if we double the number of transactions?'

12.4.3 Application Sizing
Application Sizing considers the resources required to run new or changed services, such as services under development or undergoing maintenance, or which may be purchased at the request of the customer. These predictions include information about the expected performance levels, necessary resources, and costs.

This discipline is particularly relevant during the initial product development stages. Clear information about the required hardware and other IT resources and expected costs at this stage is valuable to management. This discipline also contributes to the drafting of new or revised SLR's or SLA's.

Application Sizing can require a significant effort for large or complex environments. First, Capacity Management agrees the Service Level Requirements to be fulfilled by the service with the developers. Once the service has reached the hand over and acceptance stage, its performance is compared against the agreed service level targets to ensure they can be achieved.

One of the outputs from Application Sizing is the effect of workload variation. This can be used to predict what the needed capacity will be, if for instance the number of users grow by 25%. Other workload characteristics could be the capacity requirements over time (peaks per day/week/year and future growth.)

12.4.4 Monitoring
Monitoring the infrastructure components aims to ensure that the agreed service levels are achieved. Examples of resources to be monitored include CPU utilization, disk utilization, network utilization, number of licenses, etc. (i.e. there are only ten free licenses available).

12.4.5 Analysis
The monitoring data has to be analyzed. Trend analysis can be used to predict future growth and identify potential 'bottlenecks'. This may initiate efficiency improvements or the acquisition of additional IT components. Activity analysis requires a thorough understanding of the overall infrastructure, the business processes and the relationship between the elements of Business, Service and Resource Capacity Management.

12.4.6 Tuning
Tuning optimizes systems for the actual or expected workload on the basis of analyzed and interpreted monitoring data.

12.4.7 Implementation
The objective of implementation is to introduce the changed or new capacity. If this means a change, the implementation involves the Change Management process.

12.4.8 Demand Management
Demand Management aims to influence the demand for capacity. Demand Management is about controlling and influencing user demand. A simple example: a user is running a poorly-written SQL report in the middle of the day, locking the database and creating an inordinate amount of network traffic. The Capacity Manager suggests creating a job to run the report overnight so the user has it on his desk in the morning.

Demand Management provides important inputs for drawing up, monitoring and possibly adjusting both the Capacity Plan and SLA's.

Demand Management can also involve differential charging (i.e. different charges at peak and off-peak times) to influence customer and user behavior by controlling demand during periods of high usage.

12.4.9 Populating the Capacity Database (CDB)

Creating and populating the CDB means collecting and updating technical information, and business information, and all other information relevant to Capacity Management. It may not be feasible to store all capacity information in a single physical database. Network and computer system managers may use their own approaches. Often, the CDB refers to a set of databases containing the appropriate capacity information.

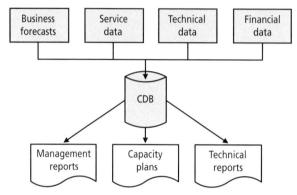

Figure 12.3 - CDB information sources

12.5 Process control

Capacity Planning is more effective when linked closely with other IT and service management planning processes, **and** with strategic (Business and IT) planning processes. Capacity Planning is one of the few processes that uses actual history to forecast futures, in terms of business expectation.

12.5.1 Critical success factors and performance indicators

The quality of the Capacity Management process depends on the following critical success factors:
- Accurate business forecasts and expectations.
- Understanding of the IT strategy and planning and its accuracy.
- Knowledge of current and future technologies.
- Cooperation with other processes.
- An ability to demonstrate cost effectiveness.

The success of Capacity Management is determined by the following key performance indicators:
- **Predictability of the customer demand** - identification of workload developments and trends over time, and the accuracy of the Capacity Plan.
- **Technology** - options for measuring the performance of all IT services, the pace of implementing new technology, and the ability to continually achieve the agreements laid down in SLA's, even when using older technology.
- **Cost** - reduction in the number of rushed purchases, reduction in unnecessary or expensive overcapacity, and the drawing up of investment plans at an early stage.
- **Operations** - reduction in the number of incidents due to performance or capacity issues, the ability to meet customer demand at all times, and the extent to which the Capacity Management process is taken seriously.

12.5.2 Management reports

The management reports provided by the Capacity Management process include, on the one hand, process control information in terms of Capacity Plan characteristics, resources used to implement the process and the progress of improvement activities, and on the other hand, exception reports about issues such as:

■ Discrepancies between actual and planned capacity.
■ Trends in the discrepancies.
■ Impact on service levels.
■ Expected increase/decrease of capacity and utilization in both the short term and long term.
■ Thresholds that, when reached, will require the possible acquisition of additional capacity.

These capacity planning and performance management reports should be made readily available to all interested people - Business, Application and IT.

12.5.3 Functions and roles

The role of the Capacity Manager is to manage the process, to ensure that the Capacity Plan is developed and maintained, and to ensure that the CDB is kept up to date.

The System, Network and Application Managers all have important supporting roles in the Capacity Management process. Not only are they responsible for assisting with the optimization of resources within their own areas, but they are also required to provide advice and assistance on technical issues within their area of specialized knowledge.

12.6 Costs and possible problems

12.6.1 Costs

The costs of setting up Capacity Management must be estimated during the preparation. The costs can be divided into:

■ Purchase of hardware and software tools such as monitoring tools, Capacity Management Database (CDB), trending and modeling tools for simulations and statistical analysis, and reporting tools.
■ Project management costs associated with the implementation of the process.
■ Personnel, training and support costs.
■ Facilities and services.

Once the process has been set up, there are recurring costs of personnel, maintenance contracts, etc.

12.6.2 Possible problems

Potential problems in Capacity Management include:

■ **Unrealistic expectations** - designers, management and customers often have unrealistic expectations, based on a lack of understanding of the technical possibilities of applications, computer systems or networks. One of the tasks of Capacity Management is to guide these expectations, for example by making designers aware of the impact of their design (e.g. for a database) on the capacity and performance. The effect of Capacity Management can also be overestimated, particularly with respect to tuning of the system and scheduling of the workload. If the operation of systems requires extensive tuning it is likely that the design of the application or database is poor. In general, tuning cannot be used to obtain a higher level of performance than the system was originally designed for. Most large systems have scheduling algorithms that are generally more effective than intervention by system managers. And of course, there is a cost associated with tuning, it makes no sense for a highly paid engineer to achieve a 3% performance improvement after a weeks' worth of effort when a hundred dollars of additional memory would produce a 10% improvement. There is a higher cost associated with system tuning: the cost of managing systems which are not, within reason, 'plain vanilla' can often be excessive. Highly 'tweaked' parameters on different boxes, applications, or databases lead to unintended consequences, and often add additional delays across all other processes, in maintenance, troubleshooting, etc.

- **Lack of appropriate information** - it is often difficult to obtain the required information for the Capacity Plan. It may be difficult to obtain reliable information about the expected workload, as the business plans are often unclear or sometimes unknown. This is also difficult for the customer, as product life cycles are getting shorter and shorter. The only solution is to make the best possible estimate and to update the estimate frequently when more information becomes available.

- **Supplier input** - if there is no historical data (for example when a new system is purchased), Capacity Management often has to depend on the information provided by suppliers. Suppliers normally use benchmarks to provide information about their systems, but because of the major differences between testing and measurement methods it is often difficult to compare information between suppliers. Also the information can often prove misleading about the actual performance of the final system solution.

- **Implementation in complex environments** - implementation in complex distributed environments is difficult because of the complexity of the solution, the magnitude of technical interfaces and the large number of performance dependencies.

- **Determining the appropriate level of monitoring** - monitoring tools often provide many options and may encourage investigations in excessive detail. When purchasing and using these tools, it should be decided in advance what level monitoring is to be required.

- **Lack of Management Support** - where the process has management visibility and expectation, support and consistency from other groups can considerably help the function and accuracy of the capacity planning function. Where management support is variable, or minimal, then this lack of enthusiasm quickly drifts down the chain of command, making access to critical and important information, and/or warning difficult to publish.

These problems are relevant to Capacity Management of computer systems as well as networks, large printing systems and PABX systems. This can be even more challenging if several units are responsible for these domains, which may lead to conflicts in Capacity Management responsibilities.

13 IT SERVICE CONTINUITY MANAGEMENT

13.1 Introduction

Many managers consider IT Service Continuity Management (ITSCM) as a luxury, for which they need no resources. However, statistics show that disruptive disasters are actually quite common.

Disaster - an event that affects a service or system such that significant effort is required to restore the original performance level.

A disaster is much more serious than an 'Incident'. A disaster is a business interruption. That means that all or part of the business is not 'in business' following a disaster. Familiar disasters include fire, lightning, water damage, burglary, vandalism and violence, large-scale power outages, and hardware failure. Additionally, terrorist attacks are becoming more common. The Internet can also lead to disasters, such as Denial of Service (DoS) attacks that disrupt the communications of an entire organization. Some companies could have prevented serious problems by thinking about and developing Business Continuity Plans. Furthermore, businesses are increasingly dependent on IT services, which means that the impact of the loss of services also increases and becomes less acceptable. In fact, for many companies, doing business is equivalent to using IT, and without IT they cannot create any revenue. It is therefore essential to consider how business continuity can be safeguarded.

Traditional contingency planning used to be part of the remit of the IT organization. However, at present IT is much more closely integrated with many aspects of the business. Where the traditional contingency planning process was primarily reactive (what to do in the event of a disaster), the new IT Service Continuity Management process emphasizes prevention, i.e. avoiding disasters.

13.2 Objectives

The objective of IT Service Continuity Management is to support the overall Business Continuity Management (BCM) by ensuring that required IT infrastructure and IT services, including support and the Service Desk, can be restored within specified time limits after a disaster. ITSCM can have a number of different aims but its scope needs to be defined on the basis of the business objectives. When assessing the risks to business continuity, decisions need to be made as to whether they are within or outside the scope of the ITSCM process.

13.2.1 Benefits

As businesses are increasingly dependent on IT services, the cost of failing to plan for business and IT service continuity, and the benefits of planning can only be identified through a risk analysis. Once the risk to the business, not just the risk to the IT services, has been identified, investments can be made measures for prevention and measures to deal with disasters, such as recovery plans. The guidelines of this chapter can be used to limit and manage the impact of disasters.

If a disaster does occur, businesses with an ITSCM process have the following benefits:
- They can manage the recovery of their systems.
- They lose less service availability time and offer better continuity to the users.
- They minimize the interruption to their business activities.

13.3 The process

13.3.1 IT Service Continuity Management activities
IT Service Continuity Management is responsible for:
- Assessing the risk and impact of the disruption of IT services following a disaster.
- Identifying services critical to the business that require additional prevention measures.
- Defining periods within which services have to be restored.
- Taking measures to prevent, detect, prepare for and mitigate the effects of disasters or to reduce their impact.
- Defining the approach to be used to restore the services.
- Developing, testing and maintaining a recovery plan with sufficient detail to survive a disaster and to restore normal services after a defined period.

As the business operations as a whole and IT are becoming more and more enmeshed, both areas are described within the ITIL scope:
- **Business Continuity Management (BCM)** covers risk analysis and management so that the organization can ensure a predetermined minimum required production capacity or provision of service at all times. BCM aims to reduce risks to an acceptable level and develops plans for restoring business activities if they are interrupted by a disaster.
- **IT Service Continuity Management (ITSCM)** is the process of dealing with disasters affecting IT services and maintaining services to allow the business to continue to operate.

IT Service Continuity Management is part of the overall Business Continuity Management and depends on the information provided by the BCM process. The availability of IT services is ensured by combining risk reduction measures (e.g. installing reliable systems) with recovery options (e.g. backup systems and redundant systems). Successful implementation of ITSCM requires the understanding, support and on-going commitment of the whole organization. In particular, the visible support of senior business managers and directors is critical to effective ITSCM.

13.3.2 Relationship with other processes
IT Service Continuity Management interacts with all the other IT Service Management processes, particularly the following:
- **Service Level Management** - provides information about the IT service obligations.
- **Availability Management** - supports ITSCM by developing and implementing prevention measures.
- **Configuration Management** - defines baseline configurations and the IT infrastructure to provide ITSCM with information about what needs to be restored after a disaster.
- **Capacity Management** - ensures that the business requirements are fully supported by the appropriate IT resources.
- **Change Management** - ensures that all ITSCM plans are correct and up-to-date by involving ITSCM in all changes that may affect prevention measures and recovery plans.

13.4 Activities
Figure 13.1 shows the ITSCM activities. The numbers refer to the subsections of section 13.4 under which the activities are described.

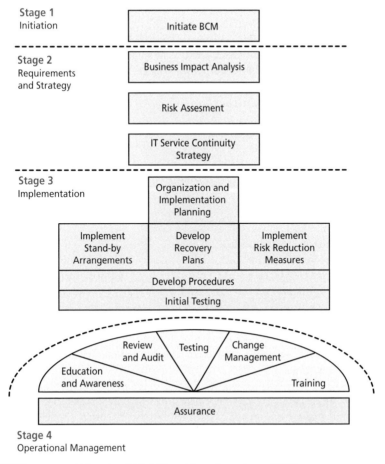

Figure 13.1 - ITSCM process model (based on OGC's BCM model, now focused upon ITSCM)

13.4.1 Defining the scope of ITSCM

The organization as a whole should be considered when initiating ITSCM, and the following activities must be undertaken:

■ **Defining the policy** - the policy should be defined as soon as possible and communicated throughout the organization so that all those concerned are aware of the need for ITSCM. Management has to demonstrate its commitment.

■ **Defining the scope and relevant areas** - insurance requirements, quality standards such as the ISO 9000 series, Security Management standards such as BS 7799, and general business policy principles are used to select the approach and methods for risk assessment and Business Impact Analysis. The appropriate management structure, with assigned responsibilities, and process structure for coping with disasters are also identified.

■ **Allocating resources** - setting up an ITSCM environment will require a significant investment in personnel and resources. Training must also be provided to ensure that personnel are prepared to implement stage 2 of the ITSCM process (Requirements and Strategy).

■ **Setting up the project organization** - it is advisable to use a formal project management method, for example PRINCE2, supported by planning software.

13.4.2 Business Impact Analysis

Before analyzing the IT services, it is advisable to identify the reasons for the company to include IT Service Continuity Management in Business Continuity Management, and to identify the potential impact of a serious disruption of services. In some cases, the business can survive for some time and the emphasis will be on **restoring services**, in other cases the business cannot operate without IT services and the emphasis will be on **prevention**. Most businesses will have to strike a balance between the two extremes.

Potential reasons for including ITSCM are:
■ Protecting business processes.
■ Protection against breaches of the law.
■ Rapid service recovery.
■ Surviving competition.
■ Maintaining market share.
■ Maintaining profitability.
■ Protecting the reputation perceived by customers.

The above reasons may well be combined. In the financial industry, such as currency trading, the loss of market information means that the business will lose money as trading (the main business process) is interrupted. Furthermore, if there is a statutory requirement to record all trading activity using a specified system, then trading can continue in the event of disruption to that system, but sooner or later a statutory requirement will be infringed and fines may be imposed. In both cases, the company may lose customers and market share.

Service analysis

Once the reasons for initiating ITSCM have been identified, an analysis is made of the IT services that are essential to the business (e.g. information systems, office applications, accounting applications, e-mail, etc.) and that must be available in accordance with the Service Level Agreements. For some nonessential services, it may be agreed to provide an emergency service with limited capacity and availability. However, service levels during disaster recovery may only be modified in agreement with the customer. For critical services, a balance has to be struck between prevention and recovery options.

Infrastructure

A service analysis is followed by an assessment of the dependencies between services and IT resources. Availability Management information is used to analyze the extent to which IT resources perform a critical function in supporting the IT services discussed earlier. Capacity Management provides information about the required capacity. It is necessary to determine the extent to which these services may be disrupted over time, from the initial loss of service to full restoration. Later, this information will be used to identify the recovery options for each service.

13.4.3 Risk assessment

There are no official disaster statistics, but some high profile events include:

Poison gas	Tokyo Metro, Japan (March 1995)
Power outage	Auckland, New Zealand (December 1997)
Earthquakes	Los Angeles, USA (January 1994)
	Kobe, Japan (January 1995)
Terrorist attacks	World Trade Center, New York, USA (February 1993)
	Bishopsgate, London, England (April 1993)

	Oklahoma City, Oklahoma, USA (April 1995)
	Docklands, London, England (February 1996)
	Manchester, England (June 1996)
	World Trade Center, New York, USA (September 2001)
Floods	Bangladesh (July 1996)
	Pakistan (August 1996)
	South East Asian tsunami (December 2004)

A risk analysis can help identify the risks that a business is exposed to. Such an analysis will provide management with valuable information by identifying the threats and vulnerabilities, and relevant prevention measures. Because maintaining a disaster recovery plan is relatively expensive, the use of prevention measures should be considered first. Once such measures have been exhausted, it is necessary to determine if there are any remaining risks that may require a Contingency plan.

Figure 13.2 shows the links between Risk Analysis and Risk Management; it is based on the **CCTA R**isk **A**nalysis and **M**anagement **M**ethod (CRAMM).

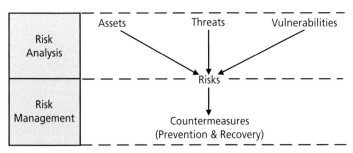

Figure 13.2 - The CCTA Risk Assessment Model

The model supports effective contingency planning by taking a phased approach.

Risk analysis
Four steps are recognized in risk analysis:
- First, the relevant **IT components** (assets) must be identified - buildings, systems, data, etc. Effective asset identification requires that the owner and the purpose of each component must be documented.
- The next step is to analyze the **threats to those assets,** and consequently to their dependencies, and to estimate the likelihood (high, medium, low) that a disaster will occur. For example the combination of an unreliable electricity power supply and an area prone to many storms.
- Next, the **vulnerabilities of those assets** are identified and classified (high, medium, and low). A lightning conductor will provide some protection against lightning strikes, but they can still seriously affect the network and the computer systems.
- Finally, the threats and vulnerabilities are evaluated in the context of the IT components, to provide an estimate of the level of the **risks**.

The scope of the ITSCM process, having been defined in stage 1, should be considered when estimating the risks. For example, minor problems would be expected to be dealt with by the service Desk and/or the Incident management process, or to be solved by Availability Management measures, and some business risks are outside the scope of ITSCM.

13.4.4 IT Service Continuity Strategy

Most businesses will aim to strike a balance between risk reduction and recovery planning. There is a distinction between risk reduction, business activity recovery actions, and IT recovery options. The relationship between risk reduction (prevention) and recovery planning (recovery options) is discussed below.

Threats can never be fully eliminated, e.g. a fire in a building nearby may also damage your building. Also, reducing one risk might increase another risk, e.g. outsourcing might increase security risks.

Prevention measures

Prevention measures can be taken on the basis of the risk analysis, having carefully considered the costs of the measures and the levels of the risks being prevented. Some measures may aim to reduce the likelihood or impact of contingencies, and therefore narrow the scope of the recovery plan. For example, measures can be taken against dust, excessively high or low temperatures, fire, leaks, power outages and burglary, leaving other risks to be covered by the recovery plan.

The **Stronghold/Fortress Approach** is the most extensive form of prevention. It eliminates most vulnerability, for example by building a bunker with its own power and water supply. However, this may introduce other vulnerabilities such as the risk of network failure, or roadblocks, as off-site recovery will now be even more difficult. The stronghold/fortress approach is suitable for large computer centers that are too complex for a recovery plan. It is vital nowadays to complement a stronghold/fortress approach with a skirmish capability, i.e., an organizational capability to go where the problem is and deal with it promptly before it spirals out of control.

Selecting recovery options

If there are some remaining risks that have not been eliminated by prevention measures, then they will have to be addressed by recovery planning. Recovery options will have to be provided as follows to ensure business continuity:

- **Personnel and accommodation** - how to deal with alternative premises, furniture, transport and travel distances, etc., and the essential staff required to support the business.
- **IT systems and networks** - recovery options are discussed below.
- **Support services** - power, water, telephone, post, and courier services.
- **Archives** - files, documents, paper-based systems, and reference materials.
- **Third-party services** - such as e-mail and Internet service providers.

There are a number of options available for the rapid recovery of IT services:

- **Do nothing** - few businesses can function effectively with this approach. It is more likely to indicate an ill-informed view. Departments which state that they can survive without IT recovery facilities may give the impression that, in their view, the lost services provided little support to the department's business functions and are, therefore, dispensable. Nevertheless, this option should be investigated for each service to see if it might be acceptable, for example, as a short-term solution.
- **Return to a manual (paper-based) system** - this option is normally unacceptable for services critical to the business, as there will be insufficient personnel with experience of using traditional systems. Furthermore, paper-based systems used in the past may no longer be available, and may be difficult to reproduce in a short period of time. However, paper-based systems may be feasible for less important, minor services. Most recovery plans include some paper-based backup routines. For example, the recovery option for a credit card terminal could be the use of paper credit card slips.

- **Reciprocal arrangements** - this option can be used if two organizations have similar hardware and agree to provide each other with facilities in the event of a disaster. For this option, the two businesses have to conclude an agreement and ensure that changes are coordinated so that both environments remain interchangeable. Capacity Management should ensure that the reserved capacity is not used for other purposes, or can be released quickly. However, this option is less attractive in today's distributed computing environments where there is a greater demand for individual processing power and high availability systems, such as ATMs and on-line banking.
- **Gradual recovery (cold stand-by)** - this option can be used by businesses that can manage without IT services for some time, for example 72 hours. It provides an empty computer room at an agreed fixed facility, or a mobile computer room delivered to the business's site, the portable facility. The computer room is provided with electrical power, air-conditioning, net-work facilities, and telephone connections. This recovery option can be provided under contract with an external supplier. Separate agreements will have to be made with suppliers of IT components to ensure that they can be delivered quickly. The advantage of this approach is that the facility is always available. The benefits and costs are different for fixed and portable facilities and relate to issues such as:
  - *Distance to the facility:* few providers offer fixed facilities. These may be remote, a disadvantage which is avoided by the use of a portable facility.
  - *Time:* fixed facility locations are only available for a limited period.
  - *Delay:* in either case, the delivery of the required computer hardware may take some time.
  - *Network:* it is often difficult to provide appropriate network facilities. Connections for a portable facility could be provided in the building used for normal operations.
- **Intermediate recovery (warm stand-by)** - this option provides access to a similar operational environment where the services can continue normally after a short changeover period (24-72 hours). There are three versions of this option:
  - *Internal:* (mutual fallback) if the business has several sites or has dedicated test environments that can be used for production. This option provides full recovery with a minimum changeover time. Organizations with several distributed systems often use a variation on this approach, where part of the required capacity is reserved on each system. This spare capacity is monitored by Capacity Management (similar to the reciprocal arrangement recovery option).
  - *External:* a commercial service offered by third-party recovery organizations, to several customers. The costs are divided between the customers and depend on the required hardware and software and the agreed period during which the facility is provided (e.g. 16 weeks). These arrangements are often made to bridge the period needed to set up a cold stand-by facility. This approach is relatively expensive and the facility is likely to be some distance away.
  - *Mobile:* the infrastructure for this option is provided ready-for-use in a trailer. The trailer serves as a computer room and provides environmental control facilities such as air-conditioning. The IT organization must provide a place to park the trailer. Power supply, data and telecommunications connections must be available at dedicated points some distance from the building. The benefits of this option include the short response time and proximity to the business site. This option is only available for a limited number of hardware platforms. Some of the larger hardware suppliers offer this service by providing a number of trailers with standard hardware configurations. At agreed times, for example once every year, the trailer visits the business to test the recovery arrangements.
- **Immediate recovery (hot start, hot stand-by)** - this option provides an immediate or very rapid recovery of services, e.g. less than 24 hours. This can be achieved by providing an identical production environment and mirroring of the data, and possibly even mirroring of the production processes - in close cooperation with Availability Management.
- **Combinations of options** - in many cases, a Contingency plan can provide for a more expen-

sive, short term recovery option to bridge the gap between no recovery and the introduction of a longer term, cheaper option. For example, a trailer with operating computer center (mobile hot start) can provide a temporarily solution until portable facilities have been set up and the new host computers have been delivered (mobile cold start). Normal operations are restored after refurbishment of the building and moving the new host computers into the building.

13.4.5 Organization and implementation planning

Once the business strategy has been determined and choices have been made, the ITSCM has to be implemented and the plans for the IT facilities have to be developed in detail. An organization will have to be set up to implement the ITSCM process. This could include management (Crisis Manager), coordination, and recovery teams for each service.

At the highest level there should be an overall plan addressing the following issues:
- Emergency response plan.
- Damage assessment plan.
- Recovery plan.
- Vital records plan (what to do with data, including paper records).
- Crisis Management and PR plans.

All these plans are used to assess emergencies and to respond to them. It can then be decided if the business recovery process should be initiated, in which case the next level of plans has to be activated, including the:
- Accommodation and services plan.
- Computer system and network plan.
- Telecommunications plan (accessibility and links).
- Security plan (integrity of the data and networks).
- Personnel plan.
- Financial and administrative plans.

13.4.6 Prevention measures and recovery options

This is when the prevention measures and recovery options identified earlier are put into practice.

Prevention measures to reduce the impact of an incident are taken in conjunction with Availability Management, and may include:
- Use of UPS and backup power supplies.
- Fault-tolerant systems.
- Off-site storage and RAID systems, etc.

A start should also be made to introduce stand-by agreements. These should cover personnel, buildings and telecommunications. Even during the contingency period a start can be made with restoring the normal situation and ordering new IT components. Dormant contracts can be made in advance with suppliers. This means that signed orders are available for the components to be supplied at an agreed price. When the disaster occurs, the supplier can process the order without having to issue quotations. Such dormant contracts should be updated every year as prices and models will change. The Configuration Management baselines should be considered when updating these contracts.

The following activities can be carried out to set up stand-by agreements:
- Negotiating off-site recovery facilities with third parties.
- Maintaining and equipping the recovery facility.

- Purchasing and installing stand-by hardware (dormant contracts).
- Managing dormant contracts.

13.4.7 Developing plans and procedures for recovery

The recovery plans should be detailed and subject to formal Change control, and should identify all the procedures needed to support them. These issues need to be communicated to all
those involved in, or affected, by the plans. A typical recovery-planning problem relates to
changes in the infrastructure and the agreed service levels. For example, migration to a new
midrange platform could mean that, when recovery is required, there is no equivalent unit at the
backup facility for a warm, external start. For this reason, Configuration Management plays an
important role in monitoring the baseline configurations referred to in the recovery plan.

Recovery plan

The recovery plan should include all elements relevant to restoring the business activities and IT
services, including:

- **Introduction** - describes the structure of the plan and envisaged recovery facilities.
- **Updating** - discusses the procedures and agreements for maintaining the plan, and tracks
  changes to the infrastructure.
- **Routing list** - the plan is divided into sections, each specifying the actions to be undertaken
  by a specific group. The routing list shows what sections should be sent to which personnel.
- **Recovery initiation** - describes when and under what conditions the plan is invoked.
- **Contingency classification** - if the plan describes procedures for different contingencies, they
  should be described here in terms of seriousness (minor, medium, major), duration (day, week,
  weeks), and damage (minor, limited, serious).
- **Specialist sections** - the plan should be divided into sections based on the six areas and groups
  covered by the plan:
  - *Administration:* how and when is the plan invoked, which managers and personnel are
    involved, and where is the control center based?
  - *IT infrastructure:* hardware, software, and telecommunications to be provided by the recovery
    system; recovery procedures; and dormant contracts for the purchase of new IT components.
  - *Personnel:* personnel required at the recovery facility and, if the facility is located far from
    the business, transport and accommodation services.
  - *Security:* instructions for protection against burglary, fires and explosions at both the home
    site and the remote site, and information about external storage facilities such as warehous-
    es and vaults.
  - *Recovery sites:* information about contracts, personnel with specified functions, security, and
    transport.
  - *Restoration:* procedures to restore the normal situation (e.g. the building), conditions under
    which these procedures are invoked, and dormant contracts.

Procedures

The recovery plan provides a framework for drafting the procedures. It is essential to develop
effective procedures, such that anyone can undertake the recovery by following the procedures.
These should address:

- Installing and testing hardware and network components.
- Restoring applications, databases, and data.

These and other relevant procedures are attached to the recovery plan.

13.4.8 Initial testing

Initial testing of the plans, procedures and technical components involved is a critical aspect of ITSCM. Tests should be performed against defined scenarios and must have clear objectives and success criteria. Further testing is then required following major changes, and at least annually. The IT department is responsible for testing the effectiveness of the IT elements of the plans and procedures. These tests may be announced or unannounced, but involving appropriate business managers would aid mutual understanding and is more likely to gain business-level support and commitment.

13.4.9 Training and awareness

Effective training of IT and other personnel, and awareness by all personnel and the organization, are essential to the success of any IT Services Continuity process. IT personnel may have to train the non-IT personnel of business recovery teams, to ensure that they are familiar with the issues and are competent to provide support during the recovery operations. The actual contingency facilities, on-site or off-site, should also be covered by the training and tests.

13.4.10 Review and audit

Plans should be reviewed and verified regularly to ensure that they are still up-to-date. This concerns all aspects of ITSCM. In the IT area, such an audit will have to be undertaken every time there is a significant change to the IT infrastructure, such as the introduction of new systems, networks and service providers.

Audits must also be carried out if there is any change in business strategy or IT strategy. Organizations where rapid and frequent change is common could implement a regular program for verifying the ITSCM concepts. Any resulting changes to the plans and strategy must be implemented under the direction of Change Management.

13.4.11 Testing

The Recovery plan must be tested regularly, rather like an emergency drill on a ship. If everyone has to study the plan when a disaster happens then there are likely to be many problems. The test can also identify weaknesses in the plan or changes that were overlooked.

13.4.12 Change Management

Change Management plays an important role in keeping all the ITSCM plans current, and for ensuring that the impact of any change to the Recovery plan is analyzed.

13.4.13 Assurance

Assurance means verifying that the quality of the process (procedures and documents) and its deliverables are adequate to meet the business needs of the company.

13.5 Process control

Effective process control depends on critical success factors, management reports and performance indicators.

13.5.1 Critical success factors and performance indicators

The success of IT Service Continuity Management depends on:

■ An effective Configuration Management process.
■ Support and commitment throughout the organization.

- Up-to-date and effective tools.
- Dedicated training for anyone involved in the process.
- Regular tests of the recovery plan.

Performance indicators include:
- Number of identified shortcomings of the recovery plans.
- Revenue lost further to a disaster.
- Cost of the process.

13.5.2 Management reports

In the event of a disaster there will be reports about its cause and effect, and how successfully it was dealt with. Any observed weaknesses will be addressed in improvement plans.

The management reports from the ITSCM process also include evaluation reports of recovery plan tests. These are used for assurance. The process also reports about the number of changes to recovery plans as a result of significant changes elsewhere. Reports may also be issued about new threats.

13.5.3 Functions and roles

The charter of the IT Service Continuity Manager is to implement and maintain the ITSCM process, so that it fulfills the requirements of Business Continuity Management at all times, and to represent the IT Service function within Business Continuity Management.

A number of roles and responsibilities can be identified. There are also differences between the responsibilities during normal and crisis conditions.

Role	Responsibilities during normal conditions	Responsibilities during crisis conditions
Board	Initiating BCM Allocating personnel and resources Defining policies Defining process authority	Crisis management Taking corporate/business decisions
Senior management	Managing the ITSCM process Accepting plans, test reports, etc. Communicating and maintaining awareness Integrating ITSCM within BCM	Coordinating and arbitrating Providing personnel, resources and funding
Management	Undertaking risk analysis Defining deliverables Drafting contracts Managing tests, evaluations and reports	Invoking recovery and continuity mechanisms Leading teams Reporting
Team leaders and team members	Developing deliverables Negotiating services Implementing tests, evaluations and reports Developing and implementing procedures	Implementing the recovery plan

Table 13.1 - Examples of ITSCM responsibilities

13.6 Costs and possible problems

13.6.1 Costs

The major costs associated with the introduction of IT Service Continuity Management are:

- Time and costs for initiating, developing and implementing ITSCM.
- Investment associated with the results of the introduction of risk management, e.g. the need for additional hardware. These costs can be reduced if the measures are considered within the scope of Availability Management at the time of designing new configurations.
- Continuing costs of the recovery arrangements, such as fees for external hot start contracts, cost of test arrangements, and the period during which the recovery facilities are available.
- Ongoing operational costs of ITSCM, such as testing, auditing, and updating the plan.

These costs may only be incurred after making a considered choice, and comparing the potential costs associated with not having a recovery plan. Although the costs of maintaining a recovery plan may appear to be high, they are often reasonable compared with the overall expenditure on fire and theft insurance. Furthermore, effective ITSCM may reduce the cost of insurance.

13.6.2 Possible problems

When implementing the process, the following potential problems should be considered:

- **Resources** - the organization may have to provide additional capacity for a project team to develop and test the plan.
- **Commitment** - the annual costs must be included in the organization's budgets, which requires commitment.
- **Access to recovery facilities** - all of the options discussed above require regular testing of the recovery facilities. Thus, any recovery service contracts will have to provide the IT organization with regular access to the recovery facilities.
- **Estimating the damage** - some damage, such as lost reputation, may be difficult to quantify for estimating purposes.
- **Budgeting** - the need for expensive contingency facilities may not always be understood, resulting in plans being cut back.
- **No business manager commitment** - this results in a failure to develop effective ITSCM, although the customer assumes that arrangements have been made.
- **Perpetual delay** - this is where all or most parts of IT service continuity management are not yet in place and progress is continually postponed. In such cases, when inquiring about ITSCM, the response will be 'yes, we're meeting on that next week…', 'we're about to appoint a committee to do just that', etc.
- **Black Boxing** - this is where the IT service provider has abdicated responsibility, as well as given up control for ITSCM readiness: 'someone else is handling it'. Because the organization has spent a lot of money on its IT systems and services, or has outsourced a portion of its operations to a supplier, the management expects that the money they've spent will ensure their ability to recover, or that the supplier has plans in place that will help them recover after a business interruption.
- **IT department** - must be guided by the actual wishes and requirements of the business, and not by the IT department's assumptions about them.
- **Familiarity with the business** - it is essential that the business supports the development of ITSCM by identifying essential issues.
- **Lack of awareness** - it is essential that the organization as a whole is aware of the value of ITSCM. Without the awareness and support of all personnel, the process is doomed to failure.

14 AVAILABILITY MANAGEMENT

14.1 Introduction

The pace of technological development keeps increasing. Because of this, within many organizations the hardware and software that is needed keeps expanding and is becoming more diverse despite efforts to standardize. Old and new technologies have to work together. This results in additional network structures, interfaces and communications facilities. Business operations are becoming increasingly dependent on reliable technology.

A few hours of computer downtime can have a serious impact on the turnover and image of a business, particularly now that the Internet is developing into an electronic marketplace. As the competitors' businesses are only a mouse click away, customer loyalty and satisfaction are now more important than ever. This is one of the reasons why computer systems are now commonly expected to be available 7 days a week, 24 hours a day.

14.1.1 Basic concepts

Figure 14.1 illustrates the basic concepts of Availability Management.

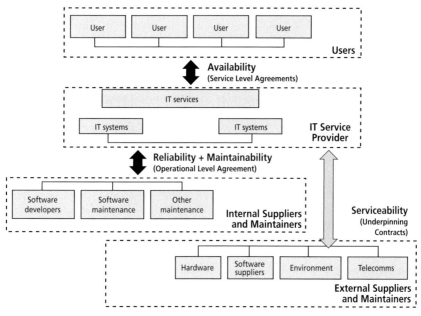

Figure 14.1 - Availability Management concepts

Availability

High availability means that the IT service is continuously available to the customer, as there is little downtime and rapid service recovery. The achieved availability is indicated by metrics. The availability of the service depends on:
- Complexity of the IT infrastructure architecture.
- Reliability of the components.
- Ability to respond quickly and effectively to faults.
- Quality of the maintenance by support organizations and suppliers.
- Quality and scope of the operational management processes.

Reliability

Adequate reliability means that the service is available for an agreed period without interruptions. This concept also includes resilience. The reliability of a service increases if downtime can be prevented. Reliability is calculated using statistics. The reliability of a service is determined by a combination of the following factors:

■ Reliability of the components used to provide the service.
■ Ability of a service or component to operate effectively despite failure of one or more subsystems (resilience).
■ Preventive maintenance to prevent downtime.

Maintainability

Maintainability and recoverability relate to the activities needed to keep the service in operation and to restore it when it fails. This includes preventive maintenance and scheduled inspections. These concepts include the following activities:

■ Taking measures to prevent faults.
■ Detecting faults.
■ Making a diagnosis, including automatic diagnosis by components themselves.
■ Resolving the fault.
■ Recovery after a fault.
■ Restoring the service.

Serviceability

Serviceability relates to contractual obligations of external service providers (contractors, third parties). The contracts define the support to be provided for the outsourced services. As this only concerns a part of the IT service, the term does not refer to the overall availability of the service. If a contractor is responsible for the service as a whole - for example when a Facilities Management contract is concluded - then serviceability and availability are synonymous.

Effective Availability Management requires a thorough understanding of both the business and the IT environment. It is important to be aware that availability cannot simply be 'bought'. Availability has to be included in the design and implementation from the initial design stage. Finally, availability depends on the complexity of the infrastructure, the reliability of the components, the professionalism of the IT organization and its contractors, and the quality of the process itself.

14.2 Objectives

The objective of Availability Management is to provide a cost-effective and defined level of availability of the IT service that enables the business to reach its objectives.

This means that the demands of the customer (the business) have to be aligned with what the IT infrastructure and IT organization is able to offer. If there is a difference between supply and demand then Availability Management will have to provide a solution. Furthermore, Availability Management ensures that the achieved availability levels are measured, and, where necessary, improved continuously. This means that the process includes both proactive and reactive activities.

The following premises must be taken into account when developing the process:

■ The introduction of Availability Management is essential for obtaining a high degree of customer satisfaction. Availability and reliability determine to a large extent how the customers perceive the service provided by an organization.
■ There will always be faults, despite a high degree of availability. Availability Management is

largely responsible for a professional response to such undesirable situations.

■ The design of the process demands not only a thorough understanding of IT, but also an appreciation of the processes and services of the customer. The objectives can be realized by combining these two aspects.

Availability Management has a broad scope and includes both new and existing services to customers, relationships with internal and external suppliers, all infrastructure components (hardware, software, networks, etc.) and organizational aspects which may affect availability, such as the expertise of personnel, management processes, and procedures and tools.

14.2.1 Benefits

The major benefit of Availability Management is that the IT services that are designed, implemented and managed, fulfill the agreed availability requirements. A thorough understanding of the business processes of the customer and IT, combined with continuously aiming to maximize the availability and customer satisfaction within the constraints can make an important contribution to realizing an effective service culture. Other benefits of Availability Management include:

■ There is a single contact and person responsible for the availability of products and services.
■ New products and services fulfill the requirements and availability standard agreed with the customer.
■ The associated costs are acceptable.
■ The availability standards are monitored continuously and improved where appropriate.
■ Appropriate corrective action is undertaken when a service is unavailable.
■ The occurrence and duration of unavailability are reduced.
■ The emphasis is shifted from remedying faults to improving service.
■ It is easier for the IT organization to prove its added value.

14.3 The process

14.3.1 Availability Management activities

Where possible, essential components are duplicated and fault detection and correction systems are used to meet high availability standards. Often, automatic fallback systems will operate in the event of a fault. However, organizational measures also need to be taken and can be provided by introducing Availability Management.

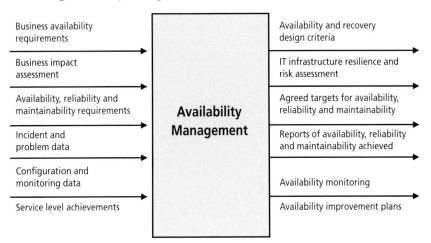

Figure 14.2 - Availability Management inputs and outputs

Availability Management can start once the business has clearly indicated its availability requirements for the service. It is an ongoing process that only ends when a service is phased out.

The **inputs** of the Availability Management process (Figure 14.2) are:
■ Business availability requirements.
■ Impact assessment for all business processes supported by IT.
■ Availability, reliability and maintainability requirements for the IT components in the infrastructure.
■ Data about faults affecting services or components, generally in the form of incident and problem records and reports.
■ Configuration and monitoring data about the services and components.
■ Achieved service levels, compared with the agreed service levels for all services covered under the SLA.

Outputs:
■ Availability and recovery design criteria for new and improved IT services.
■ Technology needed to obtain the required infrastructure resilience to reduce or eliminate the impact of faulty infrastructure components.
■ Availability, reliability and maintainability guarantees of infrastructure components required for the IT service.
■ Reports about the achieved availability, reliability and maintainability.
■ Availability, reliability and maintainability monitoring requirements.
■ An Availability Plan for the proactive improvement of the IT infrastructure.

14.3.2 Relationship with other processes

Service Level Management

Service Level Management is responsible for negotiating and managing Service Level Agreements, in which availability is one of the most important elements.

Configuration Management

Configuration Management has information about the infrastructure and can provide valuable information to Availability Management.

Capacity Management

Changes in the capacity often affect the availability of a service and changes to the availability will affect the capacity. Capacity Management has extensive information available, including information about the IT infrastructure. Thus, these two processes often exchange information about scenarios for upgrading or phasing out IT components, and about availability trends that may necessitate changes to the capacity requirements.

IT Service Continuity Management

Availability Management is not responsible for restoring business processes after a disaster. This is the responsibility of IT Service Continuity Management. ITSCM provides Availability Management with information about critical business processes. Also, in practice, many measures taken to enhance Availability also enhance IT Service Continuity, and vice versa.

Problem Management

Problem Management is directly involved in identifying and resolving the causes of actual or potential availability problems.

Incident Management

Incident Management specifies how incidents should be resolved. This process provides reports with information about recovery times, repair times, etc. This information is used to determine the achieved availability.

Security Management

Availability Management has close ties with Security Management. The three basic issues in Security Management are:
- Confidentiality.
- Integrity.
- Availability.

Security criteria have to be considered when determining availability requirements. Availability Management can provide valuable information to Security Management, particularly about new services. In ITIL the best practices on Security Management are described in the separate book 'Security Management'. Security Management is described in detail in chapter 15 of this book.

Change Management

Availability Management informs Change Management about maintenance issues related to new services and elements thereof, and initiates the Change Management process to implement changes necessitated by availability measures. Change Management informs Availability Management about scheduled changes (FSC).

14.4 Activities

Availability Management includes a number of key activities that concern planning and monitoring.

These activities are:
- **Planning**:
  - Determining the availability requirements.
  - Designing for availability.
  - Designing for recoverability.
  - Security issues.
  - Maintenance management.
  - Developing the Availability Plan.
- **Monitoring:**
  - Measuring and reporting.

These key activities are discussed below.

14.4.1 Determining the availability requirements

This activity must be undertaken before a SLA can be concluded and should address both new IT services and changes to existing services. It must be decided at the earliest possible stage if and how the IT organization can fulfill the requirements.

This activity should identify:
- Key business functions.
- Agreed definition of IT service downtime.
- Quantifiable availability requirements.

- Quantifiable impact on the business functions of unscheduled IT service downtime.
- Business hours of the customer.
- Agreements about maintenance windows.

Clearly defining the availability requirements at an early stage is essential to prevent confusion and differences in interpretation at a later stage.

The customer's requirements must be compared with what can be provided. If there is a mismatch, then the cost impact of this will have to be determined.

14.4.2 Designing for Availability
Vulnerabilities that affect the availability standards should be identified as early as possible. This will prevent excessive development costs, unplanned expenditure at later stages, Single Points Of Failure (SPOF), additional costs charged by suppliers, and delayed releases.

A good design, based on the appropriate availability standards, will make it possible to conclude effective maintenance contracts with suppliers. The design process employs a range of techniques such as Component Failure Impact Analysis (CFIA) to identify SPOF's, CRAMM (see the chapter on IT Service Continuity Management) and simulation techniques.

If the availability standards cannot be met, the best option is to determine if the design can be improved. The use of additional technology, other methods, a different release strategy, a better or different design, and development tools may provide opportunities to meet the standards.
If the requirements are particularly demanding then the use of other fault tolerance technology, other service processes (incident, problem, and Change Management), or additional Service Management resources may be considered. The financial resources available largely determine the options and choices.

14.4.3 Designing for Maintainability
As completely uninterrupted availability is rarely feasible, periods of unavailability must be considered. When an IT service is interrupted it is important that the fault is quickly and adequately solved, and that the agreed availability standards are fulfilled. Designing for recoverability involves issues such as an effective Incident Management process with appropriate escalation, communication, and backup and recovery procedures.

The tasks, responsibilities and authority should be clearly defined.

14.4.4 Key security issues
Security and reliability are closely linked. A poor information security design can affect the availability of the service. High availability can be supported by effective information security. During the planning stage, the security issues should be considered and their impact on the provision of services should be analyzed.

Some of the issues include:
- Determining who is authorized to access secure areas.
- Determining which critical authorizations may be issued.

14.4.5 Maintenance management

Normally, there will always be scheduled windows of unavailability. These periods can be used for preventive action, such as software and hardware upgrades. Changes can also be implemented during these windows. In the 24-hour economy, however, it is becoming more and more difficult to determine appropriate maintenance windows. The definition, implementation, and verification of maintenance activities have developed into major issues in Availability Management. Maintenance must be carried out when the impact on services can be minimized. This means that it must be known in advance what the maintenance objectives are, when the maintenance should be undertaken and what maintenance activities are involved (this could be based on CFIA). This information is essential for Change Management and other activities.

14.4.6 Measuring and reporting

Measuring and reporting are important Availability Management activities as they provide the basis for verifying service agreements, resolving problems, and defining proposals for improvement.

If you don't measure it, you can't manage it.
If you don't measure it, you can't improve it.
If you don't measure it, you probably don't care.
If you can't influence it, then don't measure it.

The life cycle of each incident includes the following elements:
- **Occurrence of the incident** - the time at which the user becomes aware of the fault, or when the fault is identified by other means (technically or physically).
- **Detection** - the service provider is informed of the fault. The incident status is now 'reported'. The time this took is known as the detection time.
- **Response** - the service provider needs time to respond. This is known as the response time. This time is used for diagnosis, which can then be followed by repair. The Incident Management process includes Acceptance and Registration, Classification, Matching, Analysis, and Diagnosis.
- **Repair** - the service provider restores the service or the components that caused the fault.
- **Service recovery** - the service is restored. This includes activities such as configuration and initialization, and the service is restored to the user.

Figure 14.3 illustrates the periods that can be measured.

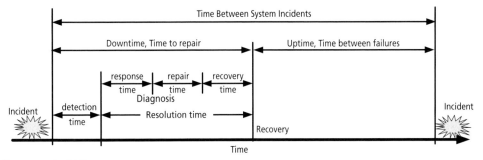

Figure 14.3 - Availability measurement

As the figure shows, the response time of the IT organization and any external contractors is one of the factors determining the downtime. As this factor can be controlled by the IT organization and directly affects the service quality, agreements about it can be included in the SLA. The measurements can be averaged to give a good impression of the relevant factors. The averages can be used to determine the achieved service levels, and to estimate the expected future availability of a service. This information can also be used to develop improvement plans.

The following metrics are commonly used in Availability Management:
- **Mean Time to Repair (MTTR)** - average time between the occurrence of a fault and service recovery, also known as the downtime. It is the sum of the detection time and the resolution time. This metric relates to the recoverability and serviceability of the service.
- **Mean Time Between Failures (MTBF)** - mean time between the recovery from one incident and the occurrence of the next incident, also known as uptime. This metric relates to the reliability of the service.
- **Mean Time Between System Incidents (MTBSI)** - mean time between the occurrences of two consecutive incidents. The MTBSI is the sum of the MTTR and MTBF.

The ratio of the MTBF and the MTBSI indicates if there are many minor faults or just a few major faults.

Availability reports may include the following metrics:
- Rate of availability (or unavailability) in terms of MTTR, MTBF and MTBSI.
- Overall uptime and downtime.
- Number of faults.
- Additional information about faults which actually or potentially result in a higher than agreed unavailability.

The problem with availability reporting is that the presented metrics may not correspond with the customer's perception. It is therefore important to report about availability from the customer's perspective. The report should primarily provide information about the availability of the service for essential business functions, application services, and the availability of the data (business view), rather than information about the availability of technical IT components. Reports should be written in a language the customer can understand.

14.4.7 Developing the Availability Plan
The Availability Plan is one of the major products of Availability Management. It is a long-term plan concerning availability over the next few years. It is not the implementation plan for Availability Management.

The plan should be a living document. Initially it should describe the current situation, and at a later stage it can be expanded to include improvement activities for existing services and guidelines, as well as plans for new services and guidelines for maintenance. A comprehensive and accurate plan requires liaison with areas such as Service Level Management, IT Service Continuity Management, Capacity Management, and Financial Management for IT Services and application development (directly or through Change Management).

14.4.8 Tools
To be efficient, Availability Management must use a number of tools for the following activities:
- Determining downtime.
- Recording historical information.
- Generating reports.
- Statistical analysis.
- Impact analysis.

Availability Management uses information from the Incident Management records, the CMDB, and the Capacity Database. Information may be stored in a dedicated Availability Management Database (AMDB).

14.4.9 Methods and techniques

There is now a broad spectrum of Availability Management methods and techniques to support planning, improvement and reporting. The most important of these are discussed below.

Component Failure Impact Analysis (CFIA)

This method uses an availability matrix with the strategic components and their roles in each service. An effective CMDB, which defines the relationships between services and production resources, can be most helpful when developing this matrix.

An example of a CFIA matrix in Figure 14.4 shows that the Configuration Items which are marked with 'X' for many services are important elements of the IT infrastructure (horizontal analysis), and that services which are frequently marked with 'X' are complex and sensitive to faults (vertical analysis). This method can also be applied to dependencies on third parties (Advanced CFIA).

Configuration Item:	Service A	Service B
PC #1	B	B
PC #2		B
Cable #1	B	B
Cable #2		B
Outlet #1	X	X
Outlet #2		X
Ethernet segment	X	X
Router	X	X
WAN link	X	X
Router	X	X
Segment	X	X
NIC	A	A
Server	B	B
System software	B	B
Application	B	B
Database	X	X

X = Fault means service is unavailable
A = Failsafe configuration
B = Failsafe, with changeover time
" " = No impact

Figure 14.4 - CFIA matrix

Fault Tree Analysis (FTA)

Fault Tree Analysis is a technique used to identify the chain of events leading to failure of an IT service. A separate tree is drawn for every service, using Boolean symbols. The tree is traversed from the bottom up. FTA distinguishes the following events:

- **Basic Events** - inputs in the diagram (circles) such as power outages and operator errors. These events are not investigated.
- **Resulting Events** - nodes in the diagram, resulting from a combination of earlier events.
- **Conditional Events** - events that only occur under certain conditions, such as an air conditioning failure.
- **Trigger Events** - events that cause other events, such as an automatic shutdown initiated by a UPS.

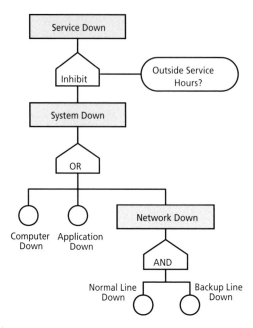

Figure 14.5 - Fault Tree Analysis

Events can be combined with logical operations, such as:
- **AND operation** - the Resulting Event will occur if all inputs occur simultaneously.
- **OR operation** - the Resulting Event will occur if one or more of the inputs occur.
- **XOR operation** - the Resulting Event will occur if only one of the inputs occurs.
- **Inhibit operation** - the Resulting Event will occur if the input conditions are not fulfilled.

CCTA Risk Analysis and Management Method (CRAMM)

CRAMM describes a means of identifying justifiable countermeasures to protect confidentiality, integrity and availability of the IT infrastructure. This method is discussed in some detail in the chapter on IT Service Continuity Management.

Availability calculations

The metrics discussed above can be used to conclude service availability agreements with the customer. These agreements are included in the Service Level Agreement. The formula below may be used to determine if the achieved availability fulfilled the agreed availability requirement:

$$\% \text{ Availability} = \frac{AST\text{-}DT}{AST} * 100\%$$

Figure 14.6 - Availability formula. [AST = Agreed service time; DT = Actual downtime during agreed service time]

The achieved uptime amounts to the difference between the agreed service time (AST) and the actual downtime during this agreed service time (DT). Example: if it were agreed that the service should have 98% availability on working days from 07.00 to 19.00 h, and the service was down for two hours during this window, then the achieved uptime (availability percentage) would be:

(5 x 12 - 2)/(5 x 12) x 100% = 96.7%

Service Outage Analysis (SOA)

SOA is a technique that can be used to identify the causes of faults, to investigate the effectiveness of the IT organization and its processes, and to present and implement proposals for improvement.

The characteristics of an SOA are:
- It has a broad scope: it is not limited to the infrastructure, but also covers processes, procedures, and cultural aspects.
- Issues are considered from the customer's perspective.
- Joint implementation by representatives of the customer and the IT organization (SOA team).

The benefits include a more efficient approach, direct communication between the customer and the supplier, and a broader base for proposals for improvement.

Technical Observation Post (TOP)

When using the TOP method, a dedicated team of IT specialists focuses on a single aspect of availability. This method may be appropriate where routine tools provide insufficient support. The TOP can also combine the expertise of designers and system managers.

The key aspects of this method are an efficient, effective and informal approach that quickly leads to results.

14.5 Process control

14.5.1 Critical success factors and performance indicators

The critical success factors for Availability Management are:
- The business must have clearly defined availability objectives and wishes.
- Service Level Management must have been set up to formalize agreements.
- Both parties must use the same definitions of availability and downtime.
- Both the business and the IT organization must be aware of the benefits of Availability Management.

The following performance indicators show the effectiveness and efficiency of Availability Management:
- Percentage availability (uptime) per service or group of users.
- Downtime duration.
- Downtime frequency.

14.5.2 Reporting

The availability reports for the customer were discussed above. The following metrics can be reported for process control:
- Detection times.
- Response times.
- Repair times.
- Recovery times.

- Successful use of appropriate methods (CFIA, CRAMM, SOA).
- Extent of process implementation: services, SLA's and customer groups covered by SLA's.

Some metrics can be determined for each service, team or infrastructure domain (network, computer center, and workstation environment).

14.5.3 Functions and roles
The organization can establish the role of Availability Manager to define and control the process. The task of the Availability Manager could include the following elements:
- Defining and developing the process in the organization.
- Ensuring that IT services are designed such that the achieved service levels (in terms of availability, reliability, serviceability, maintainability, and recoverability) correspond with the agreed service levels.
- Reporting.
- Optimizing the availability of the IT infrastructure to provide a cost-effective improvement of the service provided to the business .

14.6 Costs and possible problems

14.6.1 Costs
The costs of Availability Management include:
- Cost of implementation.
- Personnel costs.
- Facilities costs.
- Measuring and reporting tools.

Availability Management should identify the investment needed to improve the availability early. A cost/benefit analysis should be carried out in all cases. In general, the costs will rise as the required availability increases. Finding the optimum solution is an important task of Availability Management. Experience shows that the optimum can often be reached with limited resources, rather than requiring significant investment.

The discussion of the costs and benefits can be guided by asking what the costs will be if we completely ignore Availability Management and reach a situation where the agreed availability requirements are not fulfilled. This will have the following impact on the customer:
- Reduced productivity.
- Reduced turnover and profit.
- Recovery costs.
- Potential claims from third parties, etc.

The following aspects are difficult to quantify but are equally important:
- Loss of goodwill and customers.
- Loss of reputation and trust.
- Loss of personnel motivation and satisfaction.

The Availability Management process can contribute to the objectives of the IT organization in these areas by providing the required services at an acceptable and justifiable cost.

14.6.2 Possible problems

Most problems concern the organization. Problems to be expected include:
- Senior management divides responsibility for availability between several disciplines (line managers, process managers).
- Each manager feels responsible for his or her own area, and there is no overall coordination.
- IT management fails to understand the added value provided to the Incident, Problem, and Change Management processes.
- The current availability level is considered sufficient.
- There is no support for appointing a single, responsible process manager.
- The process manager does not have the required authority.

Even with sufficient management support, problems may still arise due to:
- Underestimating resources.
- Lack of effective measurement and reporting tools.
- Lack of other processes such as Service Level Management, Configuration Management, and Problem Management.

These problems can be solved with good management support, the right person with full responsibility for the process, appropriate tools, and rapid and effective resolution of existing problems.

If Availability Management is used inefficiently the following problems may arise:
- It will be difficult to define appropriate availability standards.
- It will be more difficult to guide internal and external suppliers.
- It will be difficult to compare the costs of availability and unavailability.
- If availability standards were not considered during the design, later modification to meet these standards may be many times more expensive.
- Availability standards are not fulfilled which may lead to failure to meet the business objectives.
- Customer satisfaction may be reduced.

Aiming for an excessively high availability is another potential problem. Costs will rise sharply, disproportionately to the benefits. There is always likely to be downtime. Availability Management plays an important role in resolving these undesirable events.

15 SECURITY MANAGEMENT

15.1 Introduction

Business processes can no longer operate without a supply of information. In fact, more and more business processes consist purely of one or more information systems. Information Security Management is an important activity that aims to control the provision of information and to prevent unauthorized use of information.

For many years, Information Security Management was largely ignored. However, this is changing. Security is now considered as one of the main management challenges for the coming years. The interest in this discipline is increasing because of the growing use of the Internet and e-commerce in particular. More and more businesses are opening electronic gateways into their business. This introduces the risk of intrusion, and raises some important questions for businesses. What risks do we want to cover, and what measures should we take now and in the next budgeting round? Senior Management has to take decisions and these decisions can only be taken if a thorough risk analysis is undertaken. This analysis should provide input to Security Management to determine the security requirements.

Business requirements for security affect IT service providers and should be laid down in Service Level Agreements. Security Management aims to ensure that the security aspects of services are provided at the level agreed with the customer at all times. Security is now an essential quality aspect of management.

Security Management integrates security in the IT organization from the service provider's point of view. The international standard ISO17799 provides guidance for the development, introduction and evaluation of security measures.

Security is addressed in ITIL as part of Availability Management. Security Management has become an important issue in modern IT Service Management and a separate publication is part of the ITIL book set. This book is summarized in this chapter, in-line with the ITIL structure.

15.1.1 Basic concepts

Security Management comes under the umbrella of Information Security, which aims to ensure the safety of information. **Safety** refers to not being vulnerable to known risks, and avoiding unknown risks where possible. The tool to provide this is **security**. The aim is to protect the value of the information. This value depends on confidentiality, integrity and availability:

- **Confidentiality** - protecting information against unauthorized access and use.
- **Integrity** - accuracy, completeness and timeliness of the information.
- **Availability** - the information should be accessible at any agreed time. This depends on the continuity provided by the information processing systems.

Secondary aspects include privacy (confidentiality and integrity of information relating to individuals), anonymity, and verification (being able to verify that the information is used correctly and that the security measures are effective).

15.2 Objectives

In recent decades, almost all businesses have become more dependent on information systems. The use of computer networks has also grown, not only within businesses but also between businesses and the world outside. The increasing complexity of the IT infrastructure means that businesses are now more vulnerable to technical failures, human error, intentional human acts, hackers, computer viruses, etc. This growing complexity requires a unified management approach. Security Management has important ties with other processes. Other ITIL processes, under the supervision of Security Management, carry out some security activities.

Security Management has two objectives:
■ To meet the security requirements of SLA's and external requirements further to contracts, legislation and externally imposed policies.
■ To provide a basic level of security, independent of external requirements.

Security Management is essential to maintaining the uninterrupted operation of the IT organization. It also helps to simplify Information Security Service Level Management as it is much more difficult to manage a large number of different SLA's than a limited number.

The process input is provided by the SLA's that specify security requirements, possibly supplemented by policy documents and other external requirements. The process also receives information about relevant security issues in other processes, such as security incidents.

The output includes information about the achieved implementation of the SLA's, including exception reports and routine security planning.

At present, many organizations deal with Information Security at the strategic level in information policy and information plans, and at the operational level by purchasing tools and other security products. Insufficient attention is given to the active management of Information Security, the continuous analysis and translation of policies into technical options and ensuring that the security measures continue to be effective when requirements and environments change. The consequence of this missing link between the strategic and the tactical level is that, at the tactical management level, significant investments are made in measures that are no longer relevant, at a time when new, more effective measures ought to be taken. Security Management aims to ensure that effective Information Security measures are taken at the strategic, tactical and operational levels.

15.2.1 Benefits

Information Security is not a goal in itself; it aims to serve the interests of the business or organization. Some information and information services will be more important to the organization than others. Information Security must be appropriate to the importance of the information. Striking a balance between security measures and the value of the information, and threats in the processing environment provides tailor-made security. An effective information supply, with adequate Information Security is important to an organization for two reasons:
■ **Internal reasons** - an organization can only operate effectively if correct and complete information is available when required. The level of Information Security should be appropriate for this.
■ **External reasons** - the processes in an organization create products and services that are made available to the market or society, to meet defined objectives. An inadequate information supply will lead to substandard products and services which cannot be used to meet the objectives and which will threaten the survival of the organization. Adequate Information Security is an

important condition for having an adequate information supply. The external significance of Information Security is therefore determined in part by the internal significance.

Security can provide significant added value to an information system. Effective security contributes to the continuity of the organization and helps to meet its objectives.

15.3 Process

15.3.1 Security Management activities

Organizations and their information systems change. Checklists such as the Code of Practice for Information Security Management are static and insufficiently address rapid changes in IT. For this reason, Security Management activities must be reviewed continuously to ensure their effectiveness. Security Management amounts to a never-ending cycle of plan, do, check, and act. The activities undertaken by Security Management, or undertaken in other processes under the control of Security Management are discussed below.

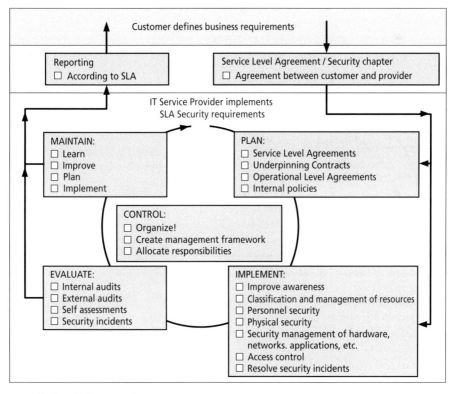

Figure 15.1 - The Security Management process

Figure 15.1 shows the Security Management cycle. The customer's requirements appear at the top right, as input to the process. The security section of the Service Level Agreement defines these requirements in terms of the security services and the level of security to be provided. The service provider communicates these agreements to the organization in the form of a Security Plan, defining the security standards or Operational Level Agreements. This plan is implemented, and the implementation is evaluated. The plan and its implementation are then updated.

Service Level Management reports about these activities to the customer. Thus, the customer and the service provider together form a complete cyclical process. The customer can modify requirements on the basis of the reports. And the service provider can adjust the plan or its implementation on the basis of these observations, or aim to change the agreements defined in the SLA. The control function appears in the middle of Figure 15.1. This diagram will now be used to discuss the Security Management activities.

15.3.2 Relationship with other processes

Security Management has links with the other ITIL processes (see Figure 15.2). This is because the other processes undertake security-related activities. These activities are carried out in the normal way, under the responsibility of the relevant process and process manager. However, Security Management gives instructions about the structure of the security-related activities to the other processes. Normally, these agreements are defined after consultation between the Security Manager and the other process managers.

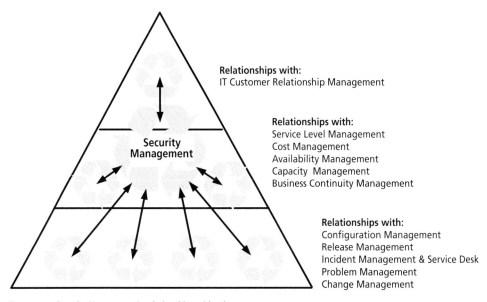

Figure 15.2 - Security Management's relationships with other processes

Configuration Management
In the context of Information Security, Configuration Management is primarily relevant because it can classify Configuration Items. This classification links the CI with specified security measures or procedures.

The classification of a CI indicates its required confidentiality, integrity and availability. This classification is based on the security requirements of the SLA. The customer of the IT organization determines the classification, as only the customer can decide how important the information or information systems are to the business processes. The customer bases the classification on an analysis of the extent to which the business processes depend on the information systems and the information. The IT organization then associates the classification with the relevant CI's. The IT organization must also implement this set of security measures for each classification level. These sets of measures can be described in procedures. Example: 'Procedure for handling storage media with personal data'. The SLA can define the sets of security measures for each classification level.

The classification system should always be tailored to the customer's organization. However, to simplify management it is advisable to aim for one unified classification system, even when the IT organization has more than one customer.

In summary, classification is a key issue. The CMDB should indicate the classification of each CI. This classification links the CI with the relevant set of security measures or procedure.

Incident Management
Incident Management is an important process for reporting security incidents. Depending on the nature of the incident, security incidents may be covered by a different procedure than other incidents. It is therefore essential that Incident Management recognize security incidents as such. Any incident that may interfere with achieving the SLA security requirements is classified as a security incident. It is useful to include a description in the SLA of the type of incidents to be considered as security incidents. Any incident that interferes with achieving the basic internal security level (baseline) is also always classified as a security incident.

Incidents reports are generated not only by users, but also by the management process, possibly on the basis of alarms or audit data from the systems.

It is clearly essential that Incident Management recognize all security incidents. This is to ensure that the appropriate procedures are initiated for dealing with security incidents. It is advisable to include the procedures for different types of security incidents in the SLA plans and to practice the procedure. It is also advisable to agree a procedure for communicating about security incidents. It is not unusual for panic to be created by rumors blown out of proportion. Similarly, it is not unusual for damage to result from a failure to communicate in time about security incidents. It is advisable to route all external communications related to security incidents through the Security Manager.

Problem Management
Problem Management is responsible for identifying and solving structural security failings. A problem may also introduce a security risk. In that case, Problem Management must involve Security Management in resolving the problem. Finally, the solution or workaround for a problem or known error must always be checked to ensure that it does not introduce new security problems. This verification should be based on compliance with the SLA and internal security requirements.

Change Management
Change Management activities are often closely associated with security because Change Management and Security Management are interdependent. If an acceptable security level has been achieved and is managed by the Change Management process, then it can be ensured that this level of security will also be provided after changes. There are a number of standard operations to ensure that this security level is maintained. Each RFC is associated with a number of parameters that govern the acceptance procedure. The urgency and impact parameters can be supplemented by a security parameter. If an RFC can have a significant impact on Information Security then more extensive acceptance tests and procedures will be required.

The RFC should also include a proposal for dealing with security issues. Again, this should be based on the SLA requirements and the basic level of internal security required by the IT organization. Thus, the proposal will include a set of security measures, based on the Code of Practice.

Preferably, the Security Manager (and possibly also the customer's Security Officer) should be a member of the Change Advisory Board (CAB).

Nevertheless, the Security Manager need not be consulted for all changes. Security should normally be integrated with routine operations. The Change Manager should be able to decide if they or the CAB need input from the Security Manager. Similarly, the Security Manager need not necessarily be involved in the selection of measures for the CI's covered by the RFC. This is because the framework for the relevant measures should already exist. Any questions should only relate to the way in which the measures are implemented.

Any security measures associated with a change should be implemented at the same time as the change itself, and be included in the tests. Security tests differ from normal functional tests. Normal tests aim to investigate if defined functions are available. Security tests not only address the availability of security functions, but also the absence of other, undesirable functions as these could reduce the security of the system.

In terms of security, Change Management is one of the most important processes. This is because Change Management introduces new security measures into the IT infrastructure, together with changes to the IT infrastructure.

Release Management

All new versions of software, hardware, data communications equipment, etc. should be controlled and rolled out by Release Management. This process will ensure that:
- The correct hardware and software are used.
- The hardware and software are tested before use.
- The introduction is correctly authorized using a change.
- The software is legal.
- The software is free from viruses and that viruses are not introduced during its distribution.
- The version numbers are known, and recorded in the CMDB by Configuration Management.
- The rollout is managed effectively.

This process also uses a regular acceptance procedure that should include Information Security aspects. It is particularly important to consider security aspects during testing and acceptance. This means that the security requirements and measures defined in the SLA should be complied with at all times.

Service Level Management

Service Level Management ensures that agreements about the services to be provided to customers are defined and achieved. The Service Level Agreements should also address security measures. The objective is to optimize the level of service provided.

Service Level Management includes a number of related security activities, in which Security Management plays an important role:
1. Identification of the security needs of the customer. Naturally, determining the security needs is the responsibility of the customer as these needs are based on their business interests.
2. Verifying the feasibility of the customer's security requirements.
3. Proposing, discussing and defining the security level of the IT services in the SLA.
4. Identifying, developing and defining the internal security requirements for IT services (Operational Level Agreements).

5. Monitoring the security standards (OLA's).
6. Reporting on the IT services provided.

Security Management provides input and support to Service Level Management for activities 1-3. Security Management carries out activities 4 and 5. Security Management and other processes provide input for activity 6. The Service Level Manager and the Security Manager decide in consultation who actually undertakes the activities.

When defining a SLA it is normally assumed that there is a general basic level of security (baseline). Additional security requirements of the customer should be clearly defined in the SLA.

Availability Management
Availability Management addresses the technical availability of IT components in relation to the availability of the service. The quality of availability is assured by continuity, maintainability and resilience. Availability Management is the most important process related to availability. As many security measures benefit both availability and the security aspects confidentiality and integrity, effective coordination of the measures between Availability Management, IT Service Continuity Management, and Security Management is essential.

Capacity Management
Capacity Management is responsible for the best possible use of IT resources, as agreed with the customer. The performance requirements are based on the qualitative and quantitative standards defined by Service Level Management. Almost all the activities of Capacity Management affect availability and therefore also Security Management.

IT Service Continuity Management
IT Service Continuity Management ensures that the impact of any contingencies is limited to the level agreed with the customer. Contingencies need not necessarily turn into disasters. The major activities are defining, maintaining, implementing, and testing the contingency plan, and taking preventive action. Because of the security aspects, there are ties with Security Management. On the other hand, failure to fulfill the basic security requirements may be considered itself as a contingency.

15.3.3 The Security section of the Service Level Agreement
The Service Level Agreement (SLA) defines the agreements with the customer. The Service Level Management process is responsible for the SLA (see also Chapter 10). The SLA is the most important driver for all ITIL processes.

The IT organization indicates to what extent the requirements of the SLA are achieved, including security requirements. The security elements addressed in the SLA should correspond to the security needs of the customer. The customer should identify the significance of all business processes (see Figure 15.3).

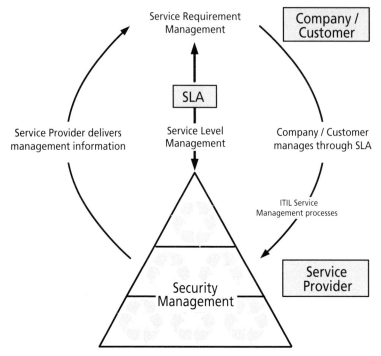

Figure 15.3 - Relationships between the processes

These business processes depend on IT services, and therefore on the IT organization. The customer determines the security requirements (SLA Information Security requirements, not included in Figure 15.3) on the basis of a risk analysis. Figure 15.4 shows how the security elements of the SLA are defined.

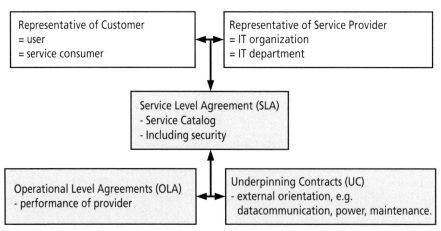

Figure 15.4 - Developing the security section of the SLA

The security elements are discussed between the representative of the customer and the representative of the service provider. The service provider compares the customer's Service Level Requirements with their own Service Catalogue, which describes their standard security measures (the Security Baseline). The customer may have additional requirements.

The customer and provider compare the Service Level Requirements and the Service Catalogue. The security section of the SLA can address issues such as the general Information Security policy, a list of authorized personnel, asset protection procedures, restrictions on copying data, etc.

15.3.4 The security section of the Operational Level Agreement

The Operational Level Agreement is another important document. It describes the services provided by the service provider. The provider must associate these agreements with responsibilities within the organization. The Service Catalogue gives a general description of the services. The Operational Level Agreement translates these and general descriptions into all services and their components, and the way in which the agreements about the service levels are assured within the organization.

Example: the Service Catalogue refers to 'managing authorizations per user and per individual'. The Operational Level Agreements details this for all relevant services provided by the IT organization. In this way, the implementation of the measure is defined for the departments providing UNIX, VMS, NT, Oracle services, etc.

Where possible, the customer's Service Level Requirements are interpreted in terms of the provider's Service Catalogue, and additional agreements are concluded where necessary. Such additional measurements exceed the standard security level.

When drafting the SLA, measurable Key Performance Indicators (KPI) and criteria must also be agreed for Security Management. KPI's are measurable parameters (metrics), and performance criteria are set at achievable levels. In some cases it will be difficult to agree on measurable security parameters. This is easier for availability, which can generally be expressed numerically. However, this is much more difficult for integrity and confidentiality. For this reason, the security section of the SLA normally describes the required measures in abstract terms. The Code of Practice for Information Security Management is used as a basic set of security measures. The SLA also describes how performance is measured. The IT organization (service provider) must regularly provide reports to the user organization (customer).

15.4 Activities

15.4.1 Control - Information Security policy and organization

The Control activity in the center of Figure 15.4 is the first subprocess of Security Management and relates to the organization and management of the process. This includes the Information Security management framework. This framework describes the subprocesses: the definition of security plans, their implementation, evaluation of the implementation, and incorporation of the evaluation in the annual security plans (action plans). The reports provided to the customer, via Service Level Management, are also addressed.

This activity defines the subprocesses, security functions, and roles and responsibilities. It also describes the organizational structure, reporting arrangements, and line of control (who instructs who, who does what, how is the implementation reported). The following measures from the Code of Practice are implemented by this activity:
- **Policy:**
  - Policy development and implementation, links with other policies.
  - Objectives, general principles and significance.

- Description of the subprocesses.
- Allocating functions and responsibilities for subprocesses.
- Links with other ITIL processes and their management.
- General responsibility of personnel.
- Dealing with security incidents.

■ **Information Security organization:**
- Management framework.
- Management structure (organizational structure).
- Allocation of responsibilities in greater detail.
- Setting up an Information Security Steering Committee.
- Information Security coordination.
- Agreeing tools (e.g. for risk analysis and improving awareness).
- Description of the IT facilities authorization process, in consultation with the customer.
- Specialist advice.
- Cooperation between organizations, internal and external communications.
- Independent Information Systems audit.
- Security principles for access by third parties.
- Information Security in contracts with third parties.

15.4.2 Plan

The Planning subprocess includes defining the security section of the SLA in consultation with Service Level Management, and the activities in the Underpinning Contracts related to security. The objectives in the SLA, which are defined in general terms, are detailed and specified in the form of an Operational Level Agreement. An OLA can be considered as the security plan for an organizational unit of the service provider, and as a specific security plan, for example for each IT platform, application and network.

The Planning subprocess not only receives input from the SLA but also from the service provider's policy principles (from the Control subprocess). Examples of these principles include: 'Every user should be uniquely identifiable', and 'A basic security level is provided to all customers, at all times.'

The Operational Level Agreements for Information Security (specific security plans) are drafted and implemented using the normal procedures. This means that, should activities be required in other processes, there will have to be coordination with these processes. Change Management using input provided by Security Management makes any required changes to the IT infrastructure. The Change Manager is responsible for the Change Management process.

The Planning subprocess is discussed with Service Level Management to define, update and comply with the security section of the SLA. The Service Level Manager is responsible for this coordination.

The SLA should define the security requirements, where possible in measurable terms. The security section of the agreement should ensure that all the customer's security requirements and standards could be verifiably achieved.

15.4.3 Implement

The Implementation subprocess aims to implement all the measures specified in the plans. The following checklist can support this subprocess.

- **Classification and management of IT resources:**
  - Providing input for maintaining the CI's in the CMDB.
  - Classifying IT resources in accordance with agreed guidelines.
- **Personnel security:**
  - Tasks and responsibilities in job descriptions.
  - Screening.
  - Confidentiality agreements for personnel.
  - Training.
  - Guidelines for personnel for dealing with security incidents and observed security weaknesses.
  - Disciplinary measures.
  - Increasing security awareness
- **Managing security:**
  - Implementation of responsibilities, implementation of job separation.
  - Written operating instructions.
  - Internal regulations.
  - Security should cover the entire life cycle; there should be security guidelines for system development, testing, acceptance, operations, maintenance and phasing out.
  - Separating the development and test environments from the production environment.
  - Procedures for dealing with incidents (handled by Incident Management).
  - Implementation of recovery facilities.
  - Providing input for Change Management.
  - Implementation of virus protection measures.
  - Implementation of management measures for computers, applications, networks and network services.
  - Handling and security of data media.
- **Access control:**
  - Implementation of access and access control policy.
  - Maintenance of access privileges of users and applications to networks, network services, computers, and applications.
  - Maintenance of network security barriers (firewalls, dial-in services, bridges and routers).
  - Implementation of measures for the identification and authentication of computer systems, workstations and PCs on the network.

15.4.4 Evaluate

An independent evaluation of the implementation of the planned measures is essential. This evaluation is needed to assess the performance and is also required by customers and third parties. The results of the Evaluation subprocess can be used to update the agreed measures in consultation with the customers, and also for their implementation. The results of the evaluation may suggest changes, in which case an RFC is defined and submitted to the Change Management process.

There are three forms of evaluation:
- **Self-assessments** - primarily implemented by the line organization of the processes.
- **Internal audits** - undertaken by internal IT auditors.
- **External audits** - undertaken by external IT auditors.

Unlike self-assessments, the same personnel that act in the other subprocesses do not undertake audits. This is to ensure that the responsibilities are separated. An Internal Audit department may undertake audits.

Evaluations are also carried out in response to security incidents.

The main activities are:
- Verifying compliance with the security policy and implementation of security plans.
- Performing security audits on IT systems.
- Identifying and responding to inappropriate use of IT resources.
- Undertaking the security aspects of other IT audits.

15.4.5 Maintenance

Security requires maintenance, as the risks change due to changes in the IT infrastructure, organization and business processes. Security maintenance includes the maintenance of the security section of the SLA and maintenance of the detailed security plans (Operational Level Agreements).

Maintenance is carried out on the basis of the results of the Evaluation subprocess and an assessment of changes in the risks. These proposals can either be introduced into the Planning subprocess, or included in the maintenance of the SLA as a whole. In either case, the proposals can result in the inclusion of activities in the annual security plan. Any changes are subject to the normal Change Management process.

15.4.6 Reporting

Reporting is not a subprocess, but an output of the other subprocesses. Reports are produced to provide information about the achieved security performance and to inform the customers about security issues. These reports are generally required under agreement with the customer. Reporting is important, both to the customer and to the service provider. Customers must be correctly informed about the efficiency of the efforts (e.g. with respect to the implementation of security measures), and the actual security measures. The customer is also informed about any security incidents. A list with some suggestions for reporting options is included below.

Examples of scheduled reports and reportable events:
- The **Planning** subprocess:
  - Reports about the extent of compliance with the SLA and agreed Key Performance Indicators for security.
  - Reports about Underpinning Contracts and any problems associated with them.
  - Reports about Operational Level Agreements (internal security plans) and the provider's own security principles (e.g. in the baseline).
  - Reports about annual security plans and action plans.
- The **Implementation** subprocess:
  - Status reports about the implementation of Information Security. This includes progress reports about the implementation of the annual security plan, possibly a list of measures which have been implemented or are yet to be implemented, training, outcome of additional risk analyses, etc.
  - A list of security incidents and responses to these incidents, optionally a comparison with the previous reporting period.
  - Identification of incident trends.
  - Status of the awareness program.
- The **Evaluation** subprocess:
  - Reports about the performance of the subprocess.
  - Results of audits, reviews, and internal assessments.
  - Warnings, identification of new threats.

Specific reports

To report on security incidents defined in the SLA, the service provider must have a direct channel of communication to a customer representative (possibly the Corporate Information Security Officer) through the Service Level Manager, Incident Manager or Security Manager. A procedure should also be defined for communication in special circumstances.

Apart from the exception in the event of special circumstances, reports are communicated through Service Level Management.

15.5 Process control

15.5.1 Critical success factors and performance indicators

The critical success factors are:
■ Full management commitment and involvement.
■ User involvement when developing the process.
■ Clear and separated responsibilities.

The Security Management performance indicators correspond with the Service Level Management performance indicators, in so far as these relate to security issues covered by the SLA.

15.5.2 Functions and roles

In small IT organizations, one person may manage several processes. While in large organizations, several persons will be working on one process, such as Security Management. In this case there is normally one person appointed as Security Manager. The Security Manager is responsible for the effective operation of the Security Management process. Their counterpart in the customer's organization is the Information Security Officer, or Corporate Information Security Officer.

15.6 Costs and possible problems

15.6.1 Costs

Securing the IT infrastructure demands personnel, and therefore money, to take, maintain and verify measures. However, failing to secure the IT infrastructure also costs money (cost of lost production; cost of replacement; damage to data, software, or hardware; loss of reputation; fines or compensation relating to failure to fulfill contractual obligations). As always, a balance will have to be struck.

15.6.2 Possible problems

The following issues are essential to the successful implementation of Security Management:
■ **Commitment** - security measures are rarely accepted immediately; resistance is more common than acceptance. Users resent losing certain privileges due to security measures, even if these facilities are not essential to their work. This is because the privileges give them a certain status. A special effort will therefore have to be made to motivate users, and to ensure that management complies with the security measures. In the field of Security Management in particular, management must set an example ('walk the talk' and 'lead by example'). If there are no security incidents, then management may be tempted to reduce the Security Management budget.

- **Attitude** - information systems are not insecure due to technical weaknesses, but due to the failure to use the technology. This is generally related to attitude and human behavior. This means that security procedures must be integrated with routine operations.
- **Awareness** - awareness, or rather communication, is a key concept. There sometimes appears to be a conflict of interest between communication and security - communication paves the road, while security creates obstacles. This means that implementing security measures requires the use of all communication methods to ensure that users adopt the required behavior.
- **Verification** - it should be possible to check and verify security. This concerns both the measures introduced, and the reasons for taking these measures. It should be possible to verify that the correct decisions have been taken in certain circumstances. For example, it should also be possible to verify the authority of the decision-makers.
- **Change Management** - frequently the verification of continued compliance with the basic level of security wanes over time when assessing changes.
- **Ambition** - when an organization wants to do everything at once, mistakes are often made. When introducing Security Management, the implementation of technical measures is much less important than organizational measures. Changing an organization requires a gradual approach and will take a long time.
- **Lack of detection systems** - new systems, such as the Internet, were not designed for security and intruder detection. This is because developing a secure system takes more time than developing an insecure system, and conflicts with the business requirements of low development costs and a short time-to-market.
- **Over-reliance on stronghold/fortress techniques** - more and more frequently security threats come from unanticipated places. Consider the first ILOVEYOU and Nimda virus attacks, and the first instance of Denial of Service (DOS) attacks. While it is important to protect information assets with traditional stronghold/fortress approaches, it has become equally important to have a skirmish capability when it comes to security events. It is analogous to needing both 'slow twitch' and 'fast twitch' muscles. The organization must have the capability to rapidly put resources on the ground where the trouble is, before that trouble has a chance to spiral out of control.

16 ICT INFRASTRUCTURE MANAGEMENT

16.1 Introduction

The quality of Information and Communications Technology Infrastructure (ICT) systems is paramount to the operation of most organizations today. ICT Infrastructure Management (ICTIM) covers all aspects of infrastructure management, from identification of business requirements through the tendering process to the testing, ongoing support and maintenance of ICT components and services. It provides the basis for the other Service Management processes.

It answers the questions:
- What is ICT infrastructure?
- What is ICT infrastructure management?
- Why is ICT infrastructure management important?

These questions are considered from two contexts: the business and ICT.

16.1.1 Business context

A number of trends have resulted in a growing need for effective and proactive ICT management. These trends include:
- The increasing dependence of businesses on ICT.
- The increasing complexity of the systems.
- The flexibility required by businesses.
- The higher demands users make of their systems.
- The increasing proportion of budgets allocated to ICT systems.
- The shorter technology life cycles.

The higher demands made of the ICT infrastructure and increased complexity are leading to higher operating costs. The Total Cost of Ownership (TCO) concept introduced by the Gartner Group covers not only the initial cost of the investment, but also the management and support costs which amount to some 60 to 90% of the overall costs. These costs are often invisible and therefore unmanageable. The various cost aspects cannot be reduced in isolation, instead we need a strategy and policy, which are delivered by ICTIM.

In addition to fulfilling its traditional operational role, the ICT organization should also be able to act as a business partner. Business partners are expected to be able to predict investments and costs and to realize the plans and projects. This means that ICT aspects must be aligned with the business strategy at an early stage, otherwise it will be impossible to do this effectively. A reactive ICT organization will lead to disproportional increases in the costs of introducing and managing ICT systems. This can only be avoided by improving internal processes and better cost management.

16.1.2 ICT context - managing ICT effectively

Effective ICT Infrastructure Management will result in clear and quantifiable results. It will lead to reliable ICT services of constant quality, which meet user needs. It will assist IT management in taking decisions on the basis of better information. It will also ensure that ICT personnel are used more effectively, as they will spend less time fire fighting. User requirements will be more effectively considered when planning upgrades, and enhancements and the available resources will be used more effectively. Problems, which may arise due to an increasing capacity or availability demand, will be recognized at an early stage. The ICT organization will be better able to monitor service levels and take appropriate action. The risk of services being inadequate is reduced. The potential of new technology to reduce costs, improve service levels or innovate business services will be recognized early.

16.1.3 ICTIM and ICT Service Management

A solid, stable and effectively managed ICT infrastructure is essential to the ITIL Service Management processes. These processes aim to translate the customer requirements to effectively structured and managed ICT services (Service Delivery) and the controlled delivery of ICT services to the users (Service Support). The figure below shows how ICTIM supports the Service Management processes.

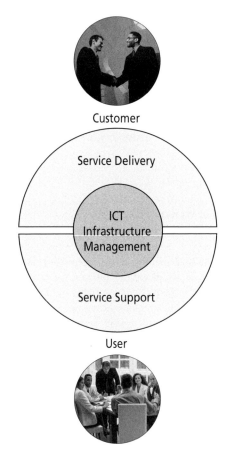

Figure 16.1 - ICTIM and its links with Service Support and Service Delivery

16.2 Objectives

The objectives of ICTIM are: to align the ICT organization with the business; reduce the overall Total Cost of Ownership of ICT and ensure the availability of a stable ICT infrastructure. This should provide the basis for managing the overall quality of ICT services in conjunction with the Service Delivery and Support processes.

16.2.1 Benefits

The benefits of ICTIM can be classified as follows:

- **Business benefits:**
  - better coordination with the business's plans and activities.
  - better business productivity through better ICT services.
  - quicker and better ICT response to new needs.
  - cost-effective delivery of ICT services.
  - lower Total Cost of Ownership.
  - planned procurement, development and deployment.
  - better management information about business processes and services.
  - better relationships with IT management.
  - better management of projects, changes and roll-outs.
- **ICT benefits:**
  - ICT services fit in better with the business needs.
  - increased effectiveness of ICT personnel when resolving incidents and problems.
  - proactive development and improvement of technology and services
  - lower risk of service failure.
  - higher capacity for implementing projects and changes.
  - better informed planning and procurement of ICT components and services.
  - better control of suppliers and their performance.

16.3 Process

16.3.1 ICT Infrastructure Management activities

ICTIM processes include identifying business needs, developing a supportive ICT strategy, policy and plans, tendering, testing, and providing, maintaining and supporting ICT resources at reasonable cost. The processes include the management and administration of the required resources, personnel, skills and training levels.

ICTIM includes four processes:

- **Design & Planning** - typically as a strategic review that is subject to revision over time which involves designing and maintaining ICT strategies and processes for the development and installation of the ICT infrastructure.
- **Deployment** - typically as individual projects which include the planning, design, build, acceptance test and roll-out of the business or ICT solutions, with the minimum adverse impact on the business processes.
- **Operations** - the routine day-to-day management and maintenance of the ICT infrastructure.
- **Technical Support** - providing a structure for the ICTIM processes supporting the other ICTIM processes.

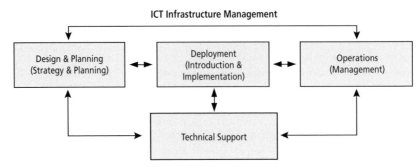

Figure 16.2 - ICTIM subprocesses

16.3.2 Relationship with other processes

ICTIM has links with all other Service Management processes. ICTIM provides the operational implementation of activities, which are planned and controlled by other processes. Some examples include:

- Introducing change (through Change and Release Management).
- Providing the infrastructure to support the implementation of applications (through Application Management).
- Providing the agreed availability, performance and support in accordance with the Service Level Agreement (SLA - for Service Level Management).
- Providing the agreed capacity (for Capacity Management).
- Securing systems in accordance with the agreed service levels (for Security Management).
- Undertaking recovery actions (for Incident and Continuity Management).
- Providing known errors at implementation(for Problem Management).

ICTIM also provides these processes with information about its own activities and performance, along with information about the characteristics and performance of the systems.

16.4 Activities

16.4.1 Design and Planning

The design and planning processes in an ICT organization result in the definition and maintenance of the strategy and policy for the development and installation of the ICT infrastructure. These processes cover all aspects of ICT, including roles and responsibilities, and also provide coordination with the Service Management processes. In this way these processes align the diverse requirements and preferences related to the ICT infrastructure, including:

- Balancing the business requirements with the costs of ICT services.
- Striking a balance between the risks and costs of innovation and the resulting competitive advantage.
- Interfacing with the infrastructure of partner organizations.
- Complying with relevant standards.
- Coordination between ICT planners and business planners.
- Strategic control of all projects, in conjunction with Service Management.

Many strategies and projects fail due to a lack of planning and a failure to monitor the implementation of the associated plans. The ICTIM processes should ensure that all those concerned are adequately informed of the strategy, policy and plans. To provide effective coordination with the business operations of the organization it is advisable to set up an ICT steering group, which includes both business and ICT managers, and which meets regularly to discuss the feasibility and progress of the strategic and project plans.

A good management system uses people, processes and resources effectively and efficiently. Effective control requires that the links between theses three aspects are transparent. The decision process is largely dependent on the information and reports provided by the processes. In turn, the processes depend on the deployment of personnel and ICT tools to provide management information. The management system should be able to integrate information from a range of technical management domains.

The management process is based on a recurring cycle:
1. Reviewing the current position, including processes, policy and external factors.
2. Defining the target state, which should result in a vision, strategy, policy and objectives.
3. Designing and implementing the plans to migrate to the target state, including results and performance indicators, followed by their implementation in projects.
4. Reviewing and evaluating progress (at the level of the organization, teams and individuals) and considering external developments.

Reviewing the current position
The review of the current position covers all aspects of the ICT organization. Strengths and weaknesses are identified, possibly through a Strength, Weakness, Opportunity and Threat (SWOT) analysis. The following aspects should be considered:
■ The ICT organization and its position in the corporate structure, culture, objectives, business services and ICT activities.
■ All aspects of IT management and planning.
■ The ICT services and their quality.
■ Personnel, skills and training levels.
■ Processes, policy and procedures.
■ All documentation aspects.
■ Geographical aspects such as locations and environments.
■ External factors such as market trends and developments.

Defining the target state
The analysis of the strengths and weaknesses of the ICT organization referred to above is used to define the mission with a timeline of several years. The identified improvements are then prioritized and included in the plans. This results in an ICT vision, strategy and objectives for the future development of the infrastructure, competencies, culture and maturity of the organization. The strategy is defined in concrete terms with measurable targets, allocated budgets, Key Performance Indicators (KPI's) and Critical Success Factors (CSF's).

Designing and implementing the plans
Designing and implementing the plans is a demanding activity with all the hallmarks of a carefully implemented program or project. The elements include:
■ Creating an ICT group which can ensure the successful implementation of the strategy.
■ Creating support for the strategy outside the ICT organization.
■ Obtaining budgets and resources for a successful implementation.
■ Developing processes and procedures to support the strategy.
■ Creating a supportive working environment and culture.

- Ensuring adequate leadership and the commitment and support of the entire IT management.
- Integrating the strategy in the routine operations of all personnel.
- Phasing out processes and structures, which are incompatible with the strategy.
- Implementing best practices and improvement programs.

Reviewing and evaluating progress of the plan

Progress monitoring is a continuous activity, which may use a Balanced Score Card (BSC) or other instruments. All ICT managers are responsible for monitoring and evaluating progress by:

- Evaluating the performance of the ICT organization.
- Evaluating the performance of the teams.
- Evaluating personal performance.
- Assessing external developments.
- Obtaining external feedback and acting on it.

16.4.2 Deployment

This process creates or modifies an ICT solution, made up of one or more technical aspects, ensuring that technical and support capabilities are in place that enable the solution to become fully operational.

Deployment ensures that the ICT solutions can be incorporated into the organization in accordance with the guidelines of the planning process. To ensure that all activities can be monitored, deployment should be implemented as a project, in cooperation with Change Management personnel. The process should ensure that all stakeholders approve the plans, after which the solution is designed and then implemented.

This process is normally implemented as a single project or in a number of consecutive stages or subprojects. Each deployment is essentially a change program or change project (compare with Change Management). It starts with developing the project plans and ends with the implemented ICT solutions.

Deployment projects progress through four stages:
- **Initiation** - defining the project objectives and business case, identifying risks, selecting stakeholders to sit on the steering group.
- **Planning** - development of the plans into a project structure, division into deliverables, detailing of the deliverables, budgeting, and determining the cycle times.
- **Execution** - design, build, testing, deployment, and hand-over of the technical and organizational components.
- **Completion** - evaluation of the project and discharge of the project team.

The execution stage progresses through the following phases:
- Design phase.
- Build phase.
- Acceptance test phase.
- Roll-out phase.
- Hand-over.

Design phase

In the design stage we have to consider existing common infrastructure services, such as network services, naming services, directory services, communication services, database services, middleware, Application Program Interfaces (APIs), etc. The intention is that further development is compatible with the de facto standards typically based upon key suppliers' products. This requires information about the design of the ICT infrastructure, which means that an adequate Configuration Management Database (CMDB) is needed

Developing the functional design needs input from the users and business plans. The acceptance criteria derived from this input are expressed in general terms and will have to be translated to clear ICT requirements. The resulting functional specification is approved by the project's steering group.

The next step is to consider the organizational aspects of the ICT solution. Both the operational management and the incorporation of Service Management processes have to be defined. For example, it will have to be considered how Incident Management will support the ICT solution, and how Availability Management will measure and monitor its availability. Additionally, responsibilities will have to be allocated and operating procedures will have to be written.

Finally, we can start with the technical design of the ICT solution. This addresses issues, which are specific to various platforms, such as configurations and component sizes. The technical design shows how the ICT solution will eventually be incorporated into the existing infrastructure.

The design phase should determine the working environments needed for each of the phases of the deployment project.

Build phase

During the build phase it is advisable to have a development environment, which is isolated from the testing, acceptance and production environments, to prevent any premature impact on operational systems. If several disciplines are working on the ICT solution during the build phase then it is advisable to structure their activities such that their development and testing activities are isolated. However, in some cases the new ICT solution will have to use the existing production environment even as it is being development. In that case, the best solution to facilitate this with the smallest possible impact will have to be selected. Change Management will play a critical part in this, as will an up-to-date CMDB.

During the build phase the documentation for the systems is written to prepare for their handover. Apart from the technical impact on the existing systems, the impact of the new systems on the ICT infrastructure capacity will also have to be considered.

The organizational aspects of the ICT solutions were already considered during the design phase. That will have resulted in a list of personnel and functions affected by the solution. The training required will then be considered during the build phase. Training will be required at several levels: specialists will require in-depth knowledge, while users only need to know how to use a particular function.

Acceptance test phase

Testing should have been conducted during the build phase. The acceptance test is carried out on the basis of a test plan approved by the steering group. The organization provides a testing team with representatives of all disciplines, including the users. A test environment with data and ICT facilities similar to the production environment will have to be provided. Preferably, this environment should be built by the testing team rather than the project team to test the build process. The information required for setting up the test environment should have been formally recorded in the CMDB and the software components taken from the DSL (Definitive Software Library). The tests follow the acceptance test scripts, which the testers also use as a guideline for documenting their comments.

The following tests may be carried out:
- **Functional tests** - to test user requirements and that the components in the technology solution work together with the common infrastructure services.
- **Performance and volume tests.**
- **Documentation checks** - to ensure all user, operational and support documentation meets predefined acceptance criteria.

The resulting test reports are used to fix any shortcomings. They also provide input for Problem Management (e.g. for known errors). Further to these reports the steering group will eventually release the environment for deployment.

Roll-out phase
The roll-out planning should start during the initiation stage of the project. The plans are written by the project team in consultation with business and IT management, change management, suppliers and other external parties.

Roll-out includes the following activities:
- **Developing the roll-out strategy** - big bang or staged transition.
- **Writing the roll-out plan** - handling release plan, migration plan, risks, back out plan.
- **Testing the roll-out** - including testing the migration and back-out plan.
- **Implementing the roll-out** - through to positive vetting that the solution meets the roll-out acceptance criteria.
- **After care period** - whilst the project team is still around to provide assistance to those involved in the management of the new solution.

Hand-over
This is the last phase during which the hand-over the documentation and operating instructions are finalized and handed over to the technical disciplines. Following the hand-over the project is evaluated, signed off and closed out. A postproject evaluation should take place with lessons learned feed into the Continuous Service Improvement Program.

16.4.3 Operations
The operational process ensures a stable and safe basis for the ICT services and compliance with the agreed service levels. The process is focused on technology, and aims to maintain the status quo by providing the best possible monitoring and management of the infrastructure services. Operations is sometimes referred to as the back-office of the ICT organization. As the operations are often carried out 24x7 and the services have to be available at all times, it is essential that there are effective operational procedures and trained, disciplined personnel. Operations is concerned with the business-related performance rather than individual technical performance. The performance of an information service should also be measured at the user's desktop, not just in the computer center.

The foundations of operations are based on the traditional monitor and control loop principle. Because the infrastructure is complex the control loop can be applied effectively to individual infrastructure services and systems. These are identified using the OSI (Open Systems Interconnection model) terms 'Managed Objects' (MO) and 'Managed Domains' (MD). Managed Objects are elements of the infrastructure which can be controlled and monitored and operates in a number of states. Managed Domains are sets of MOs to which a common Systems Management policy and practice applies.

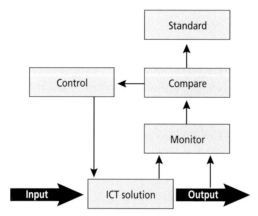

Figure 16.3 - Monitor and Control loop

Managed Objects should not be confused with Configuration Items (CIs). A CI is a static entity, which is described by details, status, management and verification. An MO is a dynamic entity, which is described by its attributes, the operations which can be performed with it, and the messages it can send.

The operational processes within the ICT organization concern not only the Managed Objects but also the interaction between them and their contribution to the delivery of ICT services. Generating and assessing events (messages from monitoring systems) is an important aspect of operations. Events are identified by Operations 24x7. They decide if they should be logged and processed as incidents and escalate them for attention where necessary.

Operations includes the following management processes:
■ Management of infrastructure events.
■ Operational control of services, components and configurations.
■ Monitoring the workload, job scheduling, resilience testing.
■ Management of the storage capacity, back-ups and service recovery.
■ Security management.
■ Management of the operational support processes.
■ Proactive operational management.

These are outlined over the following sections.

Management of infrastructure events
This is the main process in Operations, with all other operational processes arranged around it. The activities include:
■ **Event monitoring** - monitoring trends and abnormal situations affecting the infrastructure MOs.

- **Event detection** - observing alarms from MOs.
- **Event logging** - collecting and storing information about MO status transitions.
- **Event assessment and filtering** - analysis, possibly followed by choosing a resolution option.
- **Event handling** - identifying correlations between events, analysis and creating incidents.
- **Event resolution** - rectifying the abnormality and restoring services.
- **Event closure** - clearing events and closing incidents.
- **Event life cycle management** - creating and improving the resolution process.
- **Event classification** - classifying and collating events consistent with incident and problem handling procedures.
- **Event reporting** - logging, reporting and analyzing events.

Operational control of services, components and configurations
This process includes all activities related to component management, such as replacing, fixing and upgrading components. A number of these activities should use the Change Management processes, in particular as standard changes with approved work procedures and instructions, to ensure they are performed in a controlled manner and the results are visible through the CMDB.

The main activities are:
- **Installation** - including defining MO acceptance criteria.
- **De-installation** - e.g. phasing out components.
- **Distribution** - of MOs, e.g. through uploading and downloading.
- **Operational management** - including MO initialization and configuration.
- **Development and management of management tools** - including integration with ICT Service Management tools.
- **Configuration and reconfiguration** - resetting and modifying MOs.
- **Housekeeping and preventive maintenance** - all routine processes for ensuring a resilient infrastructure, including:
  - deleting log files.
  - deleting temporary files.
  - cleaning operational equipment and environments.
  - maintaining and supporting systems and tools.
  - user, file, authorization and password management.
  - preventive maintenance.
  - shift handover and reporting.
  - operational reporting.
- **Inventory and asset management** - including identification, registration and verification of operational MOs and collecting information about changes to MO configurations. This primarily concerns collecting information about the present infrastructure (e.g. using discovery tools), which can be used to verify and update the CMDB.

Workload monitoring, job scheduling and resilience testing
This process includes creating and maintaining all operational plans related to infrastructure workloads:
- Workload planning, job scheduling, controlling progress and resolving conflicts and failures.
- Output and print schedule management.
- Distribution and management of data and media, including file transmissions, backup media and physical document.
- Resilience and fail-over arrangement testing, including stand-by, alternate site operation, business continuity and disaster recovery plans.

Storage, back-ups and service recovery management

This process covers all aspects of information storage and data restores, such as:

- Storage management and storage allocation.
- System back-ups and restores.
- Information management (what is stored, on what media and where).
- Database management and administration.

Managing security

As part of Security Management this activity ensures compliance with the security policy, including:

- **Security monitoring** - including detecting and logging security exceptions and events.
- **Security control** - including physical access control to ICT infrastructure and logical security arrangements such as user authentication to control access to the ICT infrastructure.

Management of operational support processes

The management of the processes supporting operations, such as:

- **Document management** - developing and managing an Operational Document Library (ODL).
- **Logging and collecting information** on the use of operational services and infrastructure - for performance monitoring, charging, tuning and identifying trends in business transactions.
- **Information analysis** - analyzing trends in operational services and infrastructure use.
- **Developing scripts** - for automating operational control and monitoring procedures.

Proactive operational management

Documenting and managing the operational processes for process implementation and process improvement, including:

- Assessing the operational process: effectiveness, efficiency and compliance with policy.
- Internal or external audits of Operations against best practice guidelines.
- Initiating infrastructure improvement actions.
- Initiating process improvement actions.
- Operational optimization (tuning) of systems.

16.4.4 Technical Support

Technical Support consists of the process and functions that develop expertise about the current and future ICT infrastructure. It is the center of specialist expertise about all operational properties of the infrastructure, systems, management tools and configurations and undertakes research and development of new technologies.

At the other end, Technical Support is the third-line support provider and therefore an important partner of Incident Management and Problem Management. Although this is normally primarily a reactive task, Technical Support is also responsible for proactive Problem Management and undertaking impact analyses for Change Management. Technical Support deals with escalations from the Service Support processes and where necessary, communicates with external service providers and suppliers.

Technical Support also makes calculations and undertakes analysis for Capacity Management and Availability Management and plans and implements improvements, in consultation with Change Management.

Technical Support plays an important role within the Planning, Deployment and Operations processes of ICTIM. For example, Technical Support contributes to feasibility studies and developing new ICT architectures to support the design and planning process.

Processes and activities
The Technical Support processes can be divided into three functional areas:
- **Research and evaluation:**
  - analyzing the output of ICT management tools to verify if expectations are met.
  - writing reports about the performance of the infrastructure to support Capacity Management.
  - testing and evaluating infrastructure designs before deployment.
  - technical discussions with suppliers and external consultants to find the combination of features and costs.
- **Projects:**
  - designing and maintaining test environments
  - supporting infrastructure deployment
  - undertaking feasibility studies
  - secondment to project teams to provide a technical solutions
- **Business as Usual (BaU):**
  - specialist support for incidents and problems.
  - creating and maintaining the knowledge database.
  - verifying CI's to check the CMDB.
  - in depth analysis to support Availability Management.
  - maintaining and improving technical expertise and skills of support staff.
  - training other personnel on new infrastructure components.

Other activities
In addition to the processes discussed above, Technical Support includes other routine activities, such as:
- New technology research and development.
- Third-line technical support.
- Budget planning and management.
- Systems and services procurement.
- Guiding suppliers.
- Designing, planning and defining systems requirements for tenders.
- Service improvement deployment.
- Setting up Release Management processes and systems.
- Technical planning and management of administration, support, operations and tools.
- Developing operational and support documentation and procedures.

16.5 Process control

16.5.1 Critical success factors and performance indicators
A successful ICTIM structure also depends on the extent to which other Service Management processes have been structured. As the other processes are incorporated more effectively into the organization there will be fewer service interruptions which will provide the opportunity to effectively develop the last element of many actions: their operation.

Operations is often considered as the back-office of the ICT organization and has a low status. This does not provide a suitable basis for good links between Operations and the management processes. Recognizing the value of Operations will help give it a suitable place in the ICT business. In the end, ICTIM is essentially the coal face, the place where the provision of information services actually happens.

The success of ICTIM is indicated by the extent to which:
- Infrastructure activities are planned effectively.
- The infrastructure is monitored.
- Deployments are covered by roll-out plans.
- The work load is monitored.
- Jobs are scheduled.
- The storage capacity is managed.
- Back-ups are made effectively.
- Events are detected, recorded, actioned and archived.
- Security is monitored, including detecting and logging exceptions and events.
- Security is controlled, including physical access control and logical security such as user authentication.
- Operations are audited.
- Improvement actions are initiated and completed.
- Effective information is made available to Capacity Management and Availability Management.

16.5.2 Management reports
Internal management reports
ICTIM reports to the management about internal process performance, in terms of the number of jobs, intercepted security incidents, monitored systems, etc. together with information about the relevant resources. This provides information about the quality, cost and efficiency of the process. The process also reports on the qualitative and quantitative performance and volumes produced, compared with the agreed service levels.

External reports
ICTIM is the key discipline involved in planning the use of ICT with the business and reports through the ICT Steering Committee on the progress of ICTIM strategy. It relies upon Service Level Management to report on the operational performance of ICT services and on the status of day to day matters covered by service levels. Much of this information will reach Service Level Management through the information already being provided to Availability and Capacity Management.

16.5.3 Functions and roles
To ensure that the ICT organization interfaces effectively with the business processes it is advisable to develop ICTIM roles in relation to process, rather than create technology silo roles and allow them to operate as isolated technical islands. ICTIM suggests setting up an ICT Steering group (ISG) to allow business managers and ICT managers to coordinate their strategy and plans, and to steer projects.

16.6 Costs and possible problems

16.6.1 Costs

ICTIM costs include:

- Greater management time and attention for resource planning.
- More personnel, training and facilities.
- More overhead in processes, procedures and documentation.
- Procurement of additional tools, hardware and software.
- Communications strategies and publications.
- Implementing culture changes.

16.6.2 Possible problems

We can identify the following obstacles:

- Lack of management commitment.
- Inadequate resources, budgets and time.
- Resistance against working to plans.
- Lack of business strategies and policies.
- Lack of awareness of the impact on business activities.
- Great diversity of technology and applications.
- Resistance against culture change.
- Poor planning leading to ad hoc procurement.
- Poor communications and cooperation between ICT and business activities.
- Inadequate management of training and staff replacement.
- Limitations due to legacy systems and outdated technology.
- Unrealistic expectations on the side of the customer (business).
- Inadequate information, metrics and monitoring.
- Overloading personnel.
- Poor management of contracts with suppliers.
- Poor cost awareness within the company.

▐7▌ APPLICATION MANAGEMENT

17.1 Introduction

The market conditions that businesses operate in today requires them and their IT organizations to respond quickly to the challenges and implement changes.

IT organizations should not only support the required flexibility, they should enable it. This presents a major challenge to the IT organizations, which are responsible for the applications that are necessary to support the business moving forward. As applications make it possible for businesses to undertake large parts of the business processes, businesses are forced to manage their applications as corporate assets through Application Management.

17.1.1 Key concepts

Application Management is a term, which can easily lead to confusion. We have to be careful to distinguish between Application Management, application development and Service Management.
- **Application Management** is the combination of processes and activities, which describe the management of applications throughout their life cycle including operation and maintenance. This life cycle includes both application development and Service Management processes (noted below).
- **Application development** includes the planning, requirements definition, design and building or procurement of an application to be used by one or more departments in an organization to meet a particular information need. application development does not cover the deployment, operation, routine management or maintenance of applications.
- **Service Management** covers the deployment, operations, support and optimization of applications. The main objective of Service Management is to ensure that the developed and implemented applications provide the agreed service levels.

Consequently, Application Management covers all aspects of this discipline, including application development and Service Management (see figure 17.1). This comprehensive approach aims to reduce the divide between application development and Service Management. In the ITIL approach, Application Management is viewed from the perspective of a service manager who is responsible for the uninterrupted provision of IT services.

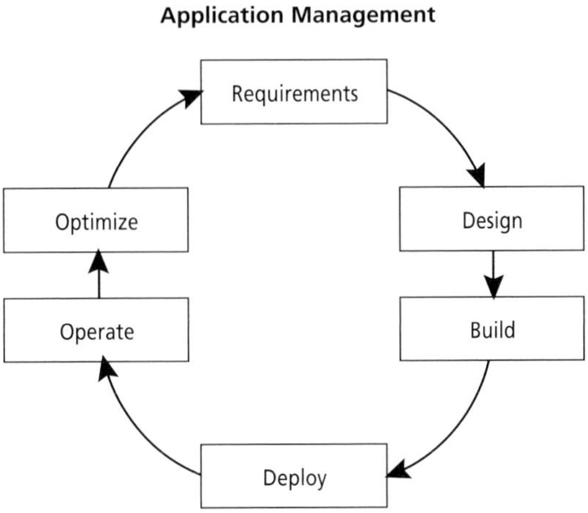

Figure 17.1 - Links between Application Management, application development and Service Management

17.2 Objectives

As discussed above, organizations should manage their applications as corporate assets. Thus, the objectives of Application Management can be described as:

Application Management is the management of applications as corporate assets to ensure that the information systems of the organization can respond flexibly to changes in the market.

These objectives can be subdivided:
■ Selecting the appropriate strategic fit between business processes and the supporting applications.
■ Coordinating the Application Management processes further to deliver the selected fit.
■ Ensuring that the IT organization can manage the applications throughout their life cycle.

17.2.1 Benefits

Application Management has a number of clear benefits:
■ The control of the IT processes in the Application Management Life Cycle in-line with the role of IT in the organization will ensure that the right investments are made by the business in its applications.
■ The use of the Strategic Alignment Objectives Model will assist the Service Manager in controlling the IT processes in the Application Management Life Cycle and in convincing the business of the added value of IT.
■ Controlling applications as corporate assets will shift the focus of the business from short-term projects to the provision of IT services.
■ The use of Key Business Drivers will facilitate the definition of test strategies.
■ Linking Key Business Drivers to process objectives and team objectives will help to develop a more customer-focused culture within the IT services organization.

17.3 The process

The Application Management process involves two sets of process:
■ One for planning and managing the portfolio and business value of applications in support of business needs along with the capabilities, frameworks and tools for effective application management.
■ The second for the development and management of each application throughout the Application Management Life Cycle.

The first of those processes 'Managing Business Value' is examined in this section and the Application Management Life Cycle is examined in the next section on 'Activities'.

The Application Management Life Cycle knows the following phases (see figure 17.1):
■ Requirements.
■ Design.
■ Build.
■ Deploy.
■ Operate.
■ Optimize.

17.3.1 Managing the Business Value

It is not technology that provides value to a business but how the technology is deployed to meet business requirements. Application support the majority of business requirements putting Application Management at the heart of planning and delivering business benefits from IT.

Aligning Business and IT

Aligning Business requirements with IT is primarily performed in the Application Management processes. There must be Business and IT management planning and review processes in place where the business owners and IT management identify the business functions (business units and departments) across the enterprise, and understand their changing business processes and the changing business objectives. This management planning process is key to aligning IT with the Business and leads to planning the development and deployment of IT applications and the supporting IT infrastructure.

The planning process should map existing and required IT services and applications against the business functions using an architectural approach.

High Level Business and IT Architecture

Business and IT architectures need to be developed to steer the development of IT to support the business functions. The scope of the architectures is represented by the Strategic Alignment Objectives Model (SAOM).

The Strategic Alignment Objectives Model is based on the principle that business processes are supported by applications, which form the major part of IT systems and IT services as shown on the right-hand side of the model below. Further to this, a relationship can be identified between the Key Business Drivers and the SLA's and OLA's as shown on the left-hand side. The nature of the relationships of the architectural components in the Strategic Alignment Objectives Model is illustrated by the entity-relationship diagram in Figure 17.2.

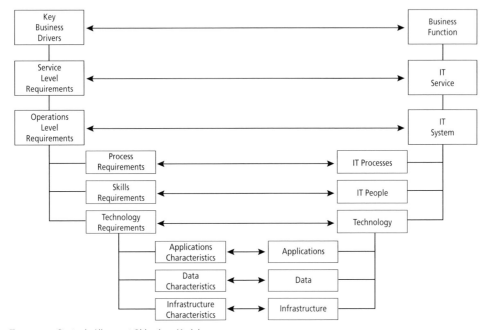

Figure 17.2 - Strategic Alignment Objectives Model

The Strategic Alignment Objectives Model provides an excellent instrument to visualize the relationships between the key components of Business functions and IT services and capabilities against the Business Drivers and down to the application requirements.

Key Business Drivers and SMART Objectives
The premise underlying Application Management Life Cycle control is related to the Key Business Drivers, which are defined as follows:

Key Business Drivers are attributes of a business process which determine the behavior and implementation of that business process, to ensure that the strategic objectives of the organization are met.

It is an ITIL best practice to define the Key Business Drivers. They control the realization of the vision and mission of the business. Their uniform use provides a common understanding of the issues, which the whole business should concentrate on. Whatever the Key Business Driver definitions used by a company, they will have some common characteristics as shown in Table 17.1.

S	Specific
M	Measurable
A	Agreed to
R	Realistic
T	Time specific

Table 17.1 - SMART business drivers

The SMART attributes above should not be limited to the Key Business Drivers but extend to the objectives, targets and requirements derived from the drivers. Although the SMART concept is hardly an innovation in setting objectives and targets (including Key Business Drivers), it is still not always consistently used. Many projects are not completed successfully as the project was based on ambiguous or ill-defined objectives.

The challenge is to link the Key Business Drivers with the Application Management Life Cycle so that it will control results of the cycle.

Portfolio Management and the Application Portfolio
Most businesses have a large number of applications supporting the business functions and in their business processes. Portfolio Management is part of the Application Management planning process which helps businesses to manage large, complex sets of applications, understanding the way they work together in sharing data and in supporting end-to-end business processes and their use of the IT infrastructure.

The Application Portfolio may be considered as an information system which stores the major application attributes and provides an architectural view of the relationships between applications. The Application Portfolio makes it possible to provide information about particular applications or suites of applications and understand the way the applications relate to one another. It enables planning of business-driven change easier and enables investment decisions to be made more quickly.

Readiness Assessment and Delivery Strategy
Many IT organizations start setting up complex applications without the ability to build and manage such applications. The planning process must make sure that creating and managing

applications is supported by a competent organization, which is able to maintain the required personnel, processes and technology.

Setting up complex applications, whether bespoke or packaged, requires planning a well-developed coordination system to enable the organization to control the cooperation between development teams and compliance with guidelines for application development and management. The introduction of new technology requires that the IT organization is flexible enough to absorb new information and embed unfamiliar technology in the organization's methods and processes. Capability assessments and maturity models, such as CMM are often used to determine the readiness of an IT organization to develop or support complex applications.

The use of third parties in the acquisition and/or support of applications provides alternative applications delivery strategies and needs consideration in the planning of the business application and application infrastructure product portfolio.

Integrating the Application Management Life Cycle
There is often a major divide between Application Developmen and application management. Under the Application Management Life Cycle approach, application development and Service Management are closely intertwined and their activities have to be coordinated.

ITIL's Application Management is primarily based on the Service Management perspective. The Service Management aspects that have a major impact on the delivery of IT services are addressed at an early phase in the Application Management Life Cycle. One of the most important aspects is the need to provide a better integration of the underlying support structures and tools throughout all life cycle phases. The information required to provide a better fit between the creation and the delivery of services includes:
■ Application components and their interdependencies
■ Planning application releases
■ Specifying alerts and events which indicate the status and performance of an application
■ Specifying the details required for monitoring the primary transactions of an application
■ Service levels
■ Operational requirements
■ Support requirements

To supplement the information related to application management it is often necessary to define how an application is related to other applications and to the application infrastructure through the Application Portfolio, application architecture and application frameworks. This will have the following benefits:
■ Mutual understanding of the dependencies between application development, infrastructure development and Service Management, to ensure that well-considered decisions are taken early in the Application Management Life Cycle.
■ Integrated application planning, from the first design outline through to deployment.
■ Capacity and performance data can be incorporated early into the life cycle so that the infrastructure can be prepared for the introduction of the application.
■ The management of the development, test and production environments is controlled, which can result in a significant reduction in the costs of defining, building, changing and phasing-out the environments.
■ Reference architectures and frameworks can be developed so that both the requirements for creating services (e.g. time-to-market) and service delivery requirements (e.g. availability) are considered.

- Developers and service managers speak a common language when defining performance indicators for phase transitions.
- Developers can consider the service managers' requirements when building applications so that they can be managed by the time they are handed over to Operations.

Traversing the Application Management Life Cycle

Given the iterative nature of application management, an application can be in several phases of different iterations of the Application Management Life Cycle at any one time. That requires disciplined version, configuration and release management. These issues are basically covered by the ITIL Service Support book. Depending on the selected development method, an application may progress more quickly through some phases than others. Similarly, an application may complete the full Application Management Life Cycle several times before deployment. However, all applications will progress through all phases of the Application Management Life Cycle several times during their life.

Organizations have to measure the effectiveness and efficiency of the progress of an application through the life cycle. Changes in processes and the flow of information between phases of the Application Management Life Cycle will affect the quality of the application. An appreciation of the primary characteristics of each phase, and how decisions in one phase affect activities in other phases are essential to a comprehensive management approach during the Application Management Life Cycle. This appreciation, and corresponding actions, largely determine the choice of methods and tools.

One also needs to consider the longevity of the Application. The effectiveness and efficiency of maintenance is affected by the quality of documentation. In turn this is influenced by the techniques, methods and tools used for analysis, design and development. Some of these can be obsolete long before the organization wishes to retire or replace the application, resulting in maintenance issues.

Alternative life cycle models

The life cycle presented here suggests an iterative approach to the Application Management Life Cycle used in development methods such as Rapid Application Development (RAD) and Rational Unified Process (RUP). There are also traditional application development methods known as the Waterfall method, which do not encourage the use iterations and incremental steps.

The primary reason for using the iterative approach is to minimize the risks associated with traditional development methods. This approach, using incremental steps, means that application requirements are delivered in small steps. The advantage is that the risk of uncertainty during the development of the application is easier to manage, and that the time-to-market of certain requirements will be reduced.

17.3.2 Relationship with other processes

Service Management processes play a significant role in every phase of the Application Management Life Cycle, which is described here using checklists.

Requirements phase

All Service Management processes should contribute in the requirements phase as this will affect the development and management of the application in later phases.

PROCESSES	ISSUES
Configuration Management	In what environment will the application operate?
Change Management	Specifying change cases.
Release Management	What elements of the application form part of the release and how is it released?
	What are the relationships between releases of different applications?
Security Management	What security management requirements will have to be complied with?
Incident Management	How do the IT and business organization deal with service interruptions?
	How are application faults dealt with?
Problem Management	How can the root causes of problems be analyzed?
Capacity Management	What is the capacity of the environment in which the application will run?
	What is the required capacity for the solution the application forms part of?
Availability Management	What are the availability requirements of the application?
Continuity Management	How long can the business operate without the IT service?
Service Level Management	What service levels are required?
Financial Management	What are the financial costs and benefits of the application?
	Who will pay for the application during the Application Management Life Cycle?

Table 17.2 - Service Management processes in the requirements phase

Design phase

During the design phase, every ITIL process should check to what extent the non-functional requirements associated with the Service Management processes are included in the design.

PROCESSES	ISSUES
Configuration Management	Did the designers observe the Configuration Management guidelines?
	To what extent does the design comply with the Configuration Management standards?
	Does the design support version management?
Change Management	Can the design accommodate changes?
	Did the designers consider the Change Management process in the organization?
Release Management	Did the designers consider the standards and tools used for releasing applications?
	To what extent will the design ensure that the application can be rapidly and efficiently introduced into the production environment?
Security Management	To what extent does the design address security and integrity?
Incident Management	Does the design ensure that the application automatically generates incidents in the event of a service interruption?
	Is the incident logging method compatible with the Incident Management tool?
	Does the design provide for automatic logging and incident detection?
Problem Management	To what extent does the application support root cause analysis?
Capacity Management	Did the designers consider the capacity planning methods used in the organization?
	How can the application performance be measured?
	Are models used to ensure that the application meets the capacity requirements?
Availability Management	Does the design accommodate the availability requirements?
	To what extent is the application compatible with current procedures?

PROCESSES	ISSUES
Continuity Management	To what extent are the continuity requirements incorporated in the design?
Service Level Management	Does the application support business recovery processes following a disaster?
	To what extent are the service levels incorporated in the design?
Financial Management	Does the design incorporate the financial specifications?

Table 17.3 - Service Management processes during the design phase

Build phase

During the build phase the various Service Management processes should demonstrably contribute to the verification of the implementation of non-functional requirements originating with Service Management. The management check list below gives some examples.

PROCESSES	ISSUES
Configuration Management	Was the application built to the Configuration Management standards?
	Does the application only use programs and tools, which have been accepted and included in the product portfolio?
Change Management	Was the normal Change Management process observed?
Release Management	Does the application support version management and Release Management?
	Was it verified if the application can easily be deployed in the production environment?
Security Management	Were the security best practices and guidelines observed?
Incident Management	Was it verified if the application can create an incident record in the Incident Management tool in the event of a service interruption?
	Was the Incident Management process tested with this Application?
Problem Management	Was it verified if the application supports root cause analysis?
Capacity Management	Was it verified if the demand and performance requirements will be fulfilled?
	Does the application provide information to the Capacity Management process? Was this tested?
	Were the stress and load tests carried out?
Availability Management	Are the availability requirements incorporated into the application? Was this tested?
	What arrangements are made to ensure that the application supports the back-up and recovery procedures of the business?
	How is the function availability affected when the application is stressed?
Continuity Management	Does the application comply with the continuity requirements of the business process? Was this verified?
Service Level Management	Was it verified if the SLA's are complied with?
Financial Management	Does the application provide the required financial information? Was this verified?

Table 17.4 - Service Management processes in the build phase

Deploy phase

The deploy phase is the last step in the life cycle before supporting the business process in the operate phase. A careful deployment involving all Service Management processes is essential to the uninterrupted provision of services.

PROCESSES	ISSUES
Configuration Management	Is the CMDB updated in every phase of the roll-out?
	Does the deployment team use an up-to-date version of the CMDB to complete the deployment?
Change Management	Is the routine Change Management process followed?
Release Management	Is the application released such that the risks are minimized?
	Does the application release include a roll-back plan?
Security Management	Are the security guidelines observed during deployment?
Incident Management	Is the Incident Management system used during deployment to record issues and incidents?
	Does the deployment team have access to Incident Management?
Problem Management	Does the deployment team know who the Problem Manager is for the deployment?
Capacity Management	Is Capacity Management involved in the deployment to check the resource use during deployment?
Availability Management	Does Availability Management check if the deployment has an adverse effect on the availability of the IT infrastructure?
	How are back-up and recovery procedures carried out during the deployment?
Continuity Management	Should the continuity plan be updated?
Service Level Management	Is Service Level Management aware of the deployment?
	Is the SLA available?
	Are current SLA's adversely affected by the deployment?
Financial Management	Is the cost of deployment included in the TCO?

Table 17.5 - Service Management processes during the deploy phase

Operate phase

During the operate phase it is not just the operators who keep the application running. It is clearly a phase in the Application Management Life Cycle in which all Service Management processes have to cooperate to provide the services in accordance with the defined requirements.

PROCESSES	ISSUES
Configuration Management	Can the operators verify if the production application is the right version and that it is correctly configured?
	Are operator instructions under version management?
Change Management	Are the operational managers involved in the deployment and do they have to approve the Change Management process?
	Are the operational managers involved in the CAB?
Release Management	Does Release Management ensure that the information required for the deployment is available to the operational managers?
	Do operational managers have access to release information before the deployment?
Security Management	Are regular security checks carried out during deployment?
Incident Management	Do the operational managers have access to the Incident Management system and can they add information to the system?
	Are operational managers aware of their responsibilities within the Incident Management process?
	Do operational managers receive feedback about their contribution to the Incident Management process?

PROCESSES	ISSUES
Problem Management	Do the operational managers assist with identifying the root causes of identified problems?
	Are there regular meetings between the Problem Manager and the operational managers?
	Do the operational managers receive regular Problem Management reports?
Capacity Management	Is application performance and demand data collected during operations?
	Is this information provided to Capacity Management?
Availability Management	How is the availability of the application measured and how is this information provided to Availability Management?
Continuity Management	Are regular recovery tests undertaken?
Service Level Management	Do the operational managers understand what they have to do to comply with the SLA?
	Do the operational managers receive regular SLA reports?
Financial Management	Do operational managers provide correct financial information such as additional activities needed for the application?

Table 17.6 - Service Management processes during the operate phase

Optimize phase

During the optimize phase all Service Management processes can contribute to the application review.

PROCESSES	ISSUES
Configuration Management	Is the CMDB used to support the review?
	Does Configuration Management advise the review team?
Change Management	Is the Change Management process used when improvements have been identified?
Release Management	Is Release Management involved in the review?
Incident Management	Does the optimization team have access to the Incident Management database so that service interruptions can be included in the review?
Problem Management	Are the known errors and identified problems known to the optimization team?
Capacity Management	Is information about Capacity Management available to the optimization team?
Availability Management	Is information about Availability Management available to the optimization team?
Continuity Management	Are there improvement to the business recovery process related to the application?
Service Level Management	Are the SLA reports available to the optimization team?
Financial Management	Is financial information available for the review?

Table 17.7 - Service Management processes in the optimize phase

17.4 Activities

The Application Management Life Cycle emphasizes the links between application development and Service Management and the activities in each phase of the life cycle to maintain these aspects. The activities are usually performed as phases under the control of a project or a release.

17.4.1 Requirements

In this phase the requirements of a new or modified application are defined on the basis of the needs of the business. The application requirements are closely related to the Key Business Drivers of the business process to be supported by the application. The following requirement types can be distinguished:

- **Functional requirements** - which describe the behavior of an application and can be expressed in terms of services, activities, tasks or functions. Functional requirements can be defined using context diagrams or use cases, such as those used in the Unified Modeling Language (UML). Currently, the use cases are generally used to describe the functional aspects of an SLA, and as a basis for functional acceptance tests.
- **Non-functional requirements** - which determine the limitations of the applications in terms of volumes, capacity, performance, manageability, operability, support and security. These requirements primarily relate to service management. The non-functional requirements should be used to define the quality attributes of an application, which then provides the basis for the production acceptance tests.
- **Usability requirements** - which ensure that the application meets the users' expectations regarding ease of use. Like the non-functional requirements, the user requirements can be used to define the quality attributes of an application.

It is important that the various requirements are tested. This is often difficult as there may not be a specific method to test abstract requirements. There may be a considerable number of requirements, and some may conflict with each other. The feasibility of the requirements can be determined through prototyping, metaplan sessions, peer reviews and presentations.

17.4.2 Design

In the design phase, the requirements provided by the business and the IT organization are translated into application characteristics. The design phase delivers not just one, but several designs. Normally the following designs are used:

- The **functional design** of the application.
- The **operational model** of the environment in which the application runs, such as the infrastructure and the systems management environment.
- The **architectural guidelines** used by an organization for application design and the operational models.

During the design phase the project manager will have to take a number of decisions to balance the available resources, the project plan and the functionality to be provided. This balance is not always obtained in projects, as a result of which the non-functional requirements are often abandoned first to remain within the budget and to be able to deliver the functionality on time. This triangle of resources can be defined with some accuracy once a number of working products has been delivered:

- The Key Business Drivers.
- The project objectives and scope.
- The functional requirements.
- The non-functional requirements.
- The application design.
- The project plan.

17.4.3 Build

In the building phase the application and operational model are prepared for deployment. Application components are coded or purchased, integrated and tested. To ensure that the management of future iterations of the Application Management Life Cycle is considered when an application is built, the development team should aim to meet both the functional and non-functional requirements.

Consistent programming guidelines

The primary reason for applying consistent programming guidelines is that it will be easier for everyone to read, understand and manage the application. Every organization should at least have a generic set of guidelines, which facilitates application maintenance and provides the developers with enough flexibility to implement the logic and functionality of the application. These programming guidelines not only make the applications easier to maintain, but also provide better opportunities for using tools to manage the applications. However, organizations should ensure that the guidelines do not become too complex or extensive. In that case the creativity of the developer would be focused on the application of the guidelines rather than meeting the functional and non-functional requirements.

Application-independent guidelines

A number of application-independent guidelines may be defined to assist the maintenance and management of an information system and its applications.
- **Application frameworks** - architectures, which identify which module or object is used for certain function and tasks of the application. An application framework makes it possible for generic tasks (which are not directly related to the business process) to be handled by a single module or object. The advantage of these frameworks is that the cost of building the information systems is greatly reduced, while at the same time making maintenance significantly easier.
- **Templates and code generation** - many development tools use templates to build applications. Developers can use these tools to modify templates to meet the requirements of the design. Other tools not only offer templates, but can also generate large sections of code further to detailed application designs. The advantage of using these tools is that they enforce standardization.
- **Built-in tools** - there should be uniformity in controlling drivers and software for generic functions such as databases and communications protocols. Applications should also provide APIs for interfacing to system management tools. There are several guidelines for incorporating such interfaces in applications.

Application testing

Testing is not simply an activity carried out after building an application, it serves as an integrated quality management instrument throughout the full Application Management Life Cycle. The test activities in the earlier phases mostly included assessments such as peer reviews and walk-throughs. When the software is built, both assessments and actual tests can be carried out.

In all phases, testing needs to be performed on the application's functionality and its non-functional aspects (non-functional aspect testing is known as 'Operability Testing').

As applications normally progress several times through the Application Management Life Cycle they will be tested on a number of occasions. Consequently, test environment management is an important, but often neglected, element of Application Management.

17.4.4 Deploy

In the deployment phase the application and the accompanying operational model are introduced into the production environment. The operational model is incorporated into the existing production environment, and the application is installed in the new environment, using standard installation procedures.

The deployment phase involves the following activities:
- Planning the deployment.
- Organizing the deployment team.
- Approving the deployment.
- Distributing applications.
- Pilot roll-outs.

A well-planned deployment will not only reduce the service interruptions, but also significantly reduce the cost of providing the services. The following issues should be considered when planning the deployment:

QUESTIONS	ISSUES
What should be deployed?	Is it clear what the application to be deployed will do, what it will consist of, and in what environment it will be deployed?
	What are the Key Business Drivers covered by the application?
	Are there critical business requirements covered by the application?
Who are the users?	What users or user communications will be affected by the deployment?
	Will these users need special training?
Where are the users based?	Are the users based in the same building as the infrastructure which the application runs on?
	If not, how will this affect logistics?
When should the deployment be completed?	Should the application be completed at a particular date, or is the deployment date flexible?
Why is the change being deployed?	Does the change relate to an identified problem or is are new functions deployed?
	Do the users understand why the change is deployed?
What is essential to a successful deployment?	When will the deployment be successful?
	What are the criteria for a completed deployment?

Table 17.8 - Questions surrounding deployment

A number of checklists and documents should be completed and approved before the deployment is allowed to start. These include:
- Deployment management checklist.
- Deployment plan and schedule.
- Back-out document.
- Sign-off document.

Approval involves the Change Management process using one or a number of Requests for Change (RFC's) with Change Advisory Board (CAB) approving the deployment of the application.

Deployment planning and back-out involves the Release Management process. The ITIL books on Service Support and ICT Infrastructure Management discuss the deployment of changes in greater detail.

17.4.5 Operate

A Gartner study indicated that 40% of service interruptions are due to operator errors and 40% to application bugs. It is therefore important that the application should largely run unattended once in production. This means that automatic start-up and shutdown scripts, reporting and recovery facilities are needed. When the operational status of an application is recovered it is important to be aware of its operational status and what components are affected. Each application includes a number of components:

- The application itself.
- Server-specific configuration details.
- Log files.
- System files.
- User-specific configuration details.
- User details.
- Network connections.

The impact of any service interruptions is minimized through effective design of the applications and the infrastructure and through a number of preventative maintenance activities taken by the operational team. These activities should be planned and documented with tools, resources and training provided, as part of the application project.

The preventative maintenance activities in respect of managing the applications and the services they provide include:

- **Daily:**
  - check the utilization level.
  - review daily problem reports.
  - review emergency change requests.
  - run database consistency checks.
  - check database server error logs.
  - monitor network performance and errors.
  - monitor client status.
  - monitor server components and service status.
  - monitor event logs of key servers.
  - monitor system performance.
  - monitor system directories.
  - make secure back-ups of the servers.
- **Weekly:**
  - attend the CAB meeting.
  - improve database performance.
  - check system directories.
  - management reports.
  - file system management.
- **Monthly:**
  - write the monthly status report.
  - hold work reviews with individual team members.
  - review the system status and performance.
  - improve system performance.
  - secure system accounts.
  - review access to server functions.
  - undertake recovery tests.

- **Ad hoc:**
    - brainstorm with the team about improvements.
    - complete feedback survey.
    - resolve reported problems.
    - initiate process improvement actions.
    - review reported security infringements.
    - improve access control.

17.4.6 Optimize

The functional, non-functional and usability requirements of all applications which have been in production should be reviewed periodically. Such a review may be initiated by a trigger such as:
- Scheduled review in relation to an Application Portfolio review or an SLA review.
- Issues detected by Problem Management.
- Changes to the business requirements.
- Changes to the infrastructure.

The review distinguishes a number of areas, such as people, business processes and technology. Table 17.9 includes an example of a review checklist.

AREA	ISSUES
People	Does the application still meet the users' needs?
	If not, what should be improved?
	Is the application intuitive?
	Do the users make unnecessary mistakes when using the application?
Business process	Has the objective of the supported business process changed, and if so, does the application still support it?
	Will a change to the organizational structure change the functional requirements of the application?
	Has there been any change in the service levels?
Technology	Are there any technical problems as a result of which the application fails to meet the agreed SLA's?
	Have any infrastructure changes been made which require changes to the application?
	What is the application performance? Is any improvement required?
	What are the availability and manageability of the application like?
	To what extent does the application support the Service Support processes?

Table 17.9 - Sample review check list

The use of an Application Portfolio can make it much easier to deal with these questions. The following decisions can be taken further to the review:
- No change required.
- The application will be changed.
- The application will be phased-out.

17.5 Process control

Application Management provides a comprehensive framework for managing the Application Portfolio in support of needs of the business functions and controlling the entire Application Management Life Cycle for each Application.

17.5.1 Management Reports and Performance indicators

Internal management reports and indicators

Application Management reports to IT management about its performance, effectiveness and costs in terms of:

- The number of applications and application components managed.
- Time dedicated to each application, specified by type of work (development, testing, maintenance, recovery, etc.)
- Remaining hours reserved for application maintenance.
- Application availability and performance data.
- Utilization levels.
- Problem reports.
- Emergency change requests.
- Completed application recovery tests.
- Resolved and outstanding problems.
- Review of security violations.
- Status of application life cycle process improvement actions.

External reports

Depending on the structure and the position of Application Management within the business, it may report to external parties typically the customer. If Service Management is properly developed, service reports will be issued regularly to the customer and there will also be regular discussions about the services provided, including applications aspects. If discussions about the applications are not yet organized by Service Management then Application Management will discuss the applications with the customer separately. This could lead to undesirable competition between departments of an IT service provider, in which case it would be advisable to combine the two IT reporting structures.

17.5.2 Functions and roles

The roles participating in the Application Management Life Cycle are the same as those in application development and Service Management. This section describes how these roles participate in the Application Management Life Cycle. The organization can use various functions to fulfill these roles, like developer, maintainer, design authority, data modeler, tester, et cetera.

Change and Configuration Management (CCM)

The Change and Configuration Management (CCM) role is responsible for Change, Release and Configuration Management, which support an application during its life cycle from design to production. The CCM role owns the CMDB, which is used throughout the Application Management Life Cycle to store and provide information about the application. The CCM role also owns the Change Management process and therefore plays an essential part in issuing and monitoring phase transition approvals during the Application Management Life Cycle.

Support

The support role is responsible for making sure that support teams can support the application once it is in production. During the requirements phase, the support role will indicate the best way to support the application in the production environment and how the service can be restored in the shortest possible time after a service interruption. During the design phase the support role advises about incorporating these requirements in the design. This advice could include: convenient access to information about the service for Service Desk personnel, automatic logging of critical information about the applications status, and providing fail-over and recovery mechanisms. The design of sophisticated help functions is also important.

Support personnel have to provide acceptance criteria for the acceptance tests. Of course, the support role can also contribute to the user acceptance tests so that users can report testing incidents through the normal Incident Management procedures. This ensures that Support personnel become familiar with the application before it enters production.

During the deployment, support personnel will assist the deployment team in dealing with incidents reported further to the implemented change. During the operations phase the support role operates as second line support and works with the application support teams to resolve service interruptions in the shortest possible time. The support role provides the optimization team with historical data about past incidents and current problems.

Operations
The Operations role is responsible for routine activities related to keeping the applications, which have reached the production environment running. Operations assists with defining the operational requirements to ensure that the application will run stably in production, with a minimum of maintenance. During the design phase, Operations ensures that the operational requirements have indeed been incorporated in the design.

During testing and deployment the role of Operations is similar to that of Support. Operations should participate actively in the product acceptance tests to ensure that the application will be stable. During deployment Operations is involved so that it can take over routine management once the application has entered production.

Operations is the most important role during the operations phase. Operations provides first line support to application incidents in liaison with the Service Desk. They are actively involved in the optimization studies to identify and initiate opportunities for operational improvement.

Security
The security role is relevant to almost all IT activities. The primary objectives of Security Management are to ensure:
■ **Data confidentiality** - only authorized users should be able to access data.
■ **Data integrity** - all authorized users should be able to rely on the correctness of the presented data.
■ **Data availability** - authorized users should be able to access data whenever they need it.

Throughout the Application Management Life Cycle, Security is responsible for providing a documented plan for the verification, storage, classification and deletion of corporate data. Legal, financial and historical data should be safely stored and archived during the required periods. This necessitates a reliable back-up and archiving process.

ICT Infrastructure Management
During the requirements phase, the ICT Infrastructure Management role (ICTIM) collects the performance and availability requirements. This extends to drafting the initial SLA's and OLA's.

During the design phase, ICTIM ensures that the capacity, availability and continuity requirements are detailed in the operational model.

During the build phase, ICTIM assists with incorporating facilities to ensure performance, availability and continuity. ICTIM supports the development team when incorporating facilities to provide the required service levels. During the deployment phase, ICTIM plans and monitors the capacity and availability of the application. ICTIM also provides third-line support to incidents.

During the operations phase ICTIM collects information about potential improvements to the application in terms of performance and availability. During the optimization phase this information is provided to the optimization team.

17.6 Costs and possible problems

17.6.1 Costs

Although the introduction of Application Management can lead to benefits, the use of these best practices in an immature organization may introduce additional costs. These costs lead to management overheads and a failure to identify the following problems at an early stage of implementing Application Management:

- Customers of an IT organization will not be prepared to discuss Key Business Drivers if they are dissatisfied about the provision of services.
- Introducing an effective exchange of information between the phases of the Application Management Life Cycle is only productive if the processes are mature enough.
- An Application Portfolio can only be effectively maintained once Configuration Management and Release Management are mature.
- It is only useful to introduce comprehensive test strategies once mature and verifiable requirements, definition methods and SLA's have been defined.
- Expertise can only be permanently embedded in the Application Management Life Cycle once the processes are mature.

17.6.2 Possible problems

Seen from an Application Management perspective, application development and Service Management have a strong interdependence. If one of them lags behind the other in terms of quality or performance this may lead to tensions, which may have an adverse effect on their cooperation.

One of the major problems, which can stand in the way of effective Application Management, is a lack of cooperation between application development and Service Management, which may be due to the customer.

If there is a tension between the two parties who, working from different angles, have to provide part of the provision of information at the request of the customer, then normally the customer will conclude two different contracts with the IT organization: one for application development and maintenance, and one for operations.

If there is effective cooperation between the two parties which do not compete with each other, they will avoid the many adverse effects that otherwise have a significant negative impact on the performance of the IT organization and of the IT services delivered to the business.

18 BUSINESS PERSPECTIVE. THE IS VIEW ON DELIVERING SERVICES TO THE BUSINESS

18.1 Introduction

It is an acknowledged fact that businesses now rely more than ever upon the delivery of appropriate IT services for their success, and indeed for their very survival.

The context of this chapter, and the associated ITIL book, is of a Business organization making use of IT Services (which could be provided internally, externally or a combination of the two). In the relationship between the Business and the IT service providers, awareness of the business perspective (the business of the clients receiving the service) is very important. The service perspective makes it important even for IT staff who are not part of the same organization (i.e. external suppliers) to understand that by delivering the service they become (at least for this part of their work) part of the business environment.

Effectively supporting an organization's vital business services requires an appreciation of how the business sees things, i.e. a Business Perspective is needed.

An appropriate Business Perspective approach helps IT to do this through a focus on:
- Establishing effective relationships between IT and business.
- Aligning the delivery of services with business practices and ensuring quality service is delivered.
- Understanding how IS (Information Systems) can add value within the business value chain.
- Incorporating the business viewpoint in every aspect of day-to-day IT activities.

18.2 Basic concepts

Developing and maintaining an appropriate Business Perspective for IS rests upon IS staff understanding that they are an integral part of the overall business environment, not a separate entity. This understanding is required across all areas of IS - Strategic, Tactical and Operational. Different attitudes and, often in larger organizations, different people, within both IS and the business, are typically involved at each of the different levels. It involves the IT department switching from a care-takers paradigm to a business partner paradigm.

Successful relationships are an essential foundation for appropriate service provision, and these relationships need to be viewed through a business perspective (see figure 18.1).

The focus of the model is on providing guidance to the service provider, in their understanding of customer attitudes and requirements, but it is also helpful in ensuring the appropriate perspective is understood by suppliers, internal and third-party, and with delivery partners.

18.2.1 Goals, scope and objectives

It is not necessary to have a dedicated group of staff concentrating on specific 'Business Perspective' responsibilities. In fact a better result is more likely to be delivered by a wide understanding and appreciation of the need for a business perspective across the entire range IT staff. So, simple targets for Business perspective tasks cannot be set, instead the results will be seen through increases in effectiveness and/or efficiency of service provision.

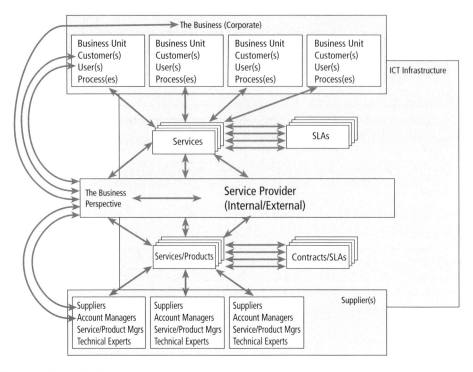

Figure 18.1 - The relationship model

18.2.2 Elements of Business perspective

The specific topics that are addressed with Business Perspective guidance are:

■ **The Value of IT** - how IT deliver benefit to the business.
■ **The Approach to business/IT alignment** - lining up disparate objectives to deliver harmonious support.
■ **Understanding the business viewpoint** - ideas on how this necessary understanding can be achieved and maintained.
■ **Managing the provision of service** - how an appropriate business perspective will affect IT Service management and other processes, such as application development and testing.
■ **Relationship management** - what is involved in building and maintaining relevant and appropriate working relationships.
■ **Roles, responsibilities and interfaces** - who will be involved, and what will they need to deliver.

The following sections in this chapter will briefly address these elements.

18.3 The value of IT

Traditionally IT was viewed as responding to stated business requirements – delivering according to pre-stated needs. But with developing IT maturity and increasing reliance on IS by the business it is now clear that IT has the opportunity to deliver real business value proactively, as understood within Porter's value chain concept.

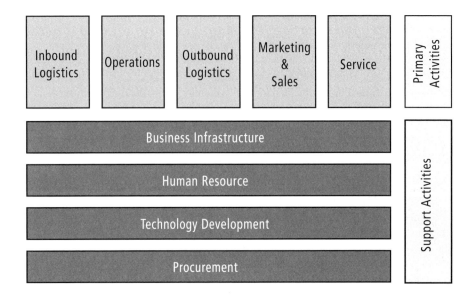

Figure 18.2 - Porter's value chain

18.3.1 Value perspective

Value can be objectively measured, typically in terms of the cost of IT provision, or in terms of extra revenue generated. But value is not just about cost but also considered subjectively, and so the perceived value will depend on the perspective of the customer. Both objective and subjective aspects of value need to be managed. By understanding both the relationships between available technologies (including knowledge and skills associated with the technology) and how business services would be affected by their deployment, for good or ill, IS are able to add genuine value.

Unfortunately, good IS is often not appreciated until its value to the business is demonstrated by damage caused from badly delivered services. Many organizations have suffered financial loss and professional embarrassment caused by failing or inappropriate IS service provision. More constructively, a formal return on investment appraisal can justify and focus IT spending and demonstrate its potential value, which can then subsequently be proved.

18.4 The approach to business/IT alignment

IS has often failed to align its services fully with business requirements. In this respect IS can seem less able than other supporting services to achieve alignment between business need and services provided. Factors that have caused, and continue to exacerbate this situation include:

- Most businesses depend more upon IS than any other (or often, every other) service and so misalignment is more damaging and more visible.
- Those working in IS still see themselves as separate from the business, and describe themselves as working in IS rather than within their employer's industry sector.
- IS does not seem able to 'take its own medicine' and fails to structure itself in an organized and integrated fashion.
- Business management often find it difficult to articulate its requirements in terms that IS can understand.

Establishing good IS alignment requires reconciliation of the IS and business cultures. The issues must be addressed at each level:

- **Strategically** - so that future IS direction is aligned with the high level objectives of the business.
- **Tactically** - so that elements such as change and business risk are properly supported, and services are designed and maintained to reflect business needs and current practices.
- **Operationally** - so that value is actually and measurably delivered.

Aligning with the business also includes a requirement to align with the financial constraints and controls in place across the business, therefore, businesses should understand there is a need to prioritize their requirements.

18.5 Understanding the Business viewpoint

IS and business people may work in the same organization yet each have a different focus. The different priorities and requirements of their jobs will mean they have different expectations and attitudes. As a supplier of IT services, those working in IT have a responsibility to ensure they understand the way the business sees things (the business perspective), rather than expecting customers to be able to specify their requirements using supplier terminology. IT will need enough awareness to understand the context of the business, but not so much that they can actually do the job of their customers! For example many business processes involve a degree of commercial risk and this acceptance of significant risks to success is not always easily understood by IS staff. Failure to understand can mean that the right degree of commercial risks are not taken by the business, because IT are too conservative in their attitudes and, in an innovative commercial environment, the business typically means that the business is disadvantaged against competitors.

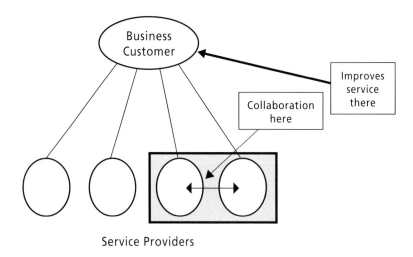

Figure 18.3 - A collaborative approach

Delivering appropriate services, and ensuring that they can be delivered, rests heavily on the quality of the relationships involved, as objective and subjective aspects of service quality affect both the reality and perception of services. In many ways the quality of the relationships developed and maintained can be more important (in terms of support given to the business) than the technical quality of the services themselves. This can be helped by IS realising they are one of several service providers supporting the business and proactively initiating direct collaboration between themselves and other service providers.

Achieving and maintaining adequate perception of the business perspective impacts upon many elements of service provision, including:

- **Service catalogue and portfolio of services** - these must be written in a way that the business can understand.
- **Informed customer** - while the bulk of translation and understanding falls upon the supplier, clearly some degree of understanding of the IT service is required by the customer and user community. The most effective degree of understanding should be established by IS and business.
- **Communication channels** - these channels should reflect the need for appropriate business understanding at each different communication level, e.g. about Service Level Management, Change Management, and Incident Management.
- **ITSM processes** - as functional silo's with specialists tend to be inward looking, the processes with their understanding of business priorities and generalistic view across the silo's are needed to translate a customer focus into internal priorities, steering and resourcing.
- **Business Impact Analysis and Business Continuity** - these must reflect the needs of, and impact upon, the business. And implementation and testing must consider how the business will be impacted under different contingency situations, and how a range of different approaches may be required from IT.

18.6 Managing the provision of service

Closer business alignment is not about a new, or separate, process of 'Business Perspective', and it is not required that there be separate dedicated staff working on achieving a Business perspective. For an IT Service provider to achieve and, crucially, to maintain appropriate business awareness requires a business aware approach across ALL IT Service Management processes and other related processes such as application maintenance and testing. This process integration with business awareness manifests itself in different ways across the processes, but has a common basis in understanding how the business acts and reacts. Examples include:

- **Service Desk** - perhaps the most obvious area for IS to express a good level of business understanding is on the Service Desk, since the communication there must be in business terms, otherwise appropriate initial data will not be collected, and the true business impact of incidents will not be captured. The service desk delivers the everyday translation channel between the business and IS perspectives.
- **Incident & Problem Management** - understanding how incidents might affect the business, in terms of their priorities and risks is essential to genuinely effective incident and problem resolution. For example, rapidly identifying and resolving errors quickly may seem the obvious priority to IS, but deferring investigation to allow a degraded service to continue during business critical periods may actually deliver more overall benefit to the business.
- **Change Management** - again the impact and benefit of the change to the vital business processes of the organization are the key drivers. For this to be realized, then IS must be aware of and understand the role of, the key business processes their IT services underpin.
- **Service Level Management** - provides the formal communication between IT and business and provides the medium for mutual documented understanding. Additionally, SLAs and SLM review meetings provide the mechanism for measuring and providing feedback on the level of perception and understanding.
- **Availability, Capacity and IT Service Continuity Management** - all rely on justifying actions because of the business benefit to be delivered, or the business risk to be avoided. The

benefits and risks can not be derived without appropriate understanding of the business practises, pressures and policies.

- **Application Management** - peripheral in many eyes to the core IT service management processes, but application development and management is vital if IT services are to be of any use at all to the business. Not only must services deliver required business functionality but they must be built and executed in such a way that the IT service management staff and processes can support the business adequately.
- **Release Management, deployment and testing** - implementation of services must accord with how the business will use a service, not how IT staff might imagine they will. This requires adequate business perspective among the staff implementing and testing.
- **Capacity management** - identifies demand and creates separate capacity pools for emerging new demands.
- **Availability Management** - identifies crucial spots in the business processes and translates these to availability demands on IS.

18.7 Supplier Relationship Management

A typical organization will have many suppliers, most of whom will provide services or products that the business uses as a commodity, supporting the business value chain but under the control of the customer. The types of suppliers and their contracts can have a decisive impact on the organizational set-up and the whole SLA framework.

For some key suppliers the relationship is more critical than for others and the quality of the service they deliver has a significant impact upon the value chain. This impacts the relationship with the IT organization on three levels:

- **Strategic** - partnering styles, such as outsourcing a significant proportion of IS provision.
- **Tactical** - relationships enabling commercial activity and business interaction.
- **Operational** - products and services, especially where a readily available alternative could be found.

In order to deliver the services, the right kinds of relationships need to be developed and maintained. Usual types of relationship include:

- **Internal supplier** - this formalizes the supply from one part of an organization to another part of the same organization.
- **Single, dual or multi-sourced supply** - the commitment to a single supplier may result from preferential rates or specialized and committed approaches within the supplier. Multiple sourcing can reduce dependence on one supplier and encourages price competition.
- **Partnering** - established at an executive level, true partnership relationships require shared strategic alliances and are based upon a shared risk.
- **Outsourcing** - increasingly common, this typically is about transferring ownership of service delivery from internal to external suppliers.

Different factors will influence the relationship, or mix of relationships chosen and a strategic positioning tool such as the profiling shown in figure 18.4 can help an organization decide on the appropriate approach.

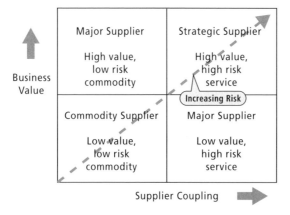

Figure 18.4 - Profiling a supplier relationship

Whatever relationships are adopted, the relationship should be underpinned by a contract or service level agreement, or an operational level agreement for internal suppliers. This formalization merely documents elements of the relationship, its success will depend also upon the human and business understanding applied to it.

The formalized relationship will address:
■ Scope and coverage
■ Documentation approach and responsibility
■ Contract management
■ Reviews and change management
■ Relationship and performance management
■ Benefits, cost and risk management
■ Performance acceptance criteria
■ Availability acceptance criteria
■ Cost criteria
■ Agreement performance, availability, and cost volume limits
■ Legal clauses

18.8 Roles, responsibilities and interfaces

It is mentioned earlier in this chapter that a truly successful business perspective alignment comes from all staff within IS having a sufficiently developed business understanding to correctly and relevantly influence their efforts.

However, notwithstanding that generic requirement, some roles can be identified as playing a crucial role in developing and maintaining the business perspective. (Note the term 'role' is used deliberately and carefully here, it is not implied that these roles equate to dedicated staff with similar job titles, instead they describe tasks that will be undertaken, sometimes by a team, more likely in association with other roles.) These roles include, among others:
■ **Overall IS management** - they will be part of the IS steering group, and possibly be an active part of setting the overall company strategy. It is essential that overall management co-ordinate and control all aspects and policy on establishing and maintaining a valid and relevant business perspective.

■ **Communications manager role** - responsible for developing and maintaining effective and efficient communication processes between IS and the business.

■ **Business Relationship Manager role** - developing effective and efficient relations with customers and suppliers, both internal and external. Often this role will be coincident with roles such as 'Service Delivery' or 'Account management'.

18.8.1 Business perspective processes

Business perspective processes are, in practice, delivered through and alongside other processes - service management and others. However the key process elements that an appropriate business perspective requires can be illustrated in a process chart as shown in figure 18.5.

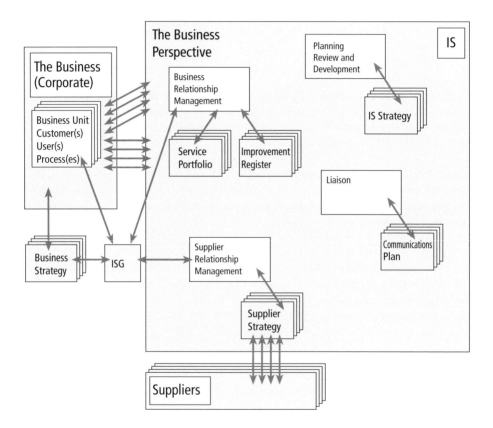

Figure 18.5 - Process chart

19 PLANNING TO IMPLEMENT SERVICE MANAGEMENT

19.1 Introduction

Introducing or improving IT Service Management (ITSM) within an organization and implementing the best practices contained within the ITIL publications described in this book requires a structured approach, that needs to take into account the following aspects:

- Where and when to begin.
- Business drivers.
- Organizational change.
- Cultural change.
- Project and Program Planning.
- Process Definition.
- Performance Improvement.

Such an implementation should be designed to contribute to Information Systems (IS) becoming better aligned with the business and to provide IT services that deliver real business benefit.

19.2 Basic Concepts

For any IT organization to be successful in delivering IT services to support a business, the full spectrum of People, Culture, Processes and Technology must be taken into account. Figure 19.1 shows how these three basic concepts relate to each other, and in what way each of them contributes to meet the business objectives.

Figure 19.1 - The People, Process, and Technology of Service Management

19.2.1 Justification

For every ITSM implementation, or program of process improvements, a clear business justification needs to be identified. The business should benefit directly or indirectly from any improved ITSM process.

Typically such benefits are reductions in the Time To Repair, reductions in the Time To Market and a better alignment between business requirements and costs. Any justification should include a specific return on investment, but should not be exclusive to all but monetary gain.

ITSM should make a difference to the whole organization by making the business processes more efficient and more effective. For example through reducing cost in IT Service Delivery, or through increasing Customer satisfaction with Service Delivery, or through more reliable IT Services to support business critical services.

19.2.2 IT Service Management Benefits

Implementing ITSM within an organization can result into financial, employee, innovative and internal benefits, as well as benefits directly affecting the business. All improvements must contribute to benefiting the business, either directly or indirectly. Benefits should be considered for each of the stakeholders. Specific benefits have to be defined in such a way that these benefits can be measured to confirm that they have been accomplished.

19.2.3 The Drivers

There are two major drivers behind ITSM implementations, improvements and change in any organization: the business and the technology. Technology investment is always predicated on supporting the business. Businesses become increasingly aware of the importance of IT to support and enable their operations and achieving their objectives. Therefore, technology developments need to be translated by the IT department into solutions for the business. This is necessary to ensure that the quality of service matches with the way the business makes use of the new technologies.

19.2.4 Which process to implement first?

'Which process should be implemented or improved first?' The real answer is, all of them, as the true value of implementing all ITSM processes is far greater than the sum of the individual processes.

However, it is recommended that the processes of greatest needs be addressed first. A detailed assessment needs to be undertaken to ascertain the strengths and weaknesses of the IT service provision. Basically, one needs to understand the problem before choosing the solution. Customer satisfaction research and a process maturity assessment may be a part of the initial investigation.

An organization should evaluate alternative approaches to implementation and improvement. Senior management commitment, resource requirements and available budget, depth of skills and knowledge in the organization, the culture of the organization and the demand for "business as usual" should be taken into account.

Because all processes interrelate with each other and in some cases are totally dependent on each other, there is no universal 'right way'. A number of different approaches have been used successfully:
- **Single process approach** - Implementing, developing or improving one process at a time. This approach is typically used in one-time improvement cases. This short term approach can deliver quick wins and provide a starting point both for wider implementation and longer-term Change Management initiatives. For example the Service Desk function and Incident Management process can show striking initial improvements when first implemented. Quick wins can be achieved by initially implementing a specific IT service, to provide a starting point for both a wider implementation and a longer-term Change Management initiative.
- **Multi process approach** - implementing, developing or improving a number of processes concurrently. This is often initiated by or involves considerable discussion with the business and customers. This approach is typically triggered and overseen by a programme for continuous service improvement, which may make use of a Strengths, Weaknesses, Opportunities and Threats (SWOT) analysis to target improvements across several processes.
- **All processes approach** - Implementing, developing or improving all the ITSM processes

simultaneously. This is accomplished most effectively by taking small steps in all processes concurrently, coordinated by one overall ITSM Continuous Service Improvement Programme (CSIP) that is supported by individual process owners with individual CSIPs for their own process. This has been shown to work successfully for organizations where there is already an inherent, high level of process inter-dependencies.

Selecting an appropriate approach
To determine which implementation approach will fit best to its situation, every organization should evaluate each of the different implementation approaches. The outcome will depend upon: senior management commitment, resource requirements, available budget, depth of experience, skills and knowledge in the organization, the culture of the organization and the demand for "business as usual".

Review Approach
The selected implementation approach should regularly be reviewed to ensure that it continues to be the appropriate approach. As organizations and their ITSM processes mature, the appropriateness of the selected approach may change. Whichever approach is selected, reviews should be scheduled frequently to fully assess its appropriateness and to adapt the implementation plans if necessary.

Quick Wins
It is important to recognize and accomplish 'quick wins' during any implementation or improvement initiative. However, long term objectives should not be jeopardized during this process.

19.2.5 The Six Stages of a Continuous Service Improvement Program (CSIP)
A recommended technique for the implementation or improvement of processes is the introduction of an overall program for Continuous Service Improvement (CSIP). Figure 19.2 outlines the six iterative key phases involved in such a program. In the remainder of this chapter every phase will be explained in greater detail.

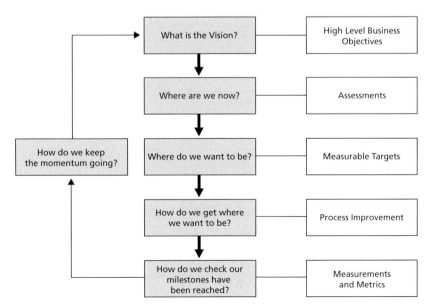

Figure 19.2 - The Six Stages of a Continuous Service Improvement Program

19.3 Stage 1: What is the vision?

An IT organization embarking on an improvement program can help position itself better for success by starting to act like a business and by creating a vision with goals, budgets and metrics. An ITSM vision is a statement of 'Where do we want to be?' mutually agreed upon between the business and IT. It describes the goal and the purpose of a CSIP.

The vision statement should clarify the program, in terms of its business and technical objectives, outline the commitment and views of senior management, and motivate people to start acting accordingly.

19.3.1 Communicating the vision

A sense of urgency identified in 'What if we do nothing?' and the personal perspective of the vision 'What's in it for me?' creates the basis of all communication to stakeholders involved in or impacted by a CSIP.

Setting Direction

The Business and IT strategies must be aligned by setting the direction of the CSIP. Clear policies and standards should be in place to ensure a consistent and continuous approach to IT service management. The IT management and tool architecture should also support the business requirements.

The key activities for setting the overall direction include:
- Analyzing business needs and how IT can enable these needs to be met.
- Establishing a Risk Management policy and ensuring that it is incorporated into the planning and decision making processes.
- Establishing an IT strategy and ensuring that it is integrated with the business strategy.
- Designing policies around the desired business outcomes and ensuring the maximum benefit is derived from investments in IT.

Success Factors

Critical to successful alignment of IT with business objectives are:
- Creating a sense of urgency.
- Having a strong coalition at the top.
- Vision and leadership in maintaining strategic direction, clear goals and measurement of goal realization.
- Acceptance of innovation and new ways of working.
- Understanding the business, its stakeholders and its environment.
- IT staff understanding the needs of the business.
- The business understanding the potential of IT.
- Information and communication available and accessible to everyone who needs it.
- Tracking of technology developments to identify opportunities for the business.
- Creating Quick-wins.
- Institutionalize the organizational changes.

19.4 Stage 2: Where are we now?

Before embarking upon a CSIP, an IT organization must be able to understand where they are today from several perspectives:
- Business drivers - the business strategy, direction, and the issues facing the business and how they impact IT.

- Technology drivers - technology developments and how these may best be deployed to support the business.
- How the business views the drivers and wants to accomplish new business benefits offered by technology.
- Do the business and IT have a common view of IT's current role, maturity, and quality of IT Service Delivery relative to these drivers?
- What are the views and needs of stakeholders?
- Is there a clear answer to 'What if we do nothing?'.

A clear understanding of the current organization helps determine the scale, complexity and effort required to achieve the vision.

19.4.1 IT Organizational Maturity Levels

Before embarking on a CSIP it is vital to understand the maturity level of the organization. These are represented in figure 19.3.

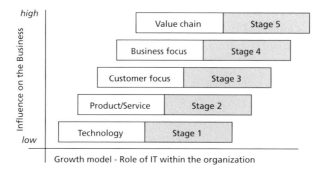

Figure 19.3 - IT Organization Growth Model

It is important to be aware that:
- Each maturity level represents a transformation of the IT organization.
- Maturing more than two levels in one CSIP iteration has a higher risk of failure.
- Not all IT organizations need to be at the highest level – the required maturity depends on the business needs of IT.

Transition to the next maturity level is more than implementing ITIL best practice, requiring a combination of the following elements to change:
- **Vision and strategy** - overall direction relating to the role and position of IT within the business.
- **Mission** - objectives and goals of IT to realize the strategy.
- **Processes** - procedures to achieve goals and objectives.
- **People** - skills and abilities to perform the processes.
- **Technology** - infrastructure to enable the processes.
- **Culture** - behavior and attitude in the business to IT.

The results of an assessment can determine the level of maturity in the IT Organization. They will also help to answer the following questions:
- How big is the gap between the current role of IT and the required role?
- How did the gap develop? What are our in-capabilities?
- Is IT being managed by goals that reflect business needs? Is there a clear set of goals relating to the CSIP?

- Are the right processes and procedures in place to realize the goals, including measurements to show improvements?
- Are the desired skill sets and competencies in place?
- Does technology enable performance of processes and delivery of metrics to support the goals?
- Do attitudes and behavior support a Customer and service focused approach to delivering IT services?

19.4.2 Stakeholders

Stakeholders can have a positive or negative impact on a CSIP, and unidentified stakeholders represent a significant risk to it. They must be identified and their needs and expectations must be understood when determining "where are we now?" and "where do we want to be?"

Figure 19.4 shows some of the major categories of stakeholders.

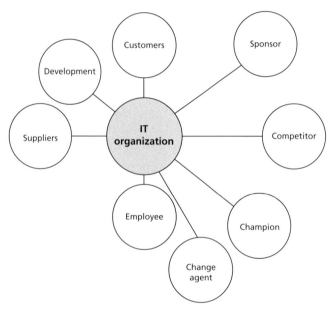

Figure 19.4 - Major Stakeholder Categories

19.4.3 Benchmarking

Through benchmarking an organization is able to compare its performance to other organizations. It can also be used to compare the performance between different business units within an organization.

Benchmarking can reveal opportunities for quick wins that may be easy to implement and do not cost much, while at the same time they provide substantial benefits by identifying opportunities for improved process effectiveness, cost reduction, or staff synergy. The costs of successful benchmarking can be repaid through the improvements realized.

People Assessment

It is necessary to understand the current ways that people work together and how their skills and competencies are being deployed. Including the organization's culture in an assessment is a critical success factor that should not be overlooked. Organizational culture is the whole of the ideas, corporate values, beliefs, practices, expectations about behaviour and daily habits that are shared by the employees in an organization.

To ensure adequate attention is being given to cultural aspects in a CSIP, it is important to understand the culture in an organization, how the culture may be affected by an ITSM improvement initiative and what effect culture may have as a 'barrier' to accomplishing organizational change. Underestimating the effect of culture will, if nothing worse, always result in the organization slipping back into its old state after the CSIP.

Process Assessment

A detailed assessment of the ITSM processes is required, as well as drilling down into each process and the related activity sets.

With fully defined and documented processes an organization's efficiency and effectiveness will improve. Continuous measurement, review and improvement of these processes will lead to higher quality processes. Quality measures may be the result of a comparison between the process quality and predetermined norms.

Process outputs need to conform to operational norms derived from business objectives. Whenever outputs conform to a predetermined norm, the process can be considered effective. When activities are also carried out with minimum effort, the process can be considered efficient. Make sure to incorporate process-measurement results into regular management reports.

The following ITSM Process Maturity Framework (based on SEI Capability Maturity Model, Paulk et al, 1991) can be used to undertake the assessment.

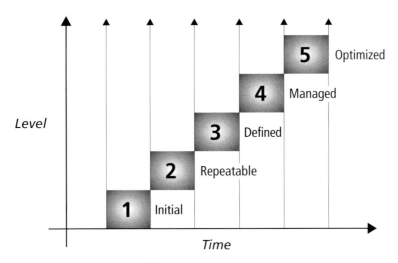

Figure 19.5 - The ITSM Process Maturity Framework

This model can be used as a framework to assess the maturity of each of the ITSM processes individually, or ITSM as a whole. The ITSM Process Maturity Framework depends on the extent to which the IT Organization Growth Model (Figure 19.3), is being embraced by the organization, since the process maturity depends on organizational maturity.

Each level of process maturity is dependent on a combination of elements. Therefore, to be fully effective, a review needs to assess aspects such as:

■ Vision and steering.
■ Process.
■ People.
■ Technology.
■ Culture.

The major characteristics of each level of process maturity are:

■ **Initial** (Level 1) - Process has been recognized; little or no process management activities; no importance, no resources or no awareness within the organization. Also described as 'ad hoc' or even 'chaotic'.
■ **Repeatable** (Level 2) - Process has been recognized; low importance, few resources or little awareness within the operation. Activities related to the process are uncoordinated, irregular, without direction and focuses on process effectiveness.
■ **Defined** (Level 3) - Process has been recognized, but no formal agreement, acceptance or recognition of its role has been accomplished within the IT organization; there is a process owner; the focus is on the efficiency as well as the effectiveness of the process. Reports and results are stored for future reference.
■ **Managed** (Level 4) - The process has been recognized completely and has been accepted throughout IT. There is a service focus; which is proactive with documented and established interfaces. Dependencies with other IT processes have been identified.
■ **Optimizing** (Level 5) - The process has been recognized completely with strategic objectives and goals. It is aligned to the overall strategic business. The IT goals have now become 'institutionalized'.

Tool Assessment

An inventory should be made of the existing toolsets, their usage and their support for the primary areas for improvement that are being considered should be taken. Very often there is a range of tools throughout various organizational departments, and all too often there is little integration or sharing of data between these tools. Tools that are being used to support specific processes may not meet the new functional requirements. Their data structures and data handling might be inadequate to support the ITIL based workflows.

The ITSM Process Maturity Framework (Figure 19.5) can support tool assessments.

19.5 Stage 3: Where do we want to be?

Both IT and the business must agree on the role and characteristics required of the IT organization. The questions to ask are 'Is this role a nice-to-have-role?', 'Is this role a need-to-have role?' and 'What will be the consequences to both the business and the IT organization if this required role is not being accomplished?' This will help a CSIP to:

■ Establish a 'sense of urgency'.
■ Shape the 'vision' of the future IT organization for the business.
■ Understand the level of ITSM expertise needed.

19.5.1 Business Case

The business case for a CSIP is based on where the organization is today and where it needs to be in terms that describe the business impact to the 'to be' state, as well as on the 'as is' state.. Stakeholder assessments and goal setting will provide the necessary focus on results and goals.

To justify a CSIP, one should compare project costs and benefits. While costs are relatively easy to measure (people, tools, etc.), the benefits are more difficult to determine as a direct result of a CSIP. Results are not always financially quantifiable, because process-oriented projects often yield higher quality service provision, higher service levels and a more flexible organization.

A business case needs a senior sponsor who supports the CSIP and is committed to its success. Without a sponsor there is a high risk funding and resources will not be made available and that improvements will not be accomplished. The sponsor must define the basis for acceptance by the business.

19.5.2 Gap assessment report
Benchmarking and reviews lead to identification of gaps in the capabilities of the people, the process and the technology. They also uncover the potential business outcomes value if the gap is closed. A documented gap assessment facilitates the prioritization of gaps and the identification of areas for improvement.

In essence, a gap analysis identifies the risks and the opportunities for improvement for an organization. If all the processes cannot be implemented simultaneously, the organization has to decide which process or processes will provide the highest benefits for the business.

19.5.3 Setting goals and expectations
Clear goals must be set and aligned to the needs and expectations of the stakeholders. If the CSIP goals are vague or cannot be measured, ITSM may become a problem rather than a solution due to differing stakeholder expectations and the lack of demonstrable results.

19.5.4 Plan for quick wins
A CSIP can be a lengthy program of change. Quick wins must be identified and attained, not 'assumed'. This will help keeping the CSIP on track and also keeping energy and commitment levels high. Make sure to identify quick wins for each process and plan these into a CSIP. And make sure to make these quick wins visible to all the stakeholders and communicate them frequently.

19.6 Stage 4: How do we get where we want to be?
The topics to be considered during a CSIP are:
- HOW the required changes are going to be accomplished.
- WHICH items are essential to be addressed within a CSIP.

19.6.1 Where to start?
The answer to the question 'Where should we start?' depends on:
- The maturity level of the IT organization as a whole (current and future target).
- The maturity of the individual ITSM processes (current and future target).
- The strategic goals of the organization.
- The priorities based on the interrelationship of the processes.

Generally, organizations are unable to attain a high maturity level with individual ITSM processes without without having the depending processes also being implemented to a similar maturity level.

A summary of the gap analysis should be presented to a cross-functional group of key stakeholders. This group needs to understand and commit to the required improvements to close the gap before any action planning can start. Take great care to establish credibility in the assessment or benchmark and its results in order to foster management support.

19.6.2 Awareness
Good communication is required to raise an awareness of 'How do we get to where we want to be?' Stakeholders must understand how the business will benefit from more mature IT management, and why certain changes and measures are being planned. This helps removing resistance to changes in established working practises.

19.6.3 Managing Organizational Change
Implementing or improving ITSM always involves organizational change, and is in essence an organizational change programme. Many such programs fail to achieve their desired results, being prone to the difficulties encountered as people must change their orientation and the way they work. People generally do not like change; so benefits must be explained to all affected to gain their support and to ensure they break away from old working practices.

John P. Kotter, Professor of Leadership at Harvard Business School, identified 'Eight steps to ensure that transformation efforts will not fail' (see figure 19.6).

Steps		Quotes
1	create a sense of urgency	'...50% of transformations fail in this phase.' '..without motivation, people won't help and the effort goes nowhere.' '..75% of a company's management should be convinced of the need..'
2	form a guiding coalition	'..underestimating the difficulties in producing change..' '..lack of effective, strong leadership...' '..not a powerful enough guiding coalition...opposition eventually stops the change initiative..'
3	create a vision	'..without a sensible vision, a transformation effort can easily dissolve into a list of confusing, incompatible projects that can take the organization in the wrong direction, or nowhere at all...' '..an explanation of 5 minutes should obtain a reaction of 'understanding' and 'interest''
4	communicate the vision	'..without credible communication, and a lot of it, the hearts and minds of the troops are never captured.' '..make use of all communications channels.' '...let managers lead by example...'walk the talk'
5	'empowering' others to act on the vision	'..structures to underpin the vision...and removal of barriers to change' '..the more people involved, the better the outcome.' '..reward initiatives..'
6	planning for and creating short term wins	'...real transformation takes time..without short term wins, too many people give up, or join the ranks of those opposing change.' '..actively look for performance improvements and establish clear goals..' '...communicate successes.'
7	consolidating improvements and producing more change	'..until changes sink deeply into the culture new approaches are fragile and subject to regression...' '..in many cases workers revert to old practice.' '..use credibility of short term wins to tackle even bigger problems.'
8	institutionalizing new appraoches	'...show how new approaches, behaviour and attitude have helped improve performance.' '..ensure selection and promotion criteria underpin the new approach.'

Figure 19.6 - Eight main reasons why transformation efforts fail

19.6.4 Managing Cultural Change

Culture is another crucial aspect to be taken into account; it can support an implementation or it can be the source of resistance. Many organizations do not view managing cultural change as a top priority. When a CSIP starts, new organizational structure and new technology are often the main focus, while little attention is paid to organizational culture. Organizational culture affects leadership and leadership affects the chances of success of an organizational change. Culture is intangible, but has to be managed:

- Determine the existing culture.
- Define supportive behavior.
- Change undesirable culture.

Proposed organizational changes affect people and the way they feel. In times of radical changes, make sure to channel these emotions to promote changes, as they have a major impact on success. Quick wins need to be planned to build excitement so the affected staff members explore the possibilities of new situations. Improvements then become consolidated and institutionalized. Communication is not a one-time activity but an on-going requirement to ensure that the initial enthusiasm is maintained and enhanced.

Make sure to involve everyone in thinking about why an organizational change is needed and can express their views and concerns. Encouraging direct feedback makes it easier to confront the issues. Addressing issues can accelerate and make the organizational change more effective in the long run.

The organization must be committed to acting on the feedback. Resistance to change should not be ignored as this will only serve to force it 'underground'. Making resistance open, discussing and analyzing it, can identify new areas of empowerment or additional barriers that need removing.

19.6.5 Roles for implementation

The new processes and working practices are often implemented within existing organizational structures. The implementation of ITSM practices introduces new roles into an organization that may overlap traditional organizational boundaries, which may cause difficulties.

A clear definitions of accountability and responsibility are critical. Without these roles and responsibilities the new process can be unclear, and individuals may fall back into the old way of working.

19.6.6 Training

Organizations and individuals may have different opinions about the affect of training courses to get everybody informed appropriately about the new way of working. However the concept of transferring or exchanging knowledge (information) to achieve understanding and then elicit the desired response remains the same. The training often covers all the aspects including ITIL, 'soft skills', ITSM tools and processes, procedures and work instructions. Cultural aspects are often best addressed in games and simulations.

19.6.7 Process improvement

Once the processes have been defined, they should become under control first. When they are under control, they can mature to a repeatable level and then mature to a manageable level. The degrees of control over the processes should be defined, and metrics can be built in to manage the process control aspects.

Figure 19.7 shows that a process-based improvement program, such as ITSM, requires an understanding of what the processes are, of their relationship to existing organizational structures and of the ways of working. For departments to work as cross-functional teams instead of technology based silos, fundamental changes need to take place, such as:
- Across-the-board defined and repeatable cross-departmental processes need to be put in place.
- New areas of responsibilities need to be included in job descriptions.
- Values, behavior, and cultures need to be changed to become customer focused.
- Greater knowledge for staff using the complex processes.
- Integrated toolset enabling data exchange and workflow.
- Management needs to be committed to business focused IT services.
- Process owners with authority, accountable for processes, are required.

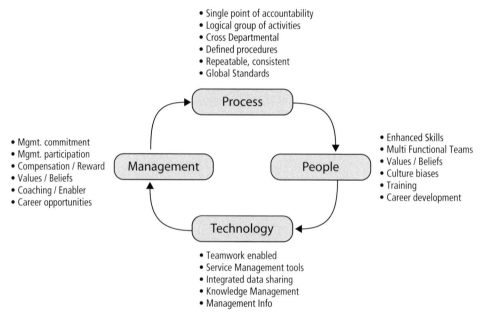

Figure 19.7 - Process re-engineering model

The processes and procedures should be simple and straightforward, and should directly support a business function. They should not exist for their own sake, but for the sake of the business goal.

19.6.8 Tool improvement
Implementation of ITSM supporting tools is essential for the success of it all. However, any tool must support the process – not the other way around. After considering the current level of process maturity and the organization's ambitions, it may be that the existing ITSM tool(s) is no longer adequate. In which case one should generate a new Statement of Requirements (SOR) and initiate the evaluation and selection process for a new or enhanced ITSM tool solution.

If no tool experience is available within the organization, it is advisable to start with a simple tool, using it as a prototype against which requirements can be documented for a more serious tool selection later in the program.

A powerful sponsorship is indispensable to most of the initiatives mentioned above.

19.7 Stage 5: How do we check if milestones have been reached?

To judge process performance, one should set clearly defined objectives with measurable targets. These targets can describe what a process should be able to achieve (output) but it can also contain maturity cretiaof the process itself such as holding audits and reviews. We can subsequently confirm that these objectives and the CSIP milestones have been reached, and that the desired service quality improvement has been accomplished.

Every time a completion of each significant phase of the CSIP has been completed, one should conduct a Post Implementation Review (PIR) to ensure that the objectives have been met. The achievements should be compared with the original goals and new improvement targets should be defined.

To confirm that CSIP milestones have been reached, Key Performance Indicators need to be monitored constantly.

19.7.1 Critical Success Factors (CSFs) and Key Performance Indicators (KPIs)

CSFs have to be taken into account within each ITSM process. KPIs should be set and measured against each process to ensure the CSFs are met. The characteristics of CSFs and KPIs are such that they cascade down from department to individual levels and establish the baseline and mechanisms for tracking the performance. Focus should be kept on a minimum number of KPI's. For example five per process. When a KPI is achieved focus can switch to new KPI's.

19.7.2 ITSM process CSFs and KPIs

CSFs and KPIs are important indicators that can be used for both the ongoing management of the ITSM efforts. They can also serve as objectives for a CSIP.

Every organization needs to agree on the applicable CSFs and KPIs. It needs to determine whether or not to gather information regarding additional CSFs and KPIs. Different metrics may be required by each stakeholder and each service management discipline. Table 19.1 shows examples of critical success factors and key performance indicators for the Change Management process.

19.7.3 Customer Satisfaction Surveys (CSS)

CSSs can be regular formal surveys and/or can be obtained by the Service Desk. Randomly selected callers can be asked a few questions on their perception of IT's service quality. Any information gathered via the Service Desk surveys should be considered as supplementary to the full CSS. Make sure to carefully consider both the wording of the questions and the actual questions being asked. Make sure to ask questions on areas that are important to the Customer and start with the most important questions. Provide the participants of the survey with copies of the results, including details of the proposed actions to address any areas for improvement.

A trend analysis should be conducted on the CSS results, to aim for continuous improvements in the customer's perception ratings to some optimal target – recognizing that in normal circumstances, improved performance, leads to increased customer expectations.

CSFs	KPIs
A repeatable process for making changes	% fewer rejected RFCs
	% reduction in unauthorized changes detected
	% of change requests implemented on time
	% reduction in average time to make changes
	% reduction in the change backlog
	% fewer changes backed out
	% reduction in changes required by previous change failures
	% increase of reports produced on schedule
Make changes quickly and accurately (business driven needs)	% reduction in the number of urgent changes
	% reduction of urgent changes causing Incidents
	% reduction of changes implemented without being tested
	% reduction of urgent, backed-out changes
	% reduction of urgent or high priority changes submitted without business justification
Protect services when making changes	Reduction in unavailability caused by changes
	% reduction in backed out changes
	% reduction of unsuccessful changes
	% reduction in changes causing incidents
	% reduction in changes impacting core services
	% increase in changes outside core service times
	% reduction in changes not referred to a CAB
	Improvement in CSS feedback on change
	% reduction in failed changes with no back-out
	% reduction in time to invoke a change freeze
Deliver process efficiency and effectiveness benefits	% efficiency improvement based on RFC volumes
	% increase in the accuracy of change estimates
	% reduction in the average cost of a change
	% reduction in change overtime(better planning)
	% reduction in the 'cost' of failed changes
	% increase of changes implemented on time
	% increase in changes implemented to budget
	% reduction of failed changes
	% reduction of backed out changes

Table 19.1 - Change Management (CSFs and KPIs)

19.8 Stage 6: How do we keep the momentum going?

The hardest part of any CSIP is maintaining the improvements that have been achieved. Make sure to take action to ensure that improvement efforts are not made in vain and that learning experiences and acquired knowledge is being retained.

Sustaining improvement will become more complex because of the continuous acceleration of the rate of change for IT. This increased demand for change will be in response to the increasing needs of the business to innovate and remain competitive. The ITIL processes support both the ability to incorporate the necessary change quickly and to continuously assess and improve the overall operational environments.

Make sure to capitalize on the success of quick wins to keep the momentum going and to instigate more changes.

19.8.1 Institutionalize the Change
Distinguish short term, mid term, and long term wins and consolidate major changes into every-day practice to ensure that the process improvements will prevail.

19.8.2 Ongoing monitoring and process reviews
The four primary reasons for measuring progress are to:

Progress towards goals and targets
Quantifying metrics is often regarded being a subjective activity. Applying an objective measurement to the current state and the end goal will help the objective to become more realistic and result into more actionable items.

Demonstrate effective use of business resources
Assuming the business is making significant investments in ITSM improvement initiatives and the CSIPs, make sure to use measurements and metrics related to the business and its usage of IT to demonstrate a return on their investments.

Provide team recognition and motivation
The initial enthusiasm for a CSIP can fade away over time whenever other initiatives arise. Make sure to keep the team, the key advocates, the sponsors, and the participants motivated to stay focused. Ensure they know they are making progress towards the key goals. Metrics will help the team understand where they are, how much they have accoplished, where they need to go, when significant milestones have been reached and when substantial barriers have been overcome.

Allow action plans to be adjusted
Make sure to use measurement information to enable the team to review and understand the results, and to make adjustments while moving forward. Any short term problems should be resolved. Long term trends can be addressed before their impacts become too severe, move around resources as needed and whenever needed instigate different approaches to future tasks.

19.8.3 Review metrics
The essentials of metrics include time, cost, quality, and effectiveness. Make sure to determine which approach to performance measurement is the most effective one for any given situation. The results may be skewed when measuring less than all the major components. Make sure to select a balanced set of metrics to prevent this problem from happening. The measurements should be done frequently to make the necessary adjustments whenever needed, but not too often to create unnecessary workloads. Also, make sure to include relevant project results and measures in employee performance reviews.

The best metrics are objective, credible, and require little downtime or processing resources. Make sure to use automated tools to gather, report, and track measurements whenever possible. Regularly review measurements and metrics in conjunction with the business for appropriateness and amend when required.

19.8.4 Ongoing quality improvement
The institutionalization phase of a CSIP enables the organization to make an inventory of all the achievements and ensure that the service improvements are embedded into every day procedures. Process improvements require to be documented to allow processes to become repeatable and to facilitate the achievement of some form of quality standard.

Auditing for improvement using KPIs is a common method of tracking metrics. Trend analysis can be done by using a 'Balanced Scorecard'. A Balanced Scorecard contributes to organizational performance management. The goals for organization performance management should include the following four perspectives:

- **Customer perspective** - relevant to most processes and particularly to SLM with documented SLA targets.
- **Internal process perspective** - include the ITIL processes.
- **Learning and growth perspective** - staffing, training and investments in software.
- **Financial perspective** - IT Financial Management covers how costs and charges are allocated to the Customer organization.

BS15000, a formal standard for IT Service Management, includes a requirement for ongoing continuous improvement.

19.8.5 Reinforcement of business and IT alignment

Make sure to continually reinforce alignment of IT to the business at all levels. Business priorities help making clear how operations affects the business, which parts are being affected and in what ways. As a result the overall business productivity will be of higher quality, and business activities will be conducted in the right order of importance. All this must be linked to the IT maturity level of the organization. Maintaining existing systems and developing new systems while responding to changing business priorities can be a difficult challenge.

19.8.6 Knowledge Management

It is important to identify the existing knowledge gaps within the organization, and to share the results of such an assessment. These knowledge gaps can be bridged by incorporating the knowledge into processes throughout the IT life cycle. The IT life cycle itself drives the prioritization of the development of knowledge and the process of sharing it. It also drives the identification and development of the necessary knowledge base prior to the moment the knowledge will be needed. Many organizations fail to recognize this need and fail to train their employees. As a result the process is halted due to a skills constraint. A lack of knowledge sharing is an activity that should be looked into prior to, during and after the application of knowledge to the task.

Throughout a CSIP, a lot of experience and information is being acquired. It is important that this knowledge is being collected, being organized and being made accessible. To ensure the ongoing success of the program, Knowledge Management techniques should be applied.

APPENDIX A **SOURCES**

The following sources for this book can be used to learn more about ITIL.

A1 Further reading

Subject	Title	Publisher	ISBN
Service Management	Service Support	OGC / TSO	0113300158
Service Management	Service Delivery	OGC / TSO	0113300174
Service Management	Security Management	OGC / TSO	011330014X
Service Management	Small-Scale Implementation	OGC/TSO	0113309805
Applications	Application Management	OGC / TSO	0113308663
Applications	Software Asset Management	OGC / TSO	0113309430
Infrastructure	ICT Infrastructure Management	OGC / TSO	0113308655
Business	Business Perspective	OGC / TSO	0113308949
Implementation	Planning to Implement Service Management	OGC / TSO	0113308779

A2 Relevant web sites

OGC	http://www.ogc.gov.uk
ITIL	http://www.itil.co.uk
EXIN	http://www.exin-exams.com
ISEB	http://www.bcs.org.uk/iseb
itSMF International	http://www.itsmf.org
ITSM PORTAL	http://en.itsmportal.net/
Loyalist College	http://www.itilexams.com
TÜV SÜD Akademie	http://www.bildung4me.de/
ISO 20000	http://www.isoiec20000certification.com/